BBC RADIO 3

The BBC presents the
119th season of Henry Wood
Promenade Concerts,
broadcasting every Prom
live on BBC Radio 3

THE PROMS
1895–2013

The Proms brings the best of classical music to a wide audience in an informal and welcoming atmosphere. From the very outset, part of the audience has stood in the central 'promenade' arena. Prom places originally cost just a shilling – similar to today's price of only £5.00. The concerts have always mixed the great classics with what Henry Wood, founder-conductor of the Proms, called his 'novelties' – in other words, rare works and premieres.

1895
The 26-year-old Henry Wood launches the Promenade Concerts with Robert Newman, manager at the newly opened Queen's Hall; Wood conducts the Proms throughout its first 50 years

1927
The BBC takes over the running of the Proms

1930
The new BBC Symphony Orchestra becomes the orchestra of the Proms, later joined by other London orchestras

1939
Proms season abandoned after only three weeks following the declaration of war

1941
The Proms moves to the Royal Albert Hall when the Queen's Hall is gutted by fire after being bombed in an air raid

1947
First televised Last Night of the Proms

1966
First non-British orchestra at the Proms: the Moscow Radio Orchestra, under Gennady Rozhdestvensky

1970
First Late Night Prom: cult pop group The Soft Machine

1996
First Proms Chamber Music series; first Prom in the Park

1998
First Blue Peter Family Prom, signalling a new commitment to events for families

2002
The Proms goes digital on BBC Four; on-demand listening begins online

2008
Proms Plus expands to precede every main evening Proms concert

2009
The Proms Family Orchestra makes its Proms debut

2012
Wallace & Gromit Prom, with specially created new animations and the unexpected premiere of a concerto for violin and dog

Clockwise from left: Henry Wood in an illustration for *Vanity Fair* (1907); Malcolm Sargent, the charismatic successor to founder-conductor Henry Wood (pictured in 1947); Robert Wyatt, drummer of The Soft Machine, at the first Late Night Prom (1970); Wallace & Gromit bring their unique antics to the Proms (2012)

BBC PROMS GUIDE 2013 CONTENTS

CONCERT LISTINGS

BOOKING

VENUE INFORMATION

BBC.CO.UK/PROMS

Join us on Facebook:
facebook.com/theproms

Follow us on Twitter:
@bbcproms (#bbcproms)

BBC Symphony Orchestra

Concerts 2013–14

An inspiring series of concerts featuring a rich and distinctive range of music including choral masterpieces, operatic treasures and stunning new works by today's leading composers.

SAKARI ORAMO

Six concerts with the BBC Symphony Orchestra's new Chief Conductor featuring symphonies by Mahler and Shostakovich and a host of exciting premieres.

BRITTEN 100

A celebration of the 100th anniversary of Britten's birth. The powerful *War Requiem* conducted by Semyon Bychkov in the Royal Albert Hall and Britten's delightful satirical opera *Albert Herring* at the Barbican, with first-rate soloists.

ELGAR ORATORIOS

Sir Andrew Davis conducts *The Dream of Gerontius* and *The Apostles* with a superb line-up of soloists including Sarah Connolly, Brindley Sherratt and Gerald Finley.

NIGHTS AT THE OPERA

Sir Harrison Birtwistle's classic re-telling of the Arthurian legend *Gawain* with Sir John Tomlinson, Britten's *Albert Herring* and Poulenc's uproarious comedy *Les Mamelles de Tirésias*.

TOTAL IMMERSION & STUNNING NEW WORKS

Day-long events devoted to Thea Musgrave and Villa-Lobos plus a celebration of Stravinsky's *The Rite of Spring*. Premieres from composers including Tristan Murail, Colin Matthews and Esa-Pekka Salonen.

A TASTE OF FRANCE

A rich array of works by French composers new and old, performed by stars of the Parisian music scene.

JOIN US AT THE BARBICAN IN SEPTEMBER

bbc.co.uk/symphonyorchestra
for full details and to sign up to our free e-newsletter

Follow us

 twitter.com/bbcso

 facebook.com/bbcso

barbican

Box Office
020 7638 8891
barbican.org.uk

BBC SINGERS

Second to none in their superb performances of a thrillingly diverse range of music, the BBC Singers bring you the very best from composers at the heart of the choral tradition and from today's brightest talents. Hear them in venues across London, the UK and beyond, on BBC Radio 3 and online.

MILTON COURT

Join the BBC Singers in the stunning surroundings of London's newest concert hall for a remarkable series of concerts featuring leading choral conductors and soloists and great repertoire.

ST PAUL'S KNIGHTSBRIDGE

A series of free concert recordings in the Victorian splendour of St Paul's Knightsbridge featuring glorious choral music from the Renaissance to the twenty-first century.

SINGERS AT SIX

Les Six at Six, *Schumann and Friends*, *Shostakovich, Stalin and Soviet Russia* and *Magyar Music*. Four early-evening concerts in St Giles Cripplegate, across the lake from the Barbican, complementing the BBC Symphony Orchestra's concert the same evening.

bbc.co.uk/singers for full details of all events, to buy tickets, to sign up for our free e-newsletter and to find out about our exciting learning projects.

Nearly all concerts are broadcast on BBC Radio 3 and streamed online via the Radio 3 website.

Follow us

 twitter.com/bbcsingers   facebook.com/bbcsingers

BBC Singers photo © Sophie Laslett

BBC RADIO 3

EDINBURGH INTERNATIONAL FESTIVAL

9 August – 1 September 2013

Don't miss the unmissable... book your trip and join us

Royal Concertgebouw Orchestra and Daniele Gatti / Opéra de Lyon / **Bang on a Can All-Stars** / Mitsuko Uchida / **Oper Frankfurt** / Pierre Laurent-Aimard and Marco Stroppa / **Bavarian Radio Symphony Orchestra and Mariss Jansons** / Mahler Symphonies 2 and 9 / **Bartók** *Bluebeard's Castle* / Verdi Requiem / **Daniil Trifonov** / Purcell *Dido and Aeneas* / **Prokofiev** *Alexander Nevsky* **conducted by Valery Gergiev** / Scottish Opera and The Opera Group *American Lulu* / **Chamber Orchestra of Europe and Yannick Nézet-Séguin** / The Sixteen / **Ian Bostridge** / Ensemble musikFabrik / **Philip Glass Ensemble** *La Belle et la Bête* / Patti Smith / **Russian National Orchestra and Mikhail Pletnev** / Beethoven *Fidelio* / **Nikolai Lugansky**…

View the full programme and book online at eif.co.uk or call 0131 473 2000 for a free copy of the Festival brochure.

·EDINBVRGH· THE CITY OF EDINBURGH COUNCIL

CREATIVE SCOTLAND ALBA | CHRUTHACHAIL

Supported by the City of Edinburgh Council and Creative Scotland. Charity No SC004694.

Backing our most precious resources.

Arts and culture.

BP Summer Big Screens brought the arts and the British public together in the unique, unforgettable setting of Trafalgar Square, as part of Metamorphosis: Titian 2012.

BP has been supporting the art and culture that inspires the British public for more than 30 years. We continue with support for the Royal Opera House, Tate Britain, the National Portrait Gallery and the British Museum.

Find out more at facebook.com/bpuk

WELCOME TO THE
2013 BBC PROMS

It's a great thrill to welcome you to the 2013 BBC Proms – a festival unique in presenting such a vast array of leading orchestras, conductors and soloists from around the world over a jam-packed eight weeks. Across more than 90 concerts – and a similar number of free events designed to extend and further enrich your Proms experience – we aim to offer a summer of music-making that allows for the most diverse and exciting musical journeys.

Among this year's highlights are the first ever performance of Wagner's four *Ring* cycle operas in a single Proms festival, a Tchaikovsky symphony cycle, the first Proms devoted to gospel music and to urban pop, the return of Doctor Who (in the 50th-birthday year of the popular TV series), two film music nights and musicians including Daniel Barenboim, Django Bates, Joshua Bell, Joseph Calleja, Fazer, Valery Gergiev, Mariss Jansons, Lorin Maazel, Laura Marling, Midori, Naturally 7, Sir Antonio Pappano, The Stranglers and Mitsuko Uchida.

Add to that a startling roster of new music – commissions and other premieres have been at the heart of the Proms over our 118-year history – and you get a sense of how the Proms is continuing to push musical boundaries and to lead our audiences to stimulating musical discoveries. The first free main-evening Prom – featuring our annual performance of Beethoven's 'Choral' Symphony – is another sign of our desire to draw new audiences to classical music.

It's a huge pleasure this year to welcome Sakari Oramo to his first Proms performances as the new Chief Conductor of the resident ensemble of the Proms, the BBC Symphony Orchestra. His love of British and new music – and of the Proms – promises exciting years ahead with him at the orchestra's helm. Marin Alsop, who made such an impact with her São Paulo orchestra last year, makes her Last Night debut, joined by star soloists Joyce DiDonato and Nigel Kennedy.

> Across more than 90 concerts
> … we aim to offer a summer
> of music-making that allows
> for the most diverse and
> exciting musical journeys.

The Proms was set up to offer the highest-quality classical music to the largest possible audience. Following the extraordinary summer of 2012 in London and across the UK, we are again looking to reach huge audiences in the Royal Albert Hall and Cadogan Hall as well as through our UK and global broadcasts. An innovation this year is the simultaneous Proms broadcasts on a number of BBC radio stations, in addition to the TV transmissions and live coverage on the BBC's home of classical music, Radio 3. Radios 1, 1Xtra, 2, 4 Extra, 6 Music and the Asian Network join us on specially selected occasions. Other opportunities too – including the BBC iPlayer and social media – have transformed our ability to reach new audiences in ways of which Proms founder-conductor Henry Wood could never even have dreamt. With another full calendar of contextual events in our popular Proms Plus series, the lunchtime, matinee and late-night series, the Proms in the Park concerts around the UK on the Last Night and lots of participation opportunities, the festival is again so much more than just the main evening concerts in the Royal Albert Hall.

For the eighth year running the Promming (standing) places are held at only £5.00. This represents extraordinary value for money. For example, to be able to hear Daniel Barenboim and his Berlin Staatsoper forces perform Wagner's *Ring* cycle for as little as

Clockwise from top left: Richard Wagner, who makes a splash in the bicentenary year of his birth, with the first complete *Ring* cycle in a single Proms festival; pre-Prom crowds gather around the Royal Albert Hall; Nigel Kennedy, who performs Vivaldi's *The Four Seasons* and returns to add sparkle to the Last Night

£20 (or less, if you buy a season ticket!) represents a once-in-a-lifetime opportunity. It is remarkable that Barenboim, one of the leading interpreters of the composer, has never conducted any of Wagner's operas in the UK. This chance at this price is only possible thanks to the BBC's running and subsidy of the Proms, made possible by the TV licence-fee payers.

British music continues to play an important part in the Proms this summer. The centenary of Benjamin Britten's birth

allows us to place his music in context, not least through including the music of his friend and contemporary Michael Tippett, still far too little heard in our concert halls. There are plenty of chances to enjoy his music, notably in a rare complete performance of his opera *The Midsummer Marriage*, conducted by longtime Proms favourite and Tippett devotee Sir Andrew Davis, who also conducts Britten's *Billy Budd*, fresh from the Glyndebourne Festival. As well as Tippett, we'll hear music ▶

Finding yourself in a good bookshop. Second only to losing yourself in one.

Waterstones

Clockwise from top left: The Doctor Who Prom invades again; pianist Mitsuko Uchida breaks her Proms absence of almost 20 years; rapper, songwriter and DJ Fazer joins the BBC Symphony Orchestra for the Urban Classic Prom; following his Beethoven symphony cycle last year, Daniel Barenboim brings his Berlin Staatsoper forces to perform Wagner's operatic epic, *The Ring*

Every concert is broadcast live on BBC Radio 3 and online and 26 are televised ... or catch them via the Proms website for seven days after broadcast.

by Malcolm Arnold, Lennox Berkeley, Imogen Holst, George Lloyd, Elizabeth Maconchy, Priaulx Rainier, Edmund Rubbra and William Walton, among others. Vaughan Williams kicks us off in grand style with his *A Sea Symphony* on the opening night and during the summer we also hear the world premiere of an orchestration the BBC has commissioned from Anthony Payne of his haunting *Four Last Songs*.

In recent years we have made a feature of British composers not celebrating particular birthdays or anniversaries and this year the spotlight falls on Granville Bantock, a significant figure in British musical life in the first part of the 20th century. In addition to other works, I hope that his *Celtic Symphony* for string orchestra and six harps will find new admirers when it receives its Proms premiere.

There are featured artists too – Proms debut artists violinist Vilde Frang and trumpeter Tine Thing Helseth appear more than once, as do British pianist Imogen Cooper and Russian conductor Vasily Petrenko – who, in addition to his National Youth Orchestra of Great Britain appearance, brings his new orchestra, the Oslo Philharmonic, for two eagerly awaited concerts in the final week of the festival. Mariss Jansons, in his 70th-birthday year, conducts two concerts with his Bavarian Radio Symphony Orchestra. His Proms appearances are always something special and it will be a thrill also to welcome back pianist Mitsuko Uchida (who appears alongside Jansons) after a Proms absence of almost 20 years.

Every concert is broadcast live on BBC Radio 3 and online and 26 are televised. If you are not able to join us in person for the Proms, there are plenty of chances to catch them wherever you are via the Proms website for seven days after broadcast. I wish you a summer full of exciting music and I hope you'll find much to enjoy in the 2013 BBC Proms. •

Roger Wright

Roger Wright
Director, BBC Proms

WELCOME | 11

BBC Symphony Chorus

Join us

The BBC Symphony Chorus is one of the UK's finest and most distinctive amateur choirs. In its appearances with the BBC Symphony Orchestra, the Chorus performs a wide range of exciting and challenging repertoire. Most performances are broadcast on BBC Radio 3.

As resident chorus for the BBC Proms, the BBC Symphony Chorus takes part in a number of concerts each season, usually including the First and Last Night. Appearances in 2013 include Tippett's *The Midsummer Marriage* with the BBC SO, BBC Singers and Sir Andrew Davis and Szymanowski's Symphony No. 3 with the BBC National Orchestra and Chorus of Wales.

Performances in the BBC SO's 2013–14 Barbican season include Elgar's *The Apostles* and *The Dream of Gerontius*, Berlioz's *L'enfance du Christ*, and Fauré's *Requiem*. In November the Chorus performs at the Royal Albert Hall and in Snape Maltings, celebrating Britten's centenary.

Would you like to join us?

If you are an experienced choral singer who would like to work on new and challenging music, as well as key choral works, then the BBC Symphony Chorus would like to hear from you. Membership is free!

To find out more about the Chorus, including details of upcoming auditions and our next Open Rehearsal, visit **bbc.co.uk/symphonychorus** or contact the Chorus Administrator.

Email: bbcsc@bbc.co.uk Tel: 020 7765 4715

Ear fresheners

B B C *Concert* ORCHESTRA

ALL AROUND
THE RING

In the bicentenary of Richard Wagner's birth, Daniel Barenboim conducts a complete cycle
of *The Ring*. **BARRY MILLINGTON** unravels the mythical and psychological forces behind
this epic undertaking, which – together with three further Wagner operas
this summer – offers a uniquely immersive view of the composer

Every new generation thrills to the power of myth and legend, especially when unfurled with the sweep of an epic. From Homer's Greek *Odyssey* to the Finnish *Kalevala*, and from King Arthur and his Knights of the Round Table to *The Lord of the Rings,* great narratives have throughout the ages captured the imagination of audiences young and old. That is one reason for the enduring appeal of Wagner's operatic tetralogy *Der Ring des Nibelungen* ('The Ring of the Nibelung'). Its story – or, rather, collection of stories – woven from ancient Norse myth, with its sword-wielding, dragon-slaying heroes, castles in the sky, magic potions, lumbering giants, scheming dwarves and self-immolating heroines, has all the ingredients of a blockbuster success.

The complex interweaving of mythical strands that makes up *The Ring* – Wagner appropriated characters and elements from the medieval Scandinavian eddas and sagas, as well as the Middle High German epic poem *Das Nibelungenlied, c*1200, welding them into a sprawling but undeniably powerful drama – resulted in a vast work beyond the resources of any existing theatre to mount. This, it has to be said, was always Wagner's intention. Almost from the start – the initial conception of *The Ring* was in 1848, the final touches made to the score in 1874 – Wagner was

thinking in terms of a special festival along the lines of those celebrated by the Greeks (spread over several days with a trilogy of dramas followed by a less serious satyr play). As with the Greek model, he wanted his audience members to assemble unencumbered by the pressures of their daily work, able to experience the drama with a fresh mind; both heart and mind were to be stimulated and nourished. The performances were, at this early stage, to be offered free of charge; no less utopian was

the idea that the theatre itself should be demolished after the performance: in one letter, Wagner even suggests that the score should also be burnt into the bargain. After a quarter of a century's struggle to complete the work, followed by equally titanic efforts to raise the necessary funds – to create a purpose-built

> Wagner was grappling with fundamental psychosexual issues that affect us all – not necessarily in our daily lives but in the world of imagination and fantasy that we also inhabit.

theatre, and to recruit and rehearse the cast and orchestra – the notion of piling the theatre and score onto Brünnhilde's funeral pyre was quietly and unsurprisingly forgotten.

As with all genuine myths, there's more to the supernatural profusion within Wagner's *Ring* than meets the eye. The characters were long ago identified as archetypes of the collective unconscious. The hero (Siegfried), the wise old man (Wotan), the great mother (Erda) all frequent this terrain; so too do ▶

Immortal sisters of Brünnhilde: the Valkyries (warrior-maidens), who swoop down dramatically from the skies in Act 3 of *Die Walküre* (the second instalment of Wagner's *The Ring*); coloured photograph printed in the magazine *Le Théâtre*, 1899

Wotan, king of the Germanic pagan gods; engraving from *Zeitgenössischen Kunstblättern* (Breitkopf und Härtel, 1900)

the Freudian/Jungian concepts of ego, id, anima/animus and shadow. 'Myth is an anonymous expression of collective truths,' Wagner's director-grandson Wieland once said and his productions of the 1960s famously explored the works from the perspective of depth psychology, giving voice to the unconscious, just as Robert Donington in his landmark study *Wagner's 'Ring' and its Symbols* (1963) brought the insights of Jungian analysis to his interpretation of the cycle. Whether or not we find this particular approach illuminating, there's no doubt that Wagner was grappling here with fundamental psychosexual issues that affect us all – not necessarily in our daily lives but in the world of imagination and fantasy that we also inhabit.

Siegfried longs to know more about the father and mother from whom he has been separated since birth, while his father Siegmund's movements are shadowed by a prowling, absent father figure of his own (Wotan) who has impossibly high hopes of him. Siegmund falls ecstatically in love with his twin sister, while the sleeping beauty whom Siegfried awakens with a kiss turns out to be his aunt. The frivolous objection to Freudian/Jungian psychoanalysis – 'but I've never had those kind of feelings for my mother/father/sibling/aunt' – misses the point. None of us is immune to the traumatic ruptures that occur at birth, in childhood and adolescence when we vie for attention with others in the family unit. Every father should be able to identify with

the torment of Wotan as he deals with his errant daughter, just as anybody who has ever experienced a forbidden or unrealisable desire will recognise similar impulses in the behaviour of characters such as Siegmund and Sieglinde.

Along with the epic conception of the drama of *The Ring* went a massive augmentation of the resources needed for an operatic performance. Where Classical symphonies were scored for double wind and brass (2 flutes, 2 oboes, 2 trumpets, etc.) and Wagner's *Lohengrin* for triple, *The Ring* calls for quadruple forces (3 flutes plus piccolo, 3 oboes plus cor anglais, 3 clarinets plus bass clarinet, 3 trumpets plus bass trumpet, and so on) together with an unprecedented body of strings (16 first violins, 16 seconds, 12 violas,

Not every opera company can muster the resources to mount a *Ring* and a production of the cycle is often viewed as something of a virility test.

12 cellos, 8 double basses), not to mention 6 harps (plus another offstage), 18 anvils, thunder machine, forging hammer and cow horns. Little wonder Wagner steered his project away from provincial theatres such as Weimar or Stuttgart. But not even the royal court theatre at Munich could do justice to it, or so Wagner felt. His chief sponsor, Ludwig II of Bavaria, frustrated with delays in the completion and mounting of the cycle, insisted – to Wagner's fury and without his co-operation – on performances there of at least the first two operas, *Das Rheingold* and *Die Walküre*, in 1869 and 1870.

Similar considerations apply today: not every company can muster the resources to mount a *Ring* and, by the same token, a production of the cycle is often viewed as something of a virility test. In this Wagner bicentenary year, fully staged productions have been lined up in a dozen or so European cities (including Paris, Frankfurt, Berlin, Bayreuth, Milan and Vienna), as well as New York, Seattle and Melbourne. Though the Royal Opera, Covent Garden, gave four performances of the cycle last autumn as an upbeat to the Wagner bicentenary, only one UK staging can be seen this year – in a converted chicken shed at Longborough in Gloucestershire (Wagner would have approved of the theatre's lowly origins). Economic ▶

THE STORY OF THE RING

A brief synopsis of the four operas

A lecherous, hunchbacked Nibelung dwarf by the name of Alberich is thwarted by a trio of cruel water-sprites, otherwise known as the Rhinemaidens. They foolishly let drop that the gold they are guarding in the depths of the waters could be forged into an all-powerful ring by one willing to give up the joys of love. In revenge, Alberich seizes the gold and makes off with it to Nibelheim, where he builds an empire based on fear, slave labour and presumably joyless procreation. Wotan, the chief god, meanwhile, has been presented with the bill for his new castle, Valhalla, built by the giants Fasolt and Fafner who are now demanding compensation in the form of Freia, the goddess of love. Hearing of the Nibelung's magic ring, which supposedly confers on its owner limitless power – a claim whose veracity is to be sorely tested over the course of the cycle – Wotan decides he wants it for himself. Descending to Nibelheim through a sulphur cleft, Wotan, with the help of his shady sidekick Loge, overpowers Alberich with a cheap trick involving a frog and seizes the ring. Alberich lays a curse on it, but in any case the ring is carried off by one of the giants, Fafner, as payment for his construction services.

Realising that he's got himself into a position ill-befitting the leader of the gods, but wishing to get the ring back, Wotan sires a hero, as one does, to help him to acquire it. That hero, Siegmund, however, blots his copybook by falling for his long-lost twin sister, Sieglinde; their union outrages Wotan's more conventionally minded consort, Fricka, who demands Siegmund's death. Sent to prepare him for it, Wotan's favourite daughter Brünnhilde, in an uprush of compassion, tries instead to defend him. As punishment she's put to sleep on a rock, surrounded by a fire. Siegmund's son, Siegfried, is the one who heroically confronts the fire to claim his bride, but when he unwisely decides to go off in search of deeds of glory, leaving Brünnhilde once again on the rock, he falls foul of another cheap little trick – this time perpetrated by Alberich's son, Hagen, who drugs the hero and sends him off to claim his own Brünnhilde to be the wife of Hagen's half-brother Gunther. Brünnhilde's fury at Siegfried's treachery leads to his murder by Hagen. Brünnhilde immolates herself on Siegfried's funeral pyre, Valhalla and all the gods go up in flames and a new order beckons.

Costume designs for Brünnhilde (*left*) and Wotan (*right*) by Carl Emil Doepler, for the first complete performance of *The Ring*, in Bayreuth, 13–17 August 1876

conditions have forced imaginative solutions such as shared productions (Berlin/Milan) and abridged versions (Dijon), as well as cancellations. Concert performances have a major role to play in such circumstances and the transferral of Daniel Barenboim's *Ring* to this summer's Proms from the Staatsoper Berlin (minus the staging) is a matter for celebration. Barenboim has established himself over the past three decades as one of the major interpreters of Wagner; many would place him right at the top of any Wagnerian superhero league. Certainly his profile in this area has remained high, not least because of his willingness to fly the Wagnerian flag in troubled waters – attempting, so far with limited success, to make it possible to perform Wagner's music in Israel. Because of the composer's undeniable anti-Semitism and

the way it was exploited by the Nazis, Wagner is clearly identified in many people's minds with that ideology. Modern directors have long since confronted the issues raised by such associations, in productions that acknowledge the impossibility of erecting a firewall between a composer's personal convictions and his art – at least in the case of Wagner.

The Ring is by no means the only work of Wagner's to grapple with big themes. Also to be heard at this summer's Proms are three operas – *Tannhäuser*, *Tristan and Isolde* and *Parsifal* – each of which tackles in its own way the kind of topics – art, politics, race, religion, sex – which it was once considered impolite to raise at dinner parties, but which most of us recognise to be the meaty issues that define the values of civilised society. Oscillating between sacred and profane love (the traditional

THE RING AND I
The pull of the ring on those around it

Why, when Wotan steals the ring from Alberich, does the latter not harness its magic powers in order to prevent him? And why, when Siegfried, disguised as Gunther, menaces Brünnhilde on her rock, can she not stop him in his tracks by brandishing the ring? The ring clearly means different things to different people. To Siegfried it's a worthless trinket, to Brünnhilde a token of love. In fact, the only character who seems to be able to use its magical properties to his advantage is Alberich, when he enslaves the Nibelungs to amass his wealth. Of course, the ring is cursed, but it could be argued that the events which unfold under that curse – Fafner killing Fasolt, Siegfried betraying Brünnhilde and being murdered – would have happened anyway, given the development of the plot.

Perhaps we should see the ring not so much as a supernatural do-it-all gadget but more as a symbol. If the lust for power and the desire to accumulate wealth corrupt the capacity to love, then the ring, which as a stage prop is a visualisation of those impulses, represents the moral conflict at the heart of the tetralogy. The mechanical details of the plot are riddled with absurdities and inconsistencies, but they do little to diminish the power of the work.

The Ride of the Valkyries: the warrior-maidens descend to transport the fallen heroes to Valhalla, home of the gods (painting dated 1876)

polarity of Madonna and whore), represented by Elisabeth and Venus respectively, *Tannhäuser* negotiates an opposition between the two, finally breaking out of the straitjacket of stereotypes. *Tristan and Isolde* is on one level another riff on the timeless theme of love and death that has served opera well since its inception four centuries ago, but it also transcends its scenario of a conventional love story to offer a profound meditation on the nature of the material world, on the metaphysics of subjectivity and on the mysteries of human existence itself. A superficial view of *Parsifal* might suggest that Wagner's final opera was a religious work that also sets out a reactionary position on sex (advocating celibacy as the solution to erotic temptation) and race (redemption of the 'lower' races by the purity of an Aryan Christ's blood). In fact, *Parsifal* contains its own critique of these tendencies: not only does it interrogate humankind's apparent need for religious belief, but it also wrestles with the issues of sex and race in ways that afford profound insights into the human condition. This year, the Proms promises a plethora of transcendental music of often unearthly beauty, but for those so inclined there's also an opportunity for a good deal of soul-searching. ●

Barry Millington is Chief Music Critic of the *London Evening Standard*, editor of *The Wagner Journal* and Co-Director of the festival Wagner 200. His new book, *Richard Wagner: The Sorcerer of Bayreuth*, was recently published by Thames & Hudson.

WAGNER AT THE PROMS

The Ring
Staatskapelle Berlin/Daniel Barenboim

Das Rheingold
PROM 14 • 22 JULY

Die Walküre
PROM 15 • 23 JULY

Siegfried
PROM 18 • 26 JULY

Götterdämmerung
PROM 20 • 28 JULY

• • •

The Mastersingers – overture
PROM 75 • 7 SEPTEMBER

Parsifal
PROM 57 • 25 AUGUST

Rienzi – overture
PROM 56 • 24 AUGUST

Tannhäuser
PROM 29 • 4 AUGUST

Tristan and Isolde
PROM 19 • 27 JULY

Wesendonck-Lieder
PROM 53 • 22 AUGUST

Exquisite dining at the Royal Albert Hall

ROYAL ALBERT HALL

The Royal Albert Hall has three stylish restaurants serving exquisite food by deliciously different caterers *"rhubarb"*. During the Proms they will be offering special promotions to Guide readers:

CODA

ELGAR

café consort

BERRY BROS & RUDD LTD
No3 BAR

Enjoy a complimentary half bottle of house wine per person when you order three courses from the à la carte menu *

Enjoy a complimentary half bottle of house wine per person when you order three courses from the à la carte menu *

Enjoy a complimentary upgrade to the 'wine and dine' package when you order a three course set menu. This includes two glasses of house wine per person.

Discover the new Berry Bros. & Rudd No3 Bar where you can enjoy Britain's oldest wine and spirit merchant's special selection of drinks such as No3 Gin & tonic.

*Offer does not apply to the set menu. Please present this advert when ordering your meal to redeem the offer. Available to people of 18 years old and above.

*Offer does not apply to the set menu. Please present this advert when ordering your meal to redeem the offer. Available to people of 18 years old and above.

Please present this advert when ordering your meal to redeem the offer. Available to people of 18 years old and above.

Located in the basement. A delicious selection of food is also available such as sharing boards and gin and tonic cured gravadlax.

Please note that pre-show dining is available to ticket holders only in Coda and the Elgar Room. Your tickets will be required to gain entry to the building. A Café Bar in the Meitar foyer at Door 12 will be newly opened from 7.30am Monday - Friday and 9.00am Saturday - Sunday without the requirement of tickets. For more details, please visit the website www.royalalberthall.com or call 0845 401 5034.

Julianne Moore

TCHAIKOVSKY AND THE
RUSSIAN SYMPHONY

As the BBC Proms presents a complete cycle of Tchaikovsky's symphonies,
DAVID FANNING credits the famously self-critical composer with putting Russia on the symphonic map

Tchaikovsky's symphonies are a tale of two halves. The first half begins in 1866, with 'Daydreams on a Wintry Road', the composer's own title for the first movement of his First Symphony, which feels much like an accompaniment to a fairy-tale sleigh-ride, albeit minus the bells, and it ends in 1875 with a boisterous Polish dance – the finale of his Third Symphony. The second half begins two years later, with an imperious blast on the horns, joined by the rest of the brass, then silenced by thunderclaps on the full orchestra, before an anxiously hyperventilating waltz; and Tchaikovsky himself confirmed what is already fairly unmistakable: that this is a drama of Fate and of Mankind's struggle to evade it. His symphonic career ended barely two months before his death, with the tragic slow finale to his Sixth Symphony ebbing into abject gloom.

Why the music sounds and feels like that, and how it gets from feelgood to despair, demands a little thought about Tchaikovsky's life and career and a lot about the position of the symphony in Russia.

In 1824, the year Beethoven completed his Ninth Symphony, the 20-year-old Mikhail Glinka – later to become known as the 'father of Russian music' – made the first of three incomplete attempts to write a symphony. He had next to nothing to build on in terms of a homeland tradition and he blamed his ultimate failure on the incompatibility between folkloric themes – which he felt to be *de rigueur* for Russia's entry into the symphonic arena – and 'Germanic' ways of working them out.

In principle the task should not have been so arduous. Beethoven himself had incorporated Ukrainian tunes in the first two of his 'Razumovsky' String Quartets and several of Haydn's symphonic themes have supposedly folk origins. But in practice the perceived tension between indigenous materials and Germanic ways of treating them remained a challenge for Russian symphonists. It took the genius of Tchaikovsky to find lasting solutions. Broadly speaking that meant either smoothing over the edges, as in the first three symphonies, or roughening them up, as in the last three.

> It took the genius of Tchaikovsky to find lasting solutions to the challenges facing Russian symphonists in the 19th century.

Tchaikovsky was helped along his symphonic path by the example of Robert Schumann, whose four completed symphonies (composed between 1841 and 1851) had narrowed the horizons of Beethoven's legacy, but at the same time packaged it in a form that was easier to emulate. Meanwhile, Tchaikovsky's own teacher Anton Rubinstein had set about establishing a professionalised concert life as well as pedagogic institutions in Russia, and Anton's brother Nikolay – also a renowned pianist, who famously rejected ►

Tchaikovsky's First Piano Concerto as unplayable – had engaged Tchaikovsky to teach at the newly founded Moscow Conservatory of Music. Although a reluctant teacher, Tchaikovsky at least had a stable position from which to compose his first three symphonies. Just as importantly, the example of Anton Rubinstein's own academically correct but imaginatively impoverished symphonies gave him something to kick against.

Tchaikovsky's First Symphony (1866, revised 1874) incorporates folk materials with consummate smoothness, but it also teases out thematic links between the outer movements, very much in the manner of Schumann's Fourth. Also on the Germanic side of the equation is the well-behaved fugal writing in the finale. In the Second Symphony of 1872 (revised 1879–80), dubbed 'The Little Russian' with reference to its Ukrainian folk materials, the folk/symphonic dichotomy is even more adroitly finessed. The five-movement Third Symphony of 1875, nicknamed the 'Polish' after its *Tempo di polacca* finale, downplays the folk element and instead attempts a more ambitious synthesis: of character-pieces (the three middle movements) and symphonic weight. Justly or otherwise, the results are less universally admired. (Henry Wood, founder-conductor of the

The Moscow Conservatory, where Tchaikovsky was a Professor of Music Theory. It has borne the name of the composer since 1940 and a monument erected in his honour in 1954 still stands outside the building today

Proms, gave the London premiere of the first three symphonies – as well as the UK premiere of *Manfred* in 1898 – and conducted all six numbered symphonies in 1902.)

Polish rhythms would find their place in the Fourth Symphony, too, but with their role greatly enhanced, since they now define the profile of the opening Fate theme, with all the menace and sense of alarm that goes with it. The midway divide between Tchaikovsky's six numbered symphonies gets sharper the closer you look at it. In the months before the Fourth (composed between May 1877 and January 1878), he had struck up a correspondence with a rich widow, Nadezhda von Meck, who became his benefactor and thereby enabled him to give up teaching at the Conservatory. Then in July 1877 he embarked on what proved to be a disastrous marriage, to his former pupil Antonina Milyukova, which brought to a head a drastic psychological crisis – much mythologised in popular

commentary but at its core quite real. In very different ways these life-events forced Tchaikovsky to define himself as a creative artist, which meant not abandoning the evocative charm and balletic grace of the first three symphonies but confronting these with opposing forces and scaling up the structures into symbolic life-and-death struggles.

A crucial enabling force in this process was the model of the programme symphony, as in Berlioz's *Symphonie fantastique* and Liszt's *A Faust Symphony*, with Tchaikovsky's application of their brazenly melodramatic elements. These did not go uncriticised. In a famous letter to von Meck – dedicatee of the Fourth Symphony – outlining how a programmatic understanding of the piece might go, the composer was full of apologies. He was on the defensive, too, in a letter to his pupil Sergey Taneyev, responding to the latter's criticism of his incorporation of balletic and humorous music. What neither man put

Nadezhda von Meck (1831–94), patroness of Tchaikovsky and dedicatee of his Fourth Symphony

Tchaikovsky worked day and night on the First Symphony to achieve 'an exellence in the tradition of great German composers', which was so much against his gift as a great melodist. But, after working 'around the rules' of the Classical form of the symphony, all his later compositions proved that he was truly unique.

GIANANDREA NOSEDA ON SYMPHONY NO. 2

I love Tchaikovsky's Second Symphony as I love all of Tchaikovsky's music! This symphony is slightly neglected compared with his more famous works, but it's no less beautiful, honest or inspired. I'm convinced that the Second Symphony will cast light on a different aspect of Tchaikovsky's personality and will help us to better know his emotions and, ultimately, his genius.

KIRILL KARABITS ON SYMPHONY NO. 3

I feel strongly that Tchaikovsky's Third is the last symphony where conflict is not the main engine to drive musical structure and development. He explores a new five-movement form, which almost gives this symphony the feel of a suite, with very aristocratic and noble-sounding first and last movements. Conducting this symphony is a joy; you simply feel that you are discovering a great work that remained unfairly overshadowed by his other symphonies.

JAC VAN STEEN ON SYMPHONY NO. 4

All great works of art demonstrate the challenge of becoming conscious of opposites. Tchaikovsky's Fourth Symphony deals with overcoming these contrasts. The first movement, born out of the chaos that is an inevitable part of this process, is concerned with darkness and fate, leading to a euphoric finale where the energy turns into light and joy.

Tchaikovsky's programme symphony *Manfred* took its inspiration from Byron's dramatic poem, a scene from which is depicted in this watercolour, *Manfred and the Alpine Witch*, by John Martin (1789–1854)

his finger on was that all the Fourth Symphony's evocations of the dance serve as means of dramatic intensification. Their material, conventionally associated with well-being, is constantly questioned – as in the first movement's nervous syncopations and slithery chromaticisms – and even assailed, by the implacable Fate theme.

Reviewing Schumann's 'Rhenish' Symphony, a work he otherwise loved, Tchaikovsky observed that 'the music of the finale, with its forcedly merry rhythm and heavy-handed jocularity, offers nothing especially interesting'. Still, as his subconscious must have recognised, forced merriment may itself be a perfectly valid mode of expression. So the extroversion of his own

Fourth Symphony finale – unlike his Violin Concerto, composed at almost exactly the same time – is exciting precisely because it is so unsure of itself. Here, rather than attempting any sort of reconciliation, a 'static' folk-song theme ('In the field a little birch-tree stood') rubs up against dynamic 'Germanic' processes (long paragraphs built on confrontation, crisis and climax), until Fate issues a crushing reality-check. Mahler and Shostakovich are just around the corner.

From now on, the ground is constantly threatening to open beneath Tchaikovsky's feet. Triumphalism teeters on a precipice, as in the finale of the Fifth Symphony (1888), and lyricism is recast as escapism, as in the first movement of the Sixth (the 'Pathétique', ▸

BBC Philharmonic

Inspiration with every note
A season of music celebrating
Manchester's contribution to musical
life with the BBC Philharmonic.
Chief Conductor Juanjo Mena

BBC Philharmonic
Season 2013/14

bbc.co.uk/philharmonic
facebook.com/bbcphilharmonic | @bbcphilharmonic

BBC RADIO 3
90 – 93 FM

Supported by
Salford City Council

THE bridgewater HALL

> What is beyond dispute is that Tchaikovsky's inner demons, allied to his supreme craft, helped to put Russia once and for all on the symphonic map.

1893). Folk materials fade further into the background; in their place we find an even more pervasive Fate theme in the Fifth and a quotation from the Orthodox Requiem in the first movement of the 'Pathétique'. Both works open in murky gloom, which the Fifth eventually vanquishes, while the Sixth sinks back into valedictory anguish. The boldness of these psychological dramas contrasts with competent but one-dimensional near-contemporary Russian symphonies by Rimsky-Korsakov, Taneyev and even the young Scriabin. It also overshadows Tchaikovsky's own more conventionally heroic programme symphony, *Manfred* (composed in 1885, in between Nos. 4 and 5).

In between his Fifth and Sixth Symphonies, Tchaikovsky conceived and drafted, but later rejected, an even more ambitious symphony, with the working title 'Life'. Here the first movement was to convey eruptiveness, the second love, the third disappointment and the fourth death. However little detailed connection there may be with the eventual 'Pathétique' Symphony, the existential resonance of those topics is clear. And if there is any doubt as to the extent to which the 'Pathétique' itself lodged in the imagination of later Russian composers, we need only consider the echoes of its final coda

at the corresponding point in Shostakovich's Fourth, or of the rushing scales of the third movement's exhilarating march-scherzo in the finale of the same composer's Tenth.

It has even been argued, not implausibly, that some of the rough-edged transitions in the 'Pathétique' look ahead even further in the Soviet symphonic tradition, to the likes of Schnittke and Shchedrin. How much any of this comes across depends to some extent on what an individual conductor chooses to highlight or downplay. What is beyond dispute is that Tchaikovsky's inner demons, allied to his supreme craft, helped to put Russia once and for all on the symphonic map. ●

David Fanning is a Professor of Music at the University of Manchester, the author of books on Nielsen, Shostakovich and Weinberg and a critic for *Gramophone* and *The Daily Telegraph*.

PETER OUNDJIAN ON SYMPHONY NO. 5

Tchaikovsky himself seems to have had a love–hate relationship with his Fifth Symphony, initially doubting not only its quality but even its sincerity. If we avoid comparisons with Bruckner or Mahler and listen to the Fifth Symphony as if for the first time, there is no doubting its greatness.

OSMO VÄNSKÄ ON SYMPHONY NO. 6

The 'Pathétique' Symphony – Tchaikovsky's testament?

XIAN ZHANG ON MANFRED

It is said among conductors that the *Manfred* symphony is a great piece only when it's done by a great conductor. I am willing to take on that challenge.

TCHAIKOVSKY SYMPHONIES AT THE PROMS

Symphony No. 1, 'Winter Daydreams'
PROM 68 • 2 SEPTEMBER

Symphony No. 2, 'Little Russian'
PROM 30 • 5 AUGUST

Symphony No. 3, 'Polish'
PROM 42 • 14 AUGUST

Symphony No. 4
PROM 16 • 24 JULY

Symphony No. 5
PROM 27 • 2 AUGUST

Symphony No. 6, 'Pathétique'
PROM 71 • 4 SEPTEMBER

Manfred
PROM 72 • 5 SEPTEMBER

• • •

MORE TCHAIKOVSKY AT THE PROMS

Eugene Onegin – Polonaise; Letter Song
PROM 46 • 17 AUGUST

Fantasy-Overture 'Romeo and Juliet'
PROM 53 • 22 AUGUST

Violin Concerto
PROM 13 • 21 JULY

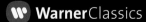

  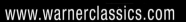

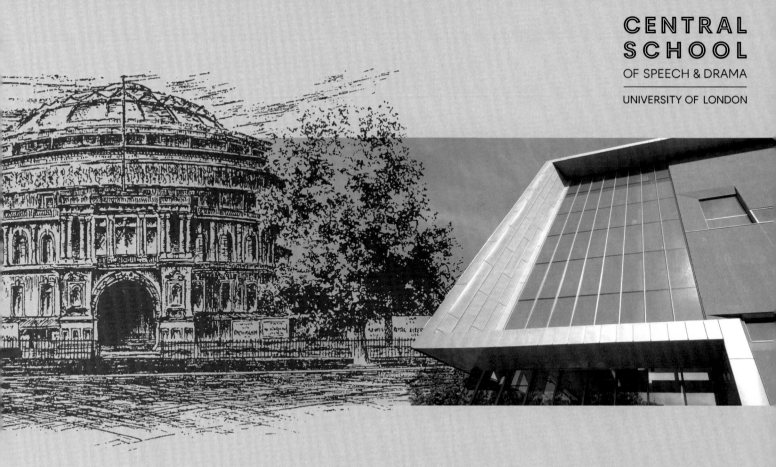

CENTRAL SCHOOL
OF SPEECH & DRAMA
UNIVERSITY OF LONDON

THE ROYAL CENTRAL SCHOOL OF SPEECH AND DRAMA FOUNDED AT THE ROYAL ALBERT HALL IN 1906

Royal Central has a powerful history and global standing. That history begins with its founder Elsie Fogerty, who believed not only in training for the theatre, but in taking drama and poetry to the disadvantaged children of the most depressed areas of London. The School remains passionately committed to engagement across all communities, developing practitioners and researchers who shape the future of theatre and performances across the UK and beyond.

Located at the Embassy Theatre in Swiss Cottage since 1957 and now a college of the University of London, Central was honoured with Royal Title in The Queen's Diamond Jubilee year in recognition of its great history and reputation as a world class institution. As well as undergraduate, postgraduate and research programmes, Royal Central offers short and business courses, and classes for young people between the ages of 6 and 17. Scholarships and bursaries for 2014 are available.

FOR FURTHER INFORMATION: 020 7722 8183 / WWW.CSSD.AC.UK / ENQUIRIES@CSSD.AC.UK

Principal: Professor Gavin Henderson CBE

A POLISH
AWAKENING

In the centenary of Witold Lutosławski's birth, the BBC Proms celebrates this great Polish composer, placing him in the context not only of his contemporaries but also of music from the royal Polish court of almost five centuries earlier. **ADRIAN THOMAS** traces a path between the two eras

Fifty years ago, the only Polish composer recognised as a world figure was Fryderyk Chopin. Yet it was already beginning to dawn on performers, audiences and critics outside Poland that a new wave of composers were creating powerful new music. Heading the list were Witold Lutosławski (1913–94), Krzysztof Penderecki (born 1933) and Henryk Mikołaj Górecki (1933–2010). This summer, the Proms celebrates the centenary of Lutosławski's birth and the 80th birthdays of Penderecki and Górecki. These three, alongside many others, including Andrzej Panufnik (whose centenary falls next year, and who left Poland for the UK in 1954), enriched the international concert repertoire in ways that were unthinkable when Lutosławski was born. As regards the other major Polish composer of the last century, Karol Szymanowski (1882–1937), it was only in the mid-1970s that his works began to achieve proper international attention.

All of these composers were shaped by history. There's nothing unusual in that, of course, except that Polish history has been exceptionally turbulent. For most of the 19th and 20th centuries, creativity across all art forms was thwarted or stifled by occupations, uprisings, wars, invasions and politics to a degree not experienced by composers in many other countries. Composers struggled to get their voices heard. Lutosławski endured more than most, yet he strove to maintain a measured distance from external pressures in order, as he said in 1980, 'to preserve a clarity of expression'. Chopin, on the other hand, as an exile in France, famously made his national heritage a central theme of his music and as such, rightly or wrongly, became emblematic of the Polish spirit.

Yet Polish music did not start or end with Chopin. During the Renaissance, Poland developed a vibrant musical culture as Cracow grew into a major European centre for trade and the arts. Foreign musicians came to work at the royal court there and Polish musicians travelled and worked abroad freely. This was a golden age in Polish culture and its music stands comparison with that elsewhere in

> For most of the 19th and 20th centuries, Polish composers struggled to get their voices heard. Lutosławski endured more than most.

Europe. Despite this, the music of the Polish Renaissance (and Polish Baroque) is still far too little-known outside Poland, so this year's Prom given by the Huelgas Ensemble is a welcome opportunity to hear not only gems such as 'Chwała tobie, Gospodzinie' (Praise to Thee, O Lord, *c*1450) – the earliest-known polyphonic piece with a Polish text, and dedicated to St Stanisław, the country's patron saint – but also the music of foreign composers who came to work in Poland.

By the time of Lutosławski's birth in 1913, such repertoire had long ceased to be a living ►

Karol Szymanowski (1882–1937), one of the first Polish composers to draw inspiration from other cultures and mingle them with his own, resulting in often opulent and exotic sound-worlds

> The exiled Chopin was revered and sentimentalised after his death in 1849 but, with the exception of composer-virtuosos such as Wieniawski and Paderewski, Poland had no cultural profile abroad.

presence in Polish culture. Indeed, one could argue that Poland had not achieved a real cultural identity since it had been partitioned and occupied at the end of the 18th century. The exiled Chopin was revered and sentimentalised after his death in 1849 but, with the exception of composer-virtuosos such as the violinist Henryk Wieniawski and the pianists Juliusz Zarębski and Ignacy Jan Paderewski, Poland had no cultural profile abroad. Thanks to recent initiatives by (largely British) independent record companies, the veil is being slowly lifted from the forgotten Polish music of the second half of the 19th century. But when Szymanowski was a student at the turn of the 20th century, he found little in Warsaw to inspire him and he sought inspiration elsewhere, initially in the German avant-garde (Richard Strauss), then in French music (Debussy and Ravel) and Mediterranean and near-Eastern culture.

During the First World War, Szymanowski sought refuge from the turmoil around him through exoticism, inspired by the Persian mystic Rumi (in the Symphony No. 3, 'The Song of the Night', 1914–16) and the fantastical poetry of his friend Tadeusz Miciński (in the Violin Concerto No. 1, 1916). Only after Poland regained independence as a nation state in 1918 did Szymanowski seek to ground his music in his native soil. This was a deliberate act of solidarity with the new Poland and he set out to establish a Polish musical identity that was independent of German culture and free of the burden of history. He recognised the dangers of isolationism, however, writing in 1920: 'Let all streams springing from universal art mingle freely with ours.' By the end of his life, Szymanowski had mingled German, French, Arabic and Polish cultures, among others, seeking the exotic wherever he looked. En route he demonstrated to younger Polish composers that it was possible to find affinities with their native folk culture ('a fertilising agent') and at the same time create fresh and vigorous music, far from what he once derided as 'the blood-clotted spectre of a polonaise or a mazurka'. Yet, for many composers of the following generation, this already felt out-of-date and, like Szymanowski 30 years earlier, they looked abroad for inspiration.

Szymanowski died before the Second World War, just as Lutosławski was writing his first major orchestral work, the *Symphonic Variations* (1936–8). This sparkling piece looks towards Stravinsky and French neo-Classicism, although there are still traces of Szymanowski's sensuous sound-world. Lutosławski was on the verge of travelling to Paris for further study in 1939 when external events intervened, not for the first time in his life. (His father and uncle had been shot by the Bolsheviks in 1918, when Lutosławski was aged only 5, and one of his brothers would die in a Soviet concentration camp not long after the start of the Second World War. He himself narrowly avoided being taken and executed in the street in Warsaw.) For most of the war he and Panufnik survived by performing piano duets in the city's cafés, making around 200 arrangements of pieces spanning Bach and Schubert to pre-war songs. The only surviving piece from their duetting is one of Lutosławski's most popular, the virtuosic *Variations on a Theme by Paganini* (1941, taking the same theme as popularised by Rachmaninov), which he rearranged and expanded in 1978, giving it a glittering orchestration.

If Lutosławski's instinctive artistic response was to sidestep the traumas of war, Panufnik was more interested in responding directly, as witnessed by his *Tragic Overture* (1942). Its pervasive rhythmic pattern connects it with the BBC's wartime 'V for Victory' Morse-code signal (or, more familiarly, with the characteristic rhythm that opens Beethoven's Fifth Symphony). The reactions

of Lutosławski and Panufnik to the onset of political interference in the arts in post-war Poland were also different. Panufnik, who had studied the scores of Anton Webern before the war, developed his motivically patterned music in ways which placed him at the forefront of young Polish composers. Even though his rarely played *Lullaby* (1947) uses a Polish folk tune, its artfully layered texture has a detached, refined quality that did not fit comfortably with the advancing Communist demands of down-to-earth Socialist Realism. Lutosławski's approach to folk music proved to be less decorative and more symphonic. In his works of the early 1950s, culminating in the ever-popular *Concerto for Orchestra* (1950–54), Lutosławski fulfilled Szymanowski's idea of folk music as a fertilising agent. For the *Concerto*, he chose 11 folk tunes from several dozen that he had carefully selected and then worked them up into one of the great orchestral showpieces. Although it is saturated with folk motifs, it somehow stands independent of its sources, while cannily going along with the Socialist Realist demand for works that traced a path from darkness to a new dawn, from conflict to resolution. The premiere of the *Concerto for Orchestra* was given by the Warsaw Philharmonic, which includes it in its appearance this summer alongside Panufnik's *Tragic Overture* and *Lullaby*, as it makes its Proms debut under its Principal Conductor Antoni Wit.

No Polish composer in 1954 anticipated that, within a couple of years, such aesthetic and stylistic shackles would be cut away and that they would be more or less free to write what they wished. In this new situation, Lutosławski was the most clear-sighted and focused on what in 1957 he called the 'tumult' of the contemporary avant-garde. By 1963,

Ignacy Jan Paderewski (1860–1941), the Polish virtuoso pianist and, later, Prime Minister: one of the few to promote his country's culture abroad during the late-19th and early 20th centuries

when he turned 50, he was beginning to be recognised internationally and his 'mature' language already marked him out as a composer of great distinction. His reputation remains undiminished today, primarily because he was able to match technique with expressivity, producing music that ranges from breathtaking delicacy to fierce immediacy.

Lutosławski's long-standing connection with British musicians began when he met Benjamin Britten and Peter Pears at the 1961 Warsaw Autumn festival, which had kick-started Polish music five years earlier. Lutosławski wrote *Paroles tissées* (1965) for Pears, who gave the premiere under the composer's baton at the Aldeburgh Festival that year. Five years later, Lutosławski completed his Cello Concerto, which had been commissioned by the Royal Philharmonic Society; its dedicatee, Mstislav Rostropovich, gave the premiere in London in October 1970. Lutosławski's work with British orchestras proved to be long-standing, fruitful and much appreciated, not least by the BBC Symphony Orchestra, with which he made his last UK appearance on the podium during the 1993 Proms, when he conducted the UK premiere of his Fourth Symphony.

Whereas *Paroles tissées* inhabits a Surrealist world (shades of Szymanowski), ▶

90 years of classical music interviews, features and reviews... at your fingertips

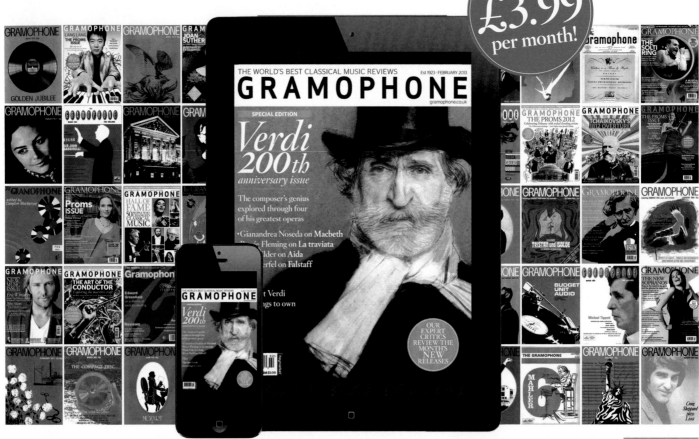

Lutoslawski's Cello Concerto encapsulates the problems facing a Polish composer who insisted that there was no programmatic element in his work, just purely musical drama. Rostropovich, however, immediately identified himself as the protagonist. As far as he was concerned, his own struggles with the Soviet authorities were paralleled in the cello's conflict with the orchestra. Try as he might, Lutosławski could not prevent others from seeing current history being reflected in some of his music. When he came to write his Piano Concerto in 1987–8, he avoided confrontation in favour of a melodic, post-Romantic fantasia that is marked, as ever, by clarity of expression.

Lutosławski was determined to pursue his own path with no obvious connections to Polish culture or history. The next generation had other ideas. Having gone through a much more dissonant and experimental trial by fire in the early 1960s, Penderecki and Górecki modified their language in the 1970s even more radically, like so many composers elsewhere. So it was that Górecki wrote his modal, slow-moving Third Symphony, 'Symphony of Sorrowful Songs', in 1976. At the time, this was a shocking departure from the avant-garde. Its connectivity with Polish history is evident in its incorporation of Polish Lenten hymns, a folk tune, quotes from Beethoven and Chopin, a folk text from the time of Silesian Uprisings after the First World War and a prayer etched on the wall of a Gestapo prison during the Second World War. The links that others have since made between Górecki's symphony and Auschwitz and the Holocaust are entirely spurious. Herein lie the pitfalls of association that Lutosławski was so anxious to avoid.

Lutosławski (*left*) during rehearsals in 1988 for his Piano Concerto with the Polish pianist Krystian Zimerman, for whom the solo part was written

Penderecki has built much of his compositional career on such external associations, especially from the memorialisation of victims of conflict. Yet since the 1970s he has also pursued the path of abstraction through symphonies, concertos and chamber music as well as drawing stylistically and aesthetically on pre-20th-century music. His *Concerto grosso* (2000–01) for three cellos and orchestra embodies this retrospective trend. If younger Polish composers do not emulate such moves, then they are simply following their own lights, just as Szymanowski, Lutosławski, Górecki and Penderecki did in their time. ●

Adrian Thomas is a specialist in Polish music. He has written many articles on Witold Lutosławski as well as books on Grażyna Bacewicz, Henryk Mikołaj Górecki and, most recently, *Polish Music since Szymanowski*. He also runs the website http://onpolishmusic.com.

POLISH MUSIC AT THE PROMS

LUTOSŁAWSKI
Cello Concerto
PROM 8 • 17 JULY

Concerto for Orchestra
PROM 55 • 23 AUGUST

Paroles tissées
PROMS SATURDAY MATINEE 4
24 AUGUST

Piano Concerto; Symphonic Variations
PROM 32 • 7 AUGUST

Variations on a Theme by Paganini
PROM 1 • 12 JULY

Partita
PROMS CHAMBER MUSIC 1 • 15 JULY

GÓRECKI
Symphony No. 3, 'Symphony of Sorrowful Songs'
PROM 71 • 4 SEPTEMBER

PANUFNIK
Lullaby; Tragic Overture
PROM 55 • 23 AUGUST

PENDERECKI
Concerto grosso
PROM 44 • 15 AUGUST

SZYMANOWSKI
Symphony No. 3, 'The Song of the Night'
PROM 9 • 18 JULY

Violin Concerto No. 1
PROM 68 • 2 SEPTEMBER

POLISH AND OTHER EUROPEAN RENAISSANCE MUSIC
Huelgas Ensemble
PROMS CHAMBER MUSIC 2 • 22 JULY

BBC SCOTTISH SYMPHONY ORCHESTRA

Donald Runnicles Chief Conductor
Ilan Volkov Principal Guest Conductor
Andrew Manze Associate Guest Conductor
Matthias Pintscher Artist-in-Association

2013 BBC PROMS APPEARANCES INCLUDE

DONALD RUNNICLES CONDUCTS

Beethoven Symphony No.5 (3 Aug)
Wagner Tannhäuser (4 Aug)

MATTHIAS PINTSCHER CONDUCTS

Pintscher Chute d'Étoiles. Hommage à Anselm Kiefer
Stravinsky The Firebird (18 Aug)

ILAN VOLKOV CONDUCTS

Frederic Anthony Rzewski Piano Concerto (19 Aug)

EDINBURGH INTERNATIONAL FESTIVAL

Volkov conducts Varèse's *Amériques*,
Berio's *Sinfonia for 8 voices and orchestra*

Runnicles conducts Verdi's *Requiem*

2013/14 SEASON INCLUDES

Thomas Hampson sings Mahler
Runnicles conducts Mozart's *Requiem*,
Mahler's Symphonies 5 and 9

Andrew Manze completes the cycle of
Vaughan Williams Symphonies

Tectonics Festival of experimental music
curated and conducted by **Ilan Volkov**

For full details please visit:
bbc.co.uk/bbcsso

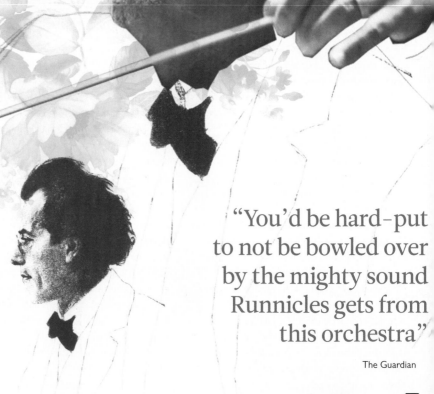

"You'd be hard-put
to not be bowled over
by the mighty sound
Runnicles gets from
this orchestra"

The Guardian

BBC RADIO 3
90 – 93FM

BBC Scotland

BBC National Orchestra of Wales

2013-14 Concert Season
with Principal Conductor Thomas Søndergård

Get Closer to the Music

**ABERYSTWYTH / BANGOR / CARDIFF
CHELTENHAM / HAVERFORDWEST
LLANDUDNO / LONDON / MARLBOROUGH
NEWTOWN / ST ASAPH / ST DAVIDS
SWANSEA / WREXHAM**

For more information visit
bbc.co.uk/now

BBC National Orchestra of Wales
Audience Line
0800 052 1812

Cyngor Celfyddydau Cymru
Arts Council of Wales

Noddir gan
Lywodraeth Cymru
Sponsored by
Welsh Government

REVEALING
BRITTEN

Though Benjamin Britten won an elevated position in society, his works often expressed a reaction to prevailing social mores and to human injustice. In the composer's centenary year, **PAUL KILDEA** reveals how Britten's music reflected the 'murky shadows' of the 20th century

The music of Benjamin Britten is one of the great Rorschach psychological tests of the 20th and 21st centuries. Confronted by these musical inkblots, audiences identify starkly divergent ideas and images, many of them straying far from Britten's intentions. This is hardly surprising: Britten was almost pathologically averse to tying up his works in a neat bow. He was far more like Henry James, an author he greatly admired, who said of his approach to writing *The Turn of the Screw*:

> Only make the reader's general vision of evil intense enough … and his own experience, his own imagination, his own sympathy (with the children) and horror (of their false friends) will supply him quite sufficiently with all the particulars. Make him think the evil, make him think it for himself, and you are released from weak specifications.

There were particulars and specifications in Britten's plots when he needed them, but mostly his works occupy the shadowy, foggy territory James describes: a world of whispers and simmering malevolence, of scraps of conversation overheard at a distance, their meaning unclear. What at first appears to be neatly sketched ends up being anything but, for there is a cumulative musical and narrative power to each work that operates almost outside the notes on the page, fuelled by the listener's fears and imagination.

None of this dramatic ambiguity characterises the Stravinsky of *The Rake's Progress*, for example, and even Richard Strauss at his most convoluted – in *Ariadne auf Naxos*, say, or *Die Frau ohne Schatten* – does not set out deliberately to confuse his audience. Yet Britten was forever shining a torch into the murky shadows of 20th-century life, even if he then balked at detailing what he found. In 1970 he told the artist Sidney Nolan he thought Western civilisation was in crisis and would meet a tragic end. He was ill by then – grey-haired and puffy-cheeked, breathless when climbing stairs or conducting big works – though he did not yet know to what extent;

his pessimism about human behaviour, however, long predated his decline in health. It underscores the *Sinfonia da Requiem* (1939–40) – a trudging funeral march for a world at war – as much as it precipitated his departure for America in 1939. 'I felt that

> Britten's works mostly occupy … a world of whispers and simmering malevolence, of scraps of conversation overheard at a distance, their meaning unclear.

Europe was finished,' he recalled long after his return to England. 'And it seemed to me that the New World was so much newer, so much readier to welcome new things.' He was not to know that the New World would disappoint him as much as the Old, probably even more. ▶

Benjamin Britten (*right*) with the tenor Peter Pears in Brooklyn Heights, New York (c1940), during the composer's period in America at the time of the Second World War

It was perhaps odd for such a socially conservative person to think this way. Because of his upbringing and schooling, Britten should have fitted well into the grand old institutions of English upper-middle-class life. Had he attended Oxford, as his teacher Frank Bridge thought he might, instead of seething his way through undergraduate studies at the Royal College of Music, he might have acclimatised himself to the British Establishment. But he was not actually wired this way. He was unengaged with postwar politics ('Politicians are so ghastly, aren't they?' he said in 1965), and was not much interested in the boisterous artistic scene to emerge in Britain from the wreckage of war. He behaved for the most part

as a classic John Stuart Mill liberal, determined to create a better world through following strict humanitarian principles, unmoved by those who did not think the same way. He was on the side of liberty against authority, a theme he explored in *Peter Grimes* (1944–5) and, in quite complex ways, in *Billy Budd* (1950–51), where Britten displays obvious sympathy for Captain Vere, even though he must kill he whom he loves and honour he whom he despises. Yet in *Grimes* he was writing on pure instinct, uncertain of the power he was wielding. But in 1960, effecting the revisions to *Budd* that would smooth its path into the repertoire, he would talk of how this instinct applied to one of his musical gods, Mozart, in

The Marriage of Figaro: 'I feel … he is writing about Figaro and his relationship with Susanna and the Countess, and is not always quite clear of the tremendous moral significance that these pieces are going to have for us.'

Ironically, Britten's social conservatism at times undermined the grand principles and moral significance of his music. Back in England from America in 1942, exposed and vulnerable as a homosexual and a conscientious objector, Britten found it almost impossible to reconcile his sexuality (and private desires) with buttoned-up contemporary mores. This left him, postwar, pulling punches in his work while others with his social conscience, but without his guilt, would have gone in for the kill. There were exceptions, of course: the *War Requiem* (1961–2) is a blistering indictment of failed politics and religious complacency, the former abetted by the latter. But mostly Britten exhibited a strange comfort in the robes and perfumes of the established church, and had done so since he was a child. *A Boy was Born* (1932–3) is a virtuosic retelling of the birth of Christ, a compilation of poems by different authors, and displays stunning narrative and musical certainty for a 19-year-old. Equally well-crafted is *The Building of the House* (1967), tossed off for the opening of Britten's beautiful new concert hall in Snape, Suffolk: a sacred psalm chosen to inaugurate a secular cathedral. And Canticle II, *Abraham and Isaac* (1952), relays at face value the story of Abraham's willingness to sacrifice his son; it was only in the *War Requiem*, in his setting of Wilfred Owen's take on this biblical story, that Britten underlined the barbarity of this scenario.

In refusing to overthrow the customs and traditions of late 19th- and early 20th-century music – as Schoenberg did or, to a lesser extent ▶

PERSONAL EXPRESSION MEETS MUSICAL PERFECTION
PIANOS AS UNIQUE AS YOU ARE

WITH STEINWAY & SONS CUSTOM PIANOS DIVISION

STEINWAY & SONS • 44 MARYLEBONE LANE • LONDON W1U 2DB
TEL: 0207 487 3391   WWW.STEINWAYHALL.CO.UK

> In depicting the complex monster Phaedra … Britten created one of his most successful dramatic characters. It was such an odd story to catch this very ill man's eye.

extent, Stravinsky – Britten showed how much he was hostage to his social conservatism. Yet in the 1930s, high on the political scraps of the decade and his intoxicating friendship with the poet W. H. Auden, he gave every indication that there was revolution on his mind. It was not simply in his desire in 1933 to study with the modernist Alban Berg, an idea that emerged from composition lessons with Frank Bridge. It was in the poetry he started reading and the music he started writing. Having demonstrated he knew his way round a string orchestra in the *Simple Symphony* (1933–4), a refashioning of juvenilia foraged from his stack of 'early horrors', in 1936 he wrote *Our Hunting Fathers*, a gruelling song-cycle full of cinematic montages and muscular vocal lines, the whole a coruscating condemnation of the hunting set and its easy cruelty. The following year it was *Variations on a Theme of Frank Bridge*, a remarkably assured essay – a tribute to his teacher and mentor as heartfelt as it was timely, given how little Bridge had thought of *Our Hunting Fathers*. Two years later he composed *Les illuminations*, a startlingly evocative setting of works by the poet Arthur Rimbaud. At exactly the same time he finished his Violin Concerto – a dramatically understated work that prefigured the pared-down textures of his music of the late 1950s and 1960s, and which, as the second-movement cadenza gives way to the plodding Passacaglia of the third movement, contains one of Britten's most breathtaking moments in the concert hall.

In all these works Britten hinted at a modernist path ultimately not taken. In fact the Violin Concerto's Passacaglia discloses what had caught his eye instead: the music of Purcell. Championing Purcell as he did from the late 1930s onwards – in realisations and arrangements, not least the Chacony in G minor of 1947–8, and in aping some of the earlier master's ideas of prosody – must have looked deliberately reactionary at the time. Perhaps. There were other principles at play, Britten gingerly stepping over all the third-rate academicians who he thought followed Purcell as chieftains of English music. But Purcell also contained a mixture of wildness and purity that appealed to Britten; after the unruly modernist experiments of the 1930s, he looked for a more authentic sound.

He became caught up in what it meant to be English and, by extension, by what it meant to be an English composer. These ideas intersected in his *Serenade for tenor, horn and strings* (1943), written for his lover Peter Pears and the brilliant horn player Dennis Brain. The bruising failure in America of his operetta *Paul Bunyan* (1939–41), based on Auden's whimsical refashioning of the folkloric origins of their adopted land, had left him wary of collaboration; instead he sought refuge in the English-language poetry of his childhood, over which Auden had no control. Britten had no great ambitions for the piece and was surprised how strongly and immediately people responded to it, but nor did he have ambitions for his masterful *Lachrymae* for viola and

The boy genius and libertine Arthur Rimbaud, a selection of whose hallucinatory poems Britten set in *Les illuminations* (detail from *Un coin de table*, 1872, by Henri Fantin-Latour)

piano (1950), composed in an instant to lure the violist William Primrose to the new Aldeburgh Festival. It takes two songs by John Dowland as its starting point, a Renaissance world he would evoke so certainly in the arrangement he made for viola and string orchestra in the last year of his life, when original composition was almost beyond him.

Almost. In 1975, a little over a year before his death, busy tidying up compositional loose ends, Britten composed for Janet Baker the cantata *Phaedra*. Like his orchestration of *Lachrymae*, *Phaedra* occupies an antiquated sound-world so suited to its subject. But in depicting the complex monster Phaedra, who attempts to seduce her husband's son and precipitates his death when he rebuffs her advance, Britten created one of his most

French actress Sarah Bernhardt (*left*) in the title-role of Racine's *Phèdre*: Britten drew on a verse translation of Racine's play for his dramatic cantata *Phaedra*, written near the end of his life for the mezzo-soprano Janet Baker

successful dramatic characters. It was such an odd story to catch this very ill man's eye, but the piece serves to remind us why, in the late 1980s, Britten emerged from the posthumous slump in his reputation, and why he is now played more than ever before: there *was* something odd about his preoccupations. 'I think if one looks back over the operas that I have written up to date,' Britten told Eric Crozier in 1960, 'one does find a kind of pattern running through them, but I must admit that I haven't been very conscious of that pattern. But I think you are quite right: there are certain conflicts which do worry me a great deal, and I want to say things about them in musical terms.' It is our response to these conflicts that has changed and which makes Britten's music so important today. •

Paul Kildea is a conductor and author, whose books include *Selling Britten* (2002) and (as editor) *Britten on Music* (2003). His biography *Benjamin Britten: A Life in the Twentieth Century* was published earlier this year.

BRITTEN AT THE PROMS

Billy Budd
PROM 60 • 27 AUGUST

A Boy was Born
PROM 70 • 3 SEPTEMBER

The Building of the House
PROM 75 • 7 SEPTEMBER

**Canticle I 'My beloved is mine';
Canticle II 'Abraham and Isaac'; A Charm of Lullabies; Master Kilby; Night-Piece (Notturno); Songs from the Chinese**
PROMS CHAMBER MUSIC 3 • 29 JULY

Chacony (Purcell, arr. Britten); Serenade for tenor, horn and strings; Variations on an Elizabethan Theme (Britten et al.)
PROMS SATURDAY MATINEE 4 • 24 AUGUST

Elegy *world premiere*; Lachrymae; Simple Symphony
PROMS SATURDAY MATINEE 5 • 31 AUGUST

Four Sea Interludes from 'Peter Grimes'
PROM 1 • 12 JULY

Les illuminations
PROM 51 • 20 AUGUST

Phaedra; Prelude and Fugue
PROMS SATURDAY MATINEE 2 • 3 AUGUST

Sinfonia da Requiem
PROM 8 • 17 JULY

Variations on a Theme of Frank Bridge; Young Apollo
PROMS SATURDAY MATINEE 3 • 10 AUGUST

Violin Concerto
PROM 67 • 1 SEPTEMBER

A COMPOSER OF
OUR TIME

Michael Tippett's works have often been overshadowed by those of his contemporary Benjamin Britten, but **OLIVER SODEN** explains why we still need Tippett's musical visions today

It seems absolutely right that, in the centenary of Britten's birth, we should honour the other colossus of 20th-century British music: Michael Tippett.

We haven't done him all that proud of late. Two feasts close together have led, perhaps understandably, to near-famine: the fact that he died at the ripe old age of 93, only seven years before his centenary celebrations in 2005, didn't leave quite enough time for Tippett's extraordinary achievements to settle. (The gap between Britten's death and centenary has been over five times as long.) So it's heartening that this summer the BBC Proms features a concert performance of Tippett's first opera, *The Midsummer Marriage*, the second of his four extraordinary symphonies and an excerpt from his creation-oratorio, the late, great, *The Mask of Time*. The early string orchestra works, which, like the Second Symphony, draw on Tippett's early interest in Baroque music and contain extraordinary explorations of rhythm and counterpoint, are also heard this season: *Fantasia Concertante on a Theme of Corelli*, *Concerto for Double String Orchestra* and *Little Music for strings*.

The Midsummer Marriage was first performed at the Royal Opera House and was initially a complete failure. Critics found Tippett's own libretto difficult and seemed not to be much moved by the music either, despite a young Joan Sutherland in the leading role. It wasn't until a 1960s revival, and a famous BBC radio broadcast that reportedly had drivers pulling off the road to listen, that the work was guaranteed a lasting place in the repertoire and audiences recognised that the score was one of almost start-to-finish rapture. Since then, music from the opera has been performed at the Proms on 15 occasions.

Initial critical opinions of Tippett's music were never unanimously positive, but were often revised as musical tastes and audiences caught up with Tippett's before-his-time experimentation and sharp changes of direction in musical technique. One critic, on hearing a 1980s revival of Tippett's opera *King Priam*, whose music of beautiful angularity had startled and confused the audience at its premiere two decades previously, sent the composer a recanting message: 'what chumps we were'.

King Priam was premiered on 29 May 1962, the day before Britten's *War Requiem*, at the same Coventry arts festival. The view arose, and has stuck, that Tippett was always in the shadow of a great rival, but this is not quite true. Tippett wrote in his autobiography that Britten had once wanted to have an affair with him and it is certain that the two, at least initially, were close friends, despite the fact that early success of the kind Britten enjoyed had eluded Tippett. In fact, Tippett's recognition only came with Britten's help.

Tippett's pacifist oratorio, *A Child of Our Time*, was premiered at London's Adelphi Theatre in 1944 but had previously languished in a drawer for years. A performance was only achieved after Britten's assistance, with Peter Pears and Joan Cross, the future stars of *Peter Grimes*, among the soloists. Indeed, Pears premiered no fewer than five of Tippett's works, often with Britten himself at the piano.

A dancer representing the hound that chases the hare in the first of the Ritual Dances in Act 2 of *The Midsummer Marriage* (Lyric Opera of Chicago production, 2005)

The last of these was in 1961, a year before Tippett dedicated his *Concerto for Orchestra* to Britten 'with affection and admiration'. (The concerto's third movement contains a clear reference to one of the Sea Interludes from *Peter Grimes*.) Britten responded in kind a year later, dedicating the church parable *Curlew River* to Tippett.

Many know Britten's cantata *Rejoice in the Lamb*, but not that Tippett sang in its first performance, nor that Britten nobly shared his commission fee with Tippett. When Tippett was imprisoned in Wormwood Scrubs in 1943 (he had refused to comply with the official terms of his conscientious objection), Britten and Pears, having previously fought on his behalf, were the first to greet him on his release. (During Tippett's imprisonment,

Britten also co-produced the first recording of the *Concerto for Double String Orchestra*.) Tippett certainly became wary of Britten's ability to fall out so spectacularly with friends and the musical paths of the two composers diverged greatly as their careers progressed. But last year's publication of the sixth and final volume of Britten's correspondence includes a final letter to Tippett, full of love and support. Tippett wrote of his devastation when Britten, 'the most purely musical person I have ever met' – and the younger of the two composers – died in 1976, leaving Tippett a further 22 years as the patriarch of British music.

In these years, Tippett travelled around the world, almost completely lost his eyesight, witnessed his work gain huge popularity outside the UK and continued to compose ▶

> There isn't always chaos in Tippett's music, but there is often struggle. Struggle with him and the stars dance.

well into his 10th decade. He produced a ravishing setting of Yeats's poem *Byzantium*, the huge creation-oratorio *The Mask of Time*, a 'Song without Words for orchestra' (*The Rose Lake*) and a fifth opera, which contained rap music and break-dancing. This absorption of different musical idioms wasn't new: his earlier work had embraced an astonishing range of influences, from the rhythms and sounds of the Indonesian gamelan ensemble in his *Triple Concerto*, to the blues and jazz of his Third Symphony and his opera *The Knot Garden*. The Symphony No. 2 was sparked by hearing a pounding ground bass of Vivaldi; and *A Child of Our Time* took wing after Tippett had the idea to include spirituals as a parallel to the Lutheran chorales in Bach's Passions. These often disparate sound-worlds are purposefully set at odds with one another, Tippett's purpose always to unite. He wrote:

> I know that my true function within a society which embraces all of us, is to continue an age-old tradition … This tradition is to create images from the depths of the imagination and to give them form whether visual, intellectual or musical … Images of vigour for a decadent period, images of calm for one too violent. Images of reconciliation for worlds torn by division. And in an age of mediocrity and shattered dreams, images of abounding, generous, exuberant beauty.

Our age continues to need Tippett's sense of music's power to reconcile and reinvigorate and his musical visions of 'abounding, generous, exuberant beauty' (and there is no better description of *The Midsummer Marriage*). This is not to say that Tippett's music is an easy ride. He questions more than he answers and never shies away from portraying the fracture and division that come before reconciliation. He was fond of quoting Nietzsche: 'one has to have chaos inside to give birth to a dancing star'. There isn't always chaos in Tippett's music, but there is often struggle. Struggle with him and the stars dance.

In Tippett's 60th-birthday celebratory publication Britten wrote to him:

> Whenever I see our names bracketed together (and they often are, I am glad to say) I am reminded of the spirit of courage and integrity, sympathy, gaiety and profound musical independence which is yours, and I am proud to call you my friend.
>
> Your devoted
> BEN.
>
> P.S. I wish your piano parts weren't so difficult.

How appropriate, then, that 2013, the year of Britten's centenary (Tippett would have been 108), will see these great composers and friends bracketed together once more. •

Oliver Soden is an actor and writer, currently working on an edition of Michael Tippett's librettos. He has worked as a researcher for the film-maker John Bridcut and lectured on Tippett and T. S. Eliot at London University. His radio broadcasts include interval features for the BBC Proms.

Tippett (*left*) pictured with Britten in 1960, whom he later described as 'the most purely musical person I have ever met'

TIPPETT AT THE PROMS

Concerto for Double String Orchestra
PROM 51 • 20 AUGUST

Fantasia concertante on a Theme of Corelli
PROMS SATURDAY MATINEE 2 • 3 AUGUST

Little Music for strings
PROMS SATURDAY MATINEE 5 • 31 AUGUST

The Mask of Time – Fanfare No. 5
PROM 51 • 20 AUGUST

The Midsummer Marriage
PROM 45 • 16 AUGUST

Symphony No. 2
PROM 26 • 1 AUGUST

NationalTheatre

South Bank, London SE1 9PX

Travelex £12 Tickets

Children of the Sun

by Maxim Gorky
in a new version by
Andrew Upton

Now playing

Maxim Gorky's darkly comic Russian classic, in a vibrant new version by Andrew Upton and directed by Howard Davies.

Othello

by William Shakespeare

Now playing

Adrian Lester, last seen at the National as Henry V, takes the title role in Shakespeare's play, opposite Rory Kinnear as Iago.

Public booking now open

Strange Interlude

by Eugene O'Neill
Playing from 28 May

Travelex £12 Tickets

The Amen Corner

by James Baldwin
Playing from 4 June

Travelex £12 Tickets

Liolà

by Luigi Pirandello
in a new version by Tanya Ronder
Playing from 21 June

020 7452 3000 No booking fe
nationaltheatre.org.uk

f national.theatre.london   🐦 nationaltheatr

BRING OUT THE
BANTOCK

Fascinated equally by Celtic folk songs and Eastern exoticism, Granville Bantock drew on a wide range of influences in his richly imagined scores. **EM MARSHALL-LUCK** profiles a unjustly neglected, mildly eccentric English composer ripe for revival

Hail to the East: Bantock sporting oriental garb in the garden of his Buckinghamshire home, mid-1930s

It is perhaps unsurprising that someone whose upbringing was so liberal that he was allowed to play cricket in the hallway and to keep snakes, rats and a monkey, would turn out to be something of an eccentric. Streaks of idiosyncrasy and romanticism coloured Bantock's life and spilled over into his music, resulting in works of lush imagery, fervent passion, extravagant opulence and, sometimes, epic proportions. His great love of myths and legends, traditions and folklore, Orientalism and Eastern culture formed the basis of the majority of his output, producing enticingly allusive works such as *Omar Khayyám, Cuchullin's Lament, The Pearl of Iran* and the *Sapphic Poem*. The last of these is a typically Romantic piece in which the soulful solo cello entwines wistfully with a radiantly sumptuous orchestral line.

Born in 1868, Granville Bantock was brought up in a professional middle-class household in London's Notting Hill and studied at the Royal Academy of Music. On graduating he founded, as editor, the *New Quarterly Musical Review* and gained invaluable conducting experience touring with the Gaiety Opera Company. In 1897 he was appointed conductor of the orchestra at the New Brighton Tower, near Liverpool, and a year later he married the artist and poet Helena von Schweitzer. Now his professional life flourished, as he transformed the scratch dance-band into a serious orchestra, establishing regular, popular concerts of wide-ranging repertoire, including much contemporary music. He also invited distinguished composers to conduct their own works, including Sibelius, Elgar and Joseph Holbrooke, with all of whom Bantock formed strong friendships; Sibelius enjoyed Bantock's hospitality on several occasions and dedicated his Third Symphony to him.

Bantock's success at New Brighton led to a difficult choice between two prestigious positions offered to him – Principal of the Birmingham and Midland Institute School of Music (on Elgar's recommendation) and a teaching post at the Royal Academy of Music. Bantock agonised but chose the former, proclaiming (in a quote from Milton's *Paradise Lost*), 'Better to reign in hell than serve in heaven!' He became a key figure in Birmingham's thriving musical life and, when he succeeded Elgar eight years later as Peyton Professor of Music at Birmingham University, he continued to raise musical standards; he also broadened the repertoire offered to students to include Elizabethan music, folk song, liturgical and contemporary music – from Parry and Stanford to Rimsky-Korsakov and Richard Strauss. He earned a knighthood in 1930 and four years later he retired from Birmingham before taking up a post at Trinity College of Music in London, where he continued to conduct, lecture, and compose.

Although he lived predominantly in the suburbs, Bantock's love of the landscape was both a passion and a vital component of his work. Like so many composers of his time (not least Elgar, Holst and Vaughan Williams), he was an avid walker, enjoyed bicycling and spent much time in the countryside. He was particularly drawn to wilder, Celtic parts of Britain and rented a couple of cottages in Wales: a corrugated iron bungalow in a disused zinc mine under the looming summit of the mountain Moelwyn Bach, reached by climbing up an old trolley shaft; and the railway manager's house for the Ffestiniog narrow-gauge line, situated right by the track. Surrounded by dense woodland, Bantock loved the isolation and privacy which allowed him to take his early morning baths under the nearby waterfall.

Scottish culture, and Hebridean folk song in particular, also influenced Bantock's music – indeed, it was in his blood, his father having descended from the Munro clan. He had been introduced by fellow composer Rutland Boughton to Marjory Kennedy-Fraser, whose collections of *Songs of the Hebrides* provided a rich source of material; major works which drew upon this included the *The Seal Woman* (a 'Celtic folk opera'), *Sea Reivers* (a 'Hebridean sea poem' depicting the adventures of ferocious Hebridean pirates) and two of his three symphonies: the *Hebridean* (No. 1) and the *Celtic* (No. 3). The latter, a haunting, late work (1940), combines the yearning and wistfulness of 'Sea-Longing', the Hebridean folk song upon

which it is based, with explosive energy and snapping, driving rhythms. In true Bantockian spirit, it is scored for string orchestra – with no fewer than six harps.

Being both extremely widely travelled and widely read no doubt stimulated Bantock's natural inventiveness and richness of imagination and he left a corpus of over 800 works. These range from piano miniatures, songs, sonatas and overtures (such as the comedy overture *Pierrot of the Minute*) to operas, ballets and a series of six tone-poems based on literary or mythological figures. *The Witch of Atlas* is the fifth of these, based on Shelley's eponymous poem. Here we find a lusciously Romantic sound-world, full of longing and yet delicately lit. Like the *Sapphic Poem* and *Celtic Symphony*, it receives its first performance at the Proms this summer.

Bantock's harmonic language is, in general, sumptuous and highly expressive, its extravagance complementing perfectly the theatricality of his melodic gestures. This characteristic is, perhaps, even more evident in his chamber music, where the smaller instrumental forces allow a greater transparency of texture. His entire output, however, displays grandiloquence of scale and an honesty of emotion, with an intensity reminiscent of Wagner and richness akin to Richard Strauss.

Bantock succumbed to pneumonia in a London hospital in 1946 – passing away, according to his son Raymond, to the portentous sound of a cockerel crowing in the distance. His ashes were scattered at the summit of his beloved Moelwyn Bach in Snowdonia. ●

Em Marshall-Luck is the Founder Director of the English Music Festival and Chairman of the Granville Bantock and Ralph Vaughan Williams societies. Her book on British composers and the countryside, *Music in the Landscape*, was published in 2011.

The Greek poet Sappho, whose erotic verse inspired Bantock's 1905 cycle of songs (*Sappho*), as well as his *Sapphic Poem* for cello and orchestra a year later (painting by John William Godward, 1861–1922)

BANTOCK AT THE PROMS

Celtic Symphony
PROM 52 • 21 AUGUST

Pierrot of the Minute
PROM 24 • 31 JULY

Sapphic Poem
PROM 16 • 24 JULY

Sea Reivers
PROM 75 • 7 SEPTEMBER

The Witch of Atlas
PROM 64 • 30 AUGUST

ORB AND
SCEPTRE

The Proms marks 60 years since the Queen's coronation with a number of works either heard on that occasion or written in honour of Elizabeth II. **FIONA MADDOCKS** rediscovers these British jewels

'A spanking march,' wrote William Walton cheerfully to a friend in January 1953, referring to his own newly completed *Orb and Sceptre*, destined for Elizabeth II's coronation later that year and, in the work's title, honouring two of the symbols of power which would be presented to the new sovereign on that ceremonial occasion. In the slightly spicy style he adopted in letters to friends, Walton added that for the previous six weeks he had indulged in 'an orgy of coronation music'.

It is hard to tell quite how enthusiastic the British composer was about the entire business. Elsewhere, in the same month, he said he had 'not been feeling in a regal mood' and that *Orb and Sceptre* had 'been making rather heavy going'. He worried that it would not be 'as good or popular as *Crown Imp.* [written in 1937 and intended for Edward VIII's coronation], and perhaps it is a warning not to tempt providence twice over. However I dare say it will improve with a little gingering up.'

Clearly he gingered it up to everyone's satisfaction. On 2 June 1953, in front of 8,000 guests and watched on television by some 20 million people across the world, the young Princess Elizabeth was crowned in Westminster Abbey. Walton was present to hear his own music featured, together with works by several of his near contemporaries, among them Holst, Ireland,

Jacob, Bax, George Butterworth, Bliss, Vaughan Williams and Elgar.

Walton had also written Elizabeth a *Coronation Te Deum* ('Lots of counter-tenors and little boys Holy-holying'). With caution in mind, however, he had turned down an invitation to supply a madrigal for *A Garland for the Queen*, a group offering, on the grounds that he 'didn't want to be accused of making a corner in the coronation music'. Having arranged a new version of the National Anthem for performance at the Royal Opera House in the same week as the coronation, he may well have thought that enough royal cap-doffing was enough.

In contrast Edmund Rubbra, hardly as inundated with regal requests as Walton, happily contributed 'Salutation' to the *Garland*, with other contributions from a long list of British composers including Tippett, Lennox Berkeley, Finzi and Rawsthorne. Rubbra also wrote an *Ode to the Queen* for voice and orchestra, consisting of three songs, 'Sound forth celestial organs', 'Fair as unshaded light' and 'Yet once again, let us our measures move'. The work receives its first Proms performance this summer. Another composite work, by Arthur Oldham, Tippett, Berkeley, Britten – whose idea it was – Humphrey Searle and Walton was *Variations on an Elizabethan Theme (Sellinger's Round)*. Britten conducted the premiere at Aldeburgh on 16 June 1953.

All these composers were in good company. The coronations of British monarchs have inspired some magnificent music over the centuries: the newly naturalised Handel (born in Germany) wrote four coronation anthems of which the most famous is *Zadok the Priest*, for the crowning of George II in 1727. Arguably Parry's most performed work, the anthem

'I was glad' – taken from Psalm 122, a text set for earlier coronations by Purcell and Boyce – provided the entrance music for Edward VII in 1902 and for George V in 1911. It has been used at all coronations since – and a few Royal weddings too, including that of Prince William and Kate Middleton in 2011.

The crowning of a monarch is not the only royal event to inspire new music, though it may be the most ceremonial. In 1930, towards the end of his life, Elgar – at the time Master of the King's Musick – wrote his *Nursery Suite* for the infant Princess Margaret, dedicating it not only to her but also to her older sister Elizabeth and their mother, then Duchess of York. The future queen was four years old when she first encountered the 22-minute work. History does not relate her view of the music but at least we know she heard it again in 1986, when Frederick Ashton choreographed a 60th-birthday ballet for her at the Royal Opera House.

Eric Coates, whose *Sleepy Lagoon* would earn immortality as the theme tune to BBC Radio 4's *Desert Island Discs*, wrote his *The Three Elizabeths* suite in the early 1940s, reviving it for use at the time of the 1953 coronation. The Lizzies in question are Elizabeth I, Elizabeth the Queen Mother and the present Queen, each of whom has a suitably atmospheric movement: 'Halcyon Days' has an air of extrovert Tudor derring-do; the slow central section has echoes of Scottish folk song and the last, called 'Youth of Britain', looks ahead to a new Elizabethan age. More than six decades on, this is its premiere at the Proms. We may be in for a right royal discovery. ●

Chief Music Critic of *The Observer*, Fiona Maddocks was founder-editor of *BBC Music Magazine*. A new edition of her biography of Hildegard of Bingen is published in July.

Elizabeth II, her husband Prince Philip and their children Prince Charles and Princess Anne on the balcony of Buckingham Palace after the coronation on 2 June 1953

The crowning of a monarch is not the only royal event to inspire new music, though it may be the most ceremonial.

CORONATION PIECES AT THE PROMS

L. Berkeley, et al. Variations on an Elizabethan Theme (Sellinger's Round)
PROMS SATURDAY MATINEE 4 • 24 AUGUST

Coates The Three Elizabeths/Elgar Nursery Suite/Walton Crown Imperial
PROM 24 • 31 JULY

Rubbra Ode to the Queen
Walton March 'Orb and Sceptre'
PROM 31 • 6 AUGUST

Birmingham International
Concert Season 2013/14

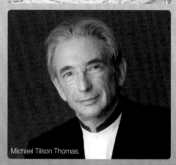

Maxim Vengerov. Photo: Naim Chidiac – courtesy of Abu Dhabi Festival 2012.

Natalie Clein. Photo: Sussie Ahlburg.

Lang Lang. Photo: Peter Hönnemann.

Sandrine Piau

Michael Tilson Thomas.

Evgeny Kissin.

Highlights include...

András Schiff

Andreas Scholl

Apollo's Fire / Sandrine Piau

Evgeny Kissin

Gustavo Dudamel / Philharmonia Orchestra

Ingrid Fliter

Joshua Bell / Academy of St Martin in the Fields

Lang Lang

Maxim Vengerov

Moscow Philharmonic Orchestra /
Yuri Simonov / Natalie Clein

Orchestra and Chorus of the Accademia Nazionale
di Santa Cecilia / Sir Antonio Pappano

Pavel Haas Quartet

San Francisco Symphony Orchestra /
Michael Tilson Thomas

The Orchestra of the Royal Opera House

Vienna Tonkünstler Orchestra / Andrés Orozco-Estrada

Vladimir Jurowski / London Philharmonic Orchestra

Zurich Chamber Orchestra / Sir Roger Norrington

For full details on all the season's events
please visit: **www.thsh.co.uk/bics-2013-14**

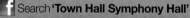
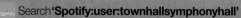 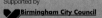

CRAVING THE
KEYBOARD

Unique in its capacity to hold its own against an entire orchestra, the piano has attracted the lion's share of concertos. **HARRIET SMITH** surveys a rich crop of works for piano and orchestra at this year's Proms, spanning Mozart to the present day

At some point in the 20th century the symphony was pronounced dead: it had come to represent all that was traditional and old-fangled. Strikingly, that fate has never befallen a similarly august and long-established genre, the piano concerto – though it has inevitably had its own ups and downs. Why is that? Could it be that the idea of pitting a lone soloist against an orchestra appeals to our inner hero? This applies to a concerto for any instrument, of course, but it's set in particularly high relief when a piano is commanding the spotlight because it's an interloper, not naturally part of an orchestra. That, and the fact that – in its modern incarnation – it's one of the few instruments that can take on a full-sized symphony orchestra and not be overwhelmed.

It's partly for these reasons that the piano concerto repertoire is huge. There's also the popularity factor – time was when any self-respecting household had a piano in its parlour. Another factor is the rich seam

of composer-pianists, and from Mozart onwards the concerto was a crucial calling card. It's no coincidence that composers as contrasted as Beethoven and Prokofiev both stopped writing piano concertos once they were no longer required for their own performance purposes. In the case of Beethoven, his encroaching deafness meant he could no longer trust himself to play with an orchestra (the last concerto he performed publicly was his Fourth). But in the space of his five piano concertos he reinvented the genre with such spectacular displays of imagination that his examples were all but unfollowable by mere mortals – no-one could match that magical chord with which the piano opens his Piano Concerto No. 4; or the seraphic slow movement of No. 3, so dramatically at odds with the frenetic outer movements.

The response of many subsequent concerto composers was to ignore Beethoven and go back instead to Mozart's rather more copyable (though no less sublime) examples; of the veritable flood of concertos that appeared during the 1830s, Mendelssohn's Piano Concerto No. 1 is a rare high point, learning from Beethoven in allowing the piano to appear almost cheekily early on in the proceedings, yet also putting the composer's inimitable stamp on the genre thanks to his propensity for fleet-fingered passagework and his gift – particularly rare, this – for equally sparkling orchestration. It was Schumann who, depressed by the rash of lesser composers churning out distinctly third-rate pieces, suggested that a 'new way' had to be found to put the concerto back on the path of greatness, offering his own example just a few years later, in which overt showmanship takes a back seat in favour of a dialogue between piano and orchestra – though no pianist would describe this work as easy!

From this point on, with Romanticism at its height, the piano concerto blossomed. The notion of the lone figure at the keyboard, who could both entrance with poetry and astound with titanic power, was very much at one with the concept of the solitary hero (or heroine) overcoming almost insurmountable odds – in this instance, outplaying a substantial orchestra – to reach a (usually) triumphant conclusion. Perhaps this is one reason why the Romantic concerto, awash with great melodies and rampant virtuosity, lived on into the 20th century, not least in the hands of Glazunov who, while not a virtuoso, was a more than adequate pianist: according to his one-time pupil Shostakovich 'he often played without removing the famous cigar from … between his third and fourth fingers … And yet he managed to play every note, absolutely everything, including the most difficult passages.' But no-one epitomised the Romantic composer-pianist better than Rachmaninov,

whose works for piano and orchestra punctuate his career. His Second Concerto was a vital step in reasserting his prowess as a composer after the disastrous premiere of his First Symphony, while also proving that there was life in the Russian concerto after Tchaikovsky (who, surprisingly, was not much of a pianist). Rachmaninov's Third continued where the Second left off, taking the genre to new heights (and lengths), its unassumingly *sotto voce* opening giving little hint of the extraordinary journey to come later in the piece. Fast-forward 25 years, to 1934, and you get the altogether edgier *Rhapsody on a Theme of Paganini*, written on the infamous theme that Lutosławski was to use for *his* variations, originally written for two pianos, which the composer played with Andrzej Panufnik in the cafés of wartime Warsaw. Virtually contemporary with this is *Young Apollo* by Britten – another stunningly gifted composer-pianist – completed in 1939. It was inspired by Keats's *Hyperion* and premiered by the composer who, in a fit of self-doubt, then withdrew it, which is why it's far less known than his Piano Concerto and his *Diversions* (for piano left hand and orchestra). The only surprise is that Britten didn't write more for his own instrument.

If Rachmaninov was a throwback to the 19th century in the sheer rhetoric of his four concertos, others were keen to bring the genre firmly into the 20th. While Stravinsky rethought texture and form, whether in the Concerto for Piano and Wind Instruments or in the late *Movements*, Prokofiev's five concertos offer a fascinating snapshot, spanning two decades from 1912 to 1932 and experimenting with structure as much as language. They also demonstrate a dawning recognition of the piano's percussive potential.

Sergey Rachmaninov, whose formidable virtuosity raised the bar for future generations of performers (painting, 1940, by Boris Chaliapin)

Despite its low-key opening, Prokofiev's Second is a humdinger of a piece, one of the hardest in the repertoire, and as vertiginously difficult for the soloist as it is a thrill a minute for the listener; the Third, initially not especially well received but long-since the most famous of the five, is packed with irritatingly catchy melodies, bright orchestration, driving rhythms and a sharp humour that is unmistakably 20th-century. It's a humour you also find in Shostakovich's Concerto for piano, trumpet and strings (1933), with its sardonic writing for solo trumpet, while he kept the following Piano Concerto No. 2 in the family, composing it for his son Maxim's 19th birthday in 1957: in many respects this is an uncharacteristically sunny piece for its time, but who can fail to respond to the slow movement, which contains one of the most heartfelt melodies of the 20th century? The Russians don't have all the best tunes, however: just think of Ravel's mercurial, ▶

Shell Classic International
2013/14

Great Orchestras
from around the world

FROM OCTOBER 2013 – JUNE 2014

World-class orchestras and stunning performance here in the heart of London at Royal Festival Hall.

Hear the **UK debut of Orchestra Mozart** with the great **Claudio Abbado** and pianist **Martha Argerich** on **1 October 2013**, and the young Venezuelan **Diego Matheuz** with pianist **Maria João Pires** on **3 October 2013**.

Marin Alsop and **São Paulo Symphony Orchestra** perform music from *West Side Story* and are joined by the famous **Swingle Singers** for Berio's *Sinfonia* on **25 October 2013**.

southbankcentre.co.uk
0844 847 9934

Michael Tilson Thomas conducts two concerts with the **San Francisco Symphony**: hear **John Adams'** high-energy *Absolute Jest* for string quartet and orchestra on **15 March 2014** and **Mahler's Third Symphony** on **16 March 2014**.

Antonio Pappano conducts the vast forces of his **Orchestra and Chorus of the Academy of Santa Cecilia**, Rome. They perform music from **Beethoven's** *Fidelio* and **Ninth Symphony** on **17 May 2014**, and **Verdi's** *Requiem* on **18 May 2014**.

The **Teresa Carreño Youth Orchestra of Venezuela** returns with **Christian Vásquez**. They perform **Stravinsky's** exotic *Firebird* and **Rimsky-Korsakov's** *Sheherazade* on **6 June 2014**, and **Tchaikovsky's Symphony No.6** *(Pathétique)* on **8 June 2014**.

Maurice Ravel, who struggled with the technical demands of his own Piano Concerto in G major

jazz-inflected G major Concerto, a work he was determined to premiere himself. Despite hours spent practising, he had to admit defeat, swapping piano stool for podium and passing the solo task to Marguerite Long, who became a major champion of the piece and no doubt gave it a much better start in life than the composer could have managed.

Following a perhaps understandable lull in the 1960s and 1970s, while composers were distracted by the possibilities of electronica, Lutosławski, late in life, found inspiration in the playing of his fellow Pole Krystian Zimerman and demonstrated very convincingly that traditional genres could sit comfortably alongside new techniques (the element of chance playing its part). And if proof were needed that the pianist-composer tradition lives on, it's in the maverick genius of Frederic Rzewski, whose newly commissioned piano concerto will be unveiled by the 75-year-old composer himself on 19 August. ●

Following periods as editor of *BBC Music Magazine* and *International Record Review* and founding editor of *International Piano Quarterly*, Harriet Smith combines her passions for music and the visual arts as a writer, editor and broadcaster, and is a regular contributor to *Gramophone* and BBC Radio 3's *CD Review*.

PIANO CONCERTOS AT THE PROMS

Addinsell Warsaw Concerto
(from 'Dangerous Moonlight')
Valentina Lisitsa *piano*
PROM 65 • 31 AUGUST

Arnold Concerto for two pianos
(three hands)
Noriko Ogawa, Kathryn Stott *pianos*
PROM 24 • 31 JULY

Beethoven Piano Concerto No. 2
Christian Ihle Hadland *piano*
PROM 69 • 3 SEPTEMBER

Beethoven Piano Concerto No. 3
Sunwook Kim *piano*
PROM 42 • 14 AUGUST

Beethoven Piano Concerto No. 4
Mitsuko Uchida *piano*
PROM 33 • 8 AUGUST

Britten Young Apollo;
Shostakovich Concerto for piano,
trumpet and strings
Barry Douglas *piano*
PROMS SATURDAY MATINEE 3
10 AUGUST

Glazunov Piano Concerto No. 2
Daniil Trifonov *piano*
PROM 41 • 13 AUGUST

Lutosławski Piano Concerto
Louis Lortie *piano*
PROM 32 • 7 AUGUST

Lutosławski Variations on
a Theme by Paganini;
Rachmaninov Rhapsody on a Theme
of Paganini Stephen Hough *piano*
PROM 1 • 12 JULY

Mendelssohn Piano Concerto No. 1
Stephen Hough *piano*
PROM 49 • 19 AUGUST

Mozart Piano Concerto No. 25
in C major, K503 Paul Lewis *piano*
PROM 23 • 30 JULY

Prokofiev Piano Concerto No. 2
Jean-Efflam Bavouzet *piano*
PROM 30 • 5 AUGUST

Prokofiev Piano Concerto No. 3
Anika Vavic *piano*
PROM 64 • 30 AUGUST

Rachmaninov Piano Concerto No. 2
Nobuyuki Tsujii *piano*
PROM 6 • 16 JULY

Rachmaninov Piano Concerto No. 3
Nikolai Lugansky *piano*
PROM 27 • 2 AUGUST

Ravel Piano Concerto in G major
Jean-Yves Thibaudet *piano*
PROM 56 • 24 AUGUST

Frederic Rzewski Piano Concerto
BBC commission: world premiere
Frederic Rzewski *piano*
PROM 50 • 19 AUGUST

Schumann Piano Concerto
Jan Lisiecki *piano*
PROM 10 • 19 JULY

Shostakovich Piano Concerto No. 2
Alexander Melnikov *piano*
PROM 55 • 23 AUGUST

Stravinsky Concerto for piano and
wind instruments; Movements
Peter Serkin *piano*
PROM 26 • 1 AUGUST

PIERINO
PASTA PIZZA RESTAURANT
37 THURLOE PLACE, LONDON SW7 2HP

Telephone 020 7581 3770

Monday to Saturday 12 noon – 11.30pm

Sunday 12 noon – 11.00pm

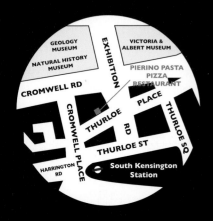

Prompt service guaranteed for you to be in time for the performance.

We are within walking distance of the Royal Albert Hall, near South Kensington tube station.

You are welcome before and after the performance.

EXPERIENCE OF SERVING GENUINE ITALIAN FOOD AND FOR
HOME-MADE PASTA AND THE BEST PIZZA IN LONDON

38 YEARS

GLYNDEBOURNE
TOUR 2013

In theatres and cinemas, exceptional opera across the country

ON STAGE

HUMPERDINCK

Hänsel und Gretel

Laurent Pelly's deliciously witty production from the 2008 Festival

DONIZETTI

L'elisir d'amore

Annabel Arden's Tour 2007 production of Donizetti's most intoxicating comedy

BRITTEN

The Rape of Lucretia

Marking Britten's centenary, a new production for Tour 2013 directed by Fiona Shaw

ON SCREEN

WAGNER

Tristan und Isolde

Nikolaus Lehnhoff's epic production recorded live at the 2007 Festival

October – December
glyndebourne.com

PHOTO: *L'ELISIR D'AMORE*, FESTIVAL 2011 © BILL COOPER

LOTTERY FUNDED   Supported using public funding by **ARTS COUNCIL ENGLAND**

NEW
MUSIC

With inspiration ranging from medieval and modern friezes to Sanskrit texts and slot machines, this year's world, UK and London premieres at the Proms draw on a wide range of influences, as **PAUL GRIFFITHS** reveals

Paul Griffiths is the author of *Modern Music and After*, recently published in its third edition. His other books include *A Concise History of Western Music* and the *New Penguin Dictionary of Music*.

THOMAS ADÈS

(BORN 1971)

Totentanz (2013)
world premiere

PROM 8 • 17 JULY

New works by Thomas Adès are rarities – three years have passed since the last – and they always surprise. This one is big, and on a big topic: the dance of death, as depicted in a 15th-century painting made for the great medieval church of St Mary in the German Baltic port of Lübeck. The original artist, working on a 30-metre roll of linen, showed death linking hands with representatives of all humanity, from pope to peasantry. This is a dance nobody can sit out.

Below the picture is a rhyming text, which Adès sets in his piece. Death issues his invitation verbally to different people in turn and most of them gloomily accept, although one or two demur.

Adès has Death's words delivered by a baritone, while a mezzo-soprano represents all the human characters obliged to join in the orchestra's dance. Dedicated to the memory of Witold Lutosławski, in his centenary year, the work unfolds as a 45-minute symphonic panoply not only of death but of life, in all its variety.

There is, however, another death in the subtext. The medieval frieze no longer exists; it was totally destroyed in 1942, when Lübeck was bombed. Adès gives voice to the figures who have gone, who speak to us – sing to us – from beyond the grave.

JULIAN ANDERSON

(BORN 1967)

Harmony (2013)
BBC commission: world premiere

PROM 1 • 12 JULY

The title is just. Julian Anderson's music sets out on voyages of discovery – be they quick tours, spangled with colour, or slow ascents – that follow the compass of harmony. This is not traditional tonality, but it works, giving his music a compelling drive and fascination. It also provides for glorious melodies along the way, as in his last Proms commission, *Heaven is Shy of Earth* (2006), a cantata of radiance and dance.

Now comes a piece made to start the season. 'It's for chorus and orchestra,' he explains, 'in which the two are blended into a seamless textural whole. The piece emerges gradually, hovers, spreads through the hall and vanishes.

'It sets a brief text by Richard Jefferies about time and eternity, in which he says that time is nothing but an illusion. This seemed to me a suitable text with which to celebrate music-making and concert-giving, as the opening work of the Proms should do. What's so magical about listening to music, or indeed playing it, is transcending everyday clock-timing and replacing it with a completely illusory musical time, which suspends our awareness of normal time altogether.

'This short work is a celebration of that and, therefore, of music itself. The final words are: "Haste not, be at rest. This now is eternity."'

GERALD BARRY

(BORN 1952)

No other people. (2008)
UK premiere

PROM 50 • 19 AUGUST

Pristine and luscious, Baroquely grand and elegantly slim, the music of the Irish composer Gerald Barry unites the most far-flung contraries. This piece, written for the RTÉ National Symphony Orchestra, Dublin, is fully characteristic.

'The title,' Barry says, 'is taken from Raymond Roussel's poem *New Impressions of Africa* and in particular from the illustrations by the hack artist Henri A. Zo. Because Roussel engaged him through a detective agency, Zo didn't know the commissioner's identity or what he was illustrating. All he received were detailed instructions for each drawing, one of which reads: "A rambler, arm raised and fingers open, dropping a pebble (still visible) down a well; he seems to cock an ear as if to listen for the splash. (No other people.)".

'I'm not aware of any direct, illustrative connection between the music and Roussel's book. But I was very struck by the everydayness of Zo's drawings. There is something poignant in his not knowing what he was illustrating. The banal images take on a mysteriousness by being placed by Roussel in his book, seeming to illustrate bizarre events unknown to Zo. They are impersonal, the people in them unaware that they lead another life in a poem of which they know nothing. Something of this is in the music.'

DJANGO BATES

(BORN 1960)

The Study of Touch (2012)
UK premiere

PROM 62 • 28 AUGUST

'The first six-note phrase of *The Study of Touch*,' Django Bates recalls, 'slunk into my head while I was walking back from the shops. I was entertained by it but didn't imagine pursuing it. I'd been expanding my Charlie Parker arrangements for the Norrbotten Big Band for some months, so by comparison this simple fragment seemed a transitory whim: just my brain's release valve giving me a break from density with a simple diatonic loop. Arriving home though, the phrase stuck with me, so I wrote it down and did pursue it. Or did it pursue me? Later, in Oslo, I heard trumpeter Nils Petter Molvaer ask someone how they were doing, using the beautifully blunt words, "Is there someone in your life whom you can touch and be touched by?" With this question he put his finger on an essential human need.'

When writing this work, Bates says he 'imagined how Petter Eldh and Peter Bruun, [his] colleagues in the trio Belovèd, would realise each note and how the trio's intensity would be transmitted to the brass and woodwind players of the Norrbotten Big Band. We often hear musicians described as having "wonderful touch". Perhaps, the simpler a piece of music, the more it requires the infinitely detailed touch of the performers if it is to reach out and move the audience.'

SIR HARRISON BIRTWISTLE

(BORN 1934)

The Moth Requiem (2012)
BBC co-commission with the Danish National Vocal Ensemble: UK premiere

PCM 5 • 12 AUGUST

New pieces by Sir Harrison Birtwistle have been appearing at the Proms regularly since the late 1960s: big orchestral scores and strange ceremonies, such as this. Delicate and dusky, like moths, it is a lament scored for 12 women's voices with three harps and an alto flute, the choice of instruments determined partly by the poems on which the music draws. These are by Robin Blaser, who wrote the libretto for Birtwistle's opera *The Last Supper*.

'Robin Blaser,' the composer explains, 'wrote a collection of moth poems about a time when he lived with some friends and they all said there was a strange sound somewhere in the house. They couldn't identify it, until in the end they discovered a large moth trapped under the strings of the piano. In trying to get out it was setting the lower strings vibrating.'

Birtwistle's harps produce that sound of resonant entrapment, while also, as often in his music, conveying the sense of something at once mysterious and definite. This is the moth's world, sullen and bright, in music that moves between dirge and dance.

Besides the Blaser poems, Birtwistle goes on, 'there are the names of extinct moths as a sort of metaphor for things which are lost'. The piece is also, in returning to a boyhood fascination with moths, an elegy for dreams unfulfilled.

BENJAMIN BRITTEN

(1913–76)

Elegy for strings (1928)
world premiere

PSM 5 • 31 AUGUST

Among the celebrations of Britten sprinkled through the Proms this year is something never heard before: an Elegy for string orchestra written in a week, during the Easter school holiday of 1928, when he was 14.

One of music's most remarkable early starters, Britten at that age had already been composing with great energy and determination for several years, progressing from songs and piano pieces to a symphony and other large orchestral scores, all composed at an astonishing pace. He had also begun taking serious lessons, with Frank Bridge, three months before writing the *Elegy*. Quite possibly it was Bridge who set him the task of trying something for orchestral strings, as well as the full-length string quartet he produced in the same month.

The *Elegy* begins sonorously and spaciously at the tempo of a funeral march, but much of it develops at faster speeds. The work also shows an enthusiastic handling of a medium to which Britten was to return on several occasions, the orchestra being divided into up to a dozen parts at times, in elaborate intertwinings that might even be said to presage, suggests Colin Matthews, who edited the score for this performance, Richard Strauss's *Metamorphosen*. The result is a bold and substantial movement in D minor, an extraordinary testimony to Britten's boyhood creativity.

DIANA BURRELL

(BORN 1948)

Blaze (2013)
BBC commission: world premiere

PCM 4 • 5 AUGUST

A composer of versatility and strength, Diana Burrell is known for her work in standard genres – concertos, choral music – as much as for her skill with unusual combinations. Whatever the resources, her music is compelling and characterful. Visual metaphors may suggest themselves: colours, architectural shapes and thrusts, which are sometimes reflected in her titles.

In 1990 she made her debut at the Proms with one such piece, *Arched Form with Bells*, commissioned for the Royal Albert Hall organ. Since then she has endeared herself to amateur pianists with her *Constellations* series, besides working on bigger projects, such as a cycle of eight pieces based on the liturgical hours, each for organ, harmonium or accordion with ensemble or electronics.

She returns to the Proms with the all-women brass ensemble tenThing, founded by the Norwegian trumpeter Tine Thing Helseth. Burrell's piece, with its appropriate title, is, she says, 'strong, bold and confident. At times the texture is dense and complex, while at other times individual instruments shine through with soaring virtuosic lines. Often the players are performing at the limits of their technique and the music gives the impression of a barely contained energy. The piece is intended to burn brightly for the whole of its duration.'

ANNA CLYNE

(BORN 1980)

Masquerade (2013)
BBC commission: world premiere

PROM 75 • 7 SEPTEMBER

Born in London, Anna Clyne has spent most of her adult life in the USA, where she has relished opportunities to work with choreographers and visual artists. At the same time, however, she has developed skills in traditional media that brought her, in 2010, an invitation to work with the Chicago Symphony Orchestra, where she remains composer-in-residence.

'*Masquerade* draws inspiration from the original mid-18th-century promenade concerts held in London's pleasure gardens. These concerts were a place where the élite mingled with the general public to enjoy a wide array of music. Other forms of entertainment included fireworks, acrobatics and masquerades. I am fascinated by the historic and sociological courtship between music and dance. Combined with costumes, masked disguises and elaborate settings, masquerades create a wonderfully exciting, yet controlled, sense of occasion and celebration. That is what I wish to evoke in my *Masquerade* through weaving exuberant and wild fanfares with gestures derived from such dance forms as the quadrille, which, after being imported to England in the early 19th century, migrated from lavish ballrooms to folk clubs.

'It is an honour to compose music for the Last Night of the Proms and I dedicate *Masquerade* to the Prommers.'

EDWARD COWIE

(BORN 1943)

Earth Music 1 – The Great Barrier Reef (2013)
BBC commission: world premiere

PROM 30 • 5 AUGUST

Edward Cowie works like a documentary film-maker. He goes to a chosen location, where he looks and listens. His eyes are his camera, his ears his microphone. He makes sketches on site, which might include drawings of animals and plants and water, with staves of music trailing through. Then he goes back home and works it all into a composition.

After a decade of composing on a smaller scale, he now returns to the orchestral canvas with the first of four planned *Earth Music* pieces, each portraying a habitat whose abundant life is under threat. The music in this case reflects his experience exploring and diving in the region of Kelso Reef, off northern Queensland, where he lived for several years. Beginning with a depiction of sunrise, the short work takes its audience on three 'dives', to see the coral growth with drifting shoals of brilliant fish, then a slow-moving manta ray and finally a contrastingly frenzied barracuda hunt. At the end calm settles over the ocean once more.

Cowie wants his listeners 'to be carried by sound into a world of dynamic and beautiful variation – to allow more than just the sense of hearing to be provoked. This is music that invites the listener to find new directions and dimensions in the delights of being in the place and space from which the music derives.'

TANSY DAVIES & JOHN WOOLRICH

(BORN 1973) / (BORN 1954)

Variations on an Elizabethan Theme (Sellinger's Round) (2013)
BBC commission: world premiere

PSM 4 • 24 AUGUST

It was Benjamin Britten's idea: a garland of variations for string orchestra on a tune from the time of the first Queen Elizabeth, put together by six composers of the new Elizabethan age to celebrate the coronation of Queen Elizabeth II. The tune he chose, an old dance, 'Sellinger's Round', as harmonised by William Byrd, was orchestrated for the occasion by Imogen Holst. The other composers invited to the gathering were Arthur Oldham, Michael Tippett, Lennox Berkeley, Humphrey Searle and William Walton. The audience for the first public performance, at Aldeburgh, was invited to identify the contributors. Nobody got them all right.

No such guessing games will be needed this year, when, to mark the 60th anniversary of the coronation, the work is revived, with additional variations by two composers who were not born when the original set was made. One of them, John Woolrich, remarks: 'I think it was Varèse who said, "No matter how original, how different a composer may seem, each has only grafted a little bit that is new onto the old plant." Here the multi-hand variations on "Sellinger's Round" is the old plant, on which I've grafted a new variation.'

PETER EÖTVÖS

(BORN 1944)

DoReMi (2012)
BBC co-commission with the Los Angeles Philharmonic and the Leipzig Gewandhaus: UK premiere

PROM 63 • 29 AUGUST

A familiar figure at the Proms in the mid-1980s when he was the BBC Symphony Orchestra's Principal Guest Conductor, Peter Eötvös has since come forward much more as a composer. The conducting no doubt helped: his sense of orchestral sound and space is extraordinary. But there is also something delightfully offbeat about his music that goes back to his youth in the Budapest avant-garde.

He acknowledges this in introducing his new piece: 'I liked the idea of returning to where I began as a youngster: putting voices above or next to each other like building blocks and finding pleasure in the variations of the successions. But, while a child is concerned with shaping, I am interested in misshaping.'

Writing a concerto for Midori, he came up with a title that is almost an anagram of her name: 'DoReMi means the beginning of music. We've learnt from nursery rhymes and ancient melodies how to create tunes with only these three notes and we can hear how a hierarchal relationship comes into being among them.

'The position of the Re in the middle is extremely sensitive; it seems to want to escape from the pressure of the two other sounds. Also, it can be pushed a semitone up or down, nearer one or the other, creating immense tension. This is where my violin concerto begins.'

PHILIP GLASS

(BORN 1937)

Symphony No. 10 (2012)
UK premiere

PROM 25 • 31 JULY

Only one of Philip Glass's 10 symphonies has been performed at the Proms before: his Seventh, four years ago. On the podium then was Dennis Russell Davies, who has been responsible for commissioning all but one of the pieces in the Glass symphonic canon, the Seventh being the exception. No. 10 came about when Davies was artistic director of the French Youth Orchestra and together they gave the work a resounding first performance in Aix-en-Provence in the summer of last year.

'I wrote it very quickly, in a month,' says Glass. 'It's the exact opposite of my Ninth,' which was a massive piece in three movements, whereas this one is compact and in five. There is no diminution in power, however. All the accumulating might of Glass's revolving phrases is there, as well as all the excitement of his harmonic shifts, not least in the firework display of the finale.

The score's exuberance may, Glass concedes, have something to do with the commission: 'The fact that I was writing for young musicians under 25 was very stimulating.'

When asked how he planned the structure, he amiably turns the question aside: 'I didn't have a plan. I've been composing since I was 15 years old, which is now 60 years ago. Nowadays I don't think about theory any more. I write as it comes.'

SOFIA GUBAIDULINA

(BORN 1931)

The Rider on the White Horse (2002)
UK premiere

PROM 41 • 13 AUGUST

When Sofia Gubaidulina made her first appearance at the Proms, in 1991, it was with one of the few large-scale compositions she had achieved, her violin concerto *Offertorium*. Since then, working through her sixties, seventies and now eighties, she has maintained an astonishing output of big pieces that speak intimately of holiness and eternity.

The Rider on the White Horse, scored for large orchestra plus organ, will certainly make a lot of noise, suiting its subject: the mounted archer, crowned and conquering, who is the first of the Four Horsemen of the Apocalypse seen by St John in the book of Revelation. The piece is almost shocking in its force, vividly portraying this gigantic and alarming figure. Adapting it from a passage in her *St John Easter*, which Valery Gergiev brought to the Proms in 2002, Gubaidulina created this version specifically for Gergiev, who conducts it here. The singers of the original have gone. The narrative, in Gubaidulina's words, has been 'more or less melted down to a single point, a kind of turning point.

'The first part,' she explains, 'corresponds to God's descent upon the earth and the Incarnation (the element earth dominates) and the last part to the transfiguration and the Ascension of Christ (everything is devoured by fire and light).'

NISHAT KHAN

(BORN 1960)

The Gate of the Moon (Sitar Concerto No. 1) (2013)
BBC commission: world premiere

PROM 39 • 12 AUGUST

One of the most acclaimed artists of the sitar, Nishat Khan returns to the Proms in what promises to be a groundbreaking collaboration with the BBC National Orchestra of Wales.

The work will be, he says, 'a commemoration of the treasures of Western classical music that ring in my psyche and my soul; my concept of life has always been harmonious, spending time with different peoples, interacting with different European cultures. The concerto opens as if introducing life from a distant universe in little flashes of orchestral light, which the sitar welcomes, seduces, cajoles, argues with, and plays with in the manner of hide and seek, culminating in a complex union.' Then come intricate, mathematically precise phrasings, where the sitar melody transforms constantly, recalling Caravaggio's deep colours against black. The following section involves interaction with different instruments. Inspiration came from the Indian tradition of masters taking an idea, developing it, giving it flourishes, then moving onto another idea or a different section.

'The finale starts in a stately manner, leading all the players into a royal gathering. Sitar and orchestra dance together like old friends, through the ornate corridors of European palaces. But, as the music progresses, the harmony is twisted by the arrival of a beautiful temptress ...'

HELMUT LACHENMANN

(BORN 1935)

Tanzsuite mit Deutschlandlied
(1979–80)
UK premiere

PROM 5 • 15 JULY

Helmut Lachenmann's music, not heard at the Proms before, offers a startling new experience. For half a century Lachenmann has been finding irregular ways of handling instruments, unexpected combinations and encounters of sound with sound and, as in his *Dance Suite with German National Anthem*, aspects of the familiar that need to be reconsidered. We hear, as he says, 'dance-type figures and musical formulae, but also songs and, in two cases, fragments of music by Bach'. However, the rhythms of waltz, gigue, tarantella and so on bring to life a musical world that is thoroughly strange: sometimes beguiling, powerful or humorous. For Lachenmann, the sheer joy of sonic discovery goes along with reflecting on life and, in this composition, on memory. How far can we go with what we are accustomed to? Can we extend our comfort zone?

'The piece,' he says, 'is an unreliable musical antique. The music jumps on rhythms as on a moving vehicle and lets itself be drawn along by them until they transform themselves or disintegrate.' The Arditti Quartet plays the role of the solo string quartet, which 'forces the orchestra into its own dimensions of sound, and is inevitably sometimes drowned, nestling into holes in the *tutti* fabric – like,' he adds comically, 'a louse in the pelt'.

GEORGE LLOYD

(1913–98)

Requiem (1998) *London premiere*
PROM 70 • 3 SEPTEMBER
HMS Trinidad March (1941, orch. 1946) *UK premiere of this version*
PROM 75 • 7 SEPTEMBER

The switchback career of George Lloyd began with a symphony in A that he wrote at the age of 19. Within the next six years he had seen two full-length operas staged in London; a third was commissioned for the Festival of Britain in 1951, along with works by Vaughan Williams and Britten.

By then, however, he was slowing down, partly in reaction to his wartime experience aboard HMS *Trinidad*, calamitously hit during an engagement in 1942. For the ship Lloyd had written a march, which will be played at the Last Night to mark his centenary.

The first public performance of his Sixth Symphony, at the 1981 Proms, a quarter-century after the work was written, was one notable mark of a Lloyd revival, and he returned to full activity as a composer. His *Requiem* followed in 1998 and was inscribed it to the memory of Diana, Princess of Wales, although Lloyd also knew it would be his own swansong. Feeling that a full orchestral setting would be beyond him, he wrote it for choir and organ, with a consolatory solo part for counter-tenor. Lloyd's work might be compared with the Fauré *Requiem* for its prevailing gentleness and for the modal touches that come from the use of plainsong melodies. The tunefulness, though, is that of this persevering late, late Romantic.

COLIN MATTHEWS

(BORN 1946)

Turning Point (2003–6)
UK premiere

PROM 21 • 29 JULY

An expert strategist of orchestral energy and sound, Colin Matthews has been called on in recent years to write works for the New York Philharmonic, the San Francisco Symphony and the Leipzig Gewandhaus Orchestra. *Turning Point* was commissioned by the Concertgebouw of Amsterdam and first performed there in 2007.

'The title,' the composer recalls, 'did not emerge until the piece was nearly finished and arose in part from the circumstances of its composition. I began it in the spring of 2003 but, having completed the first main section, I couldn't find the way to continue and put the score aside for a year while working on other projects. This first section was almost wholly fast music and when I came back to it, the continuation was even faster – a whirling scherzo-like episode. Again I found it difficult to make any further progress until I realised that what was needed was a complete change of direction, a "turning point", into music that is very slow and intense (though based entirely on the same material that was heard earlier).'

It is as if a previously unsuspected possibility, utterly still, steals over the music and fulfils it. The impression is, as Matthews puts it, 'of complex momentum countered by expressive simplicity'; it is also of abundant liveliness, on which grace descends.

DAVID MATTHEWS

(BORN 1943)

A Vision of the Sea (2013)
BBC commission: world premiere

PROM 6 • 16 JULY

A musician of landscape, holding a firm place in that long-standing English tradition, David Matthews invites us to sit and look out with him through his study window on the Kent coast. 'Most of the piece,' he says, 'was written at my house in Deal, where I am constantly aware of the sea.'

'Not for the first time,' he goes on, 'I have attempted to portray the sea in all its various moods, as I have observed them. I have included the calls of herring gulls, which I hear all day while writing, and which play a significant part in the piece. Their cry becomes in the music a descending major third, short-long.'

The dawn with which the work closes, however, comes as much from scientific study as from his own observation: 'My sunrise is based on the sound of the sun as recorded by scientists from Sheffield University and broadcast at the very end of the final programme of *A History of the World in 100 Objects*. That sound turns out to be a rising fourth, C–F, heard against a sustained harmony of those two notes.'

A Romantic aware of the troubled times in which we live, Matthews will surely also be offering a vision not only of the sea's moods but of our own, scanning it as a mirror.

JOHN MCCABE

(BORN 1939)

Joybox (2013)
BBC commission: world premiere

PROM 17 • 25 JULY

Among the most prolific composers for orchestra working in Britain today, with seven symphonies to his name, along with numerous concertos and other works, John McCabe is a champion of the broad middle way. His music is vigorous and decisive, driven by strong but irregular tonal forces in ways that might recall Nielsen or Hindemith. Vitality of colour is also characteristic, his melodies being always shaped by the particular qualities of the instruments that play them.

Works of his have been appearing at the Proms since 1975, when his lustrous orchestral song-cycle *Notturni ed alba* – a breakthrough piece – was performed. Now, for his first Proms commission, he has produced a buoyant overture for an orchestra with which he has had a long relationship: the BBC Philharmonic.

'Joybox,' he says, 'is a musical souvenir of a trip to Japan a few years ago. I was in Osaka, listening with amazement to an "entertainment centre" full of slot machines playing widely different musical jingles, all going on simultaneously but independently. Eventually I seemed to perceive a kind of musical-structural pattern to the babel of noise, and this gave me the idea for what I hope is an "entertainment" piece. Unlike those of the original, however, my patterns are constantly changing as well as coming together in different ways.'

MATTHIAS PINTSCHER

(BORN 1971)

Chute d'étoiles (2012)
London premiere

PROM 48 • 18 AUGUST

A composer whose music often has a graphic impact by virtue of its arresting gestures and subtle colour fields, Matthias Pintscher has previously been influenced by the work of visual artists. Thus it is in this concerto for two trumpets, where he responds to a powerful and immense creation by Anselm Kiefer: *Chute d'étoiles*, or 'Starfall'. Seeing this construction of great lead blocks and sheets under the glass roof of the Grand Palais in Paris, Pintscher was overwhelmed by 'the sound and the aura of the whole installation: an inspirational moment that enabled me to think further about the force of sounds I have previously developed. The musical material is melted, as it were, into lead: the entry of the solo trumpets is like the opening of two valves of a gigantic instrument made of lead.

'There is no virtuoso wrestling of the two trumpets,' he continues. 'Instead they mutually inspire each other, represent the same stance, play the same repertoire of sounds and techniques.' Nor are they in contest with the orchestra, but rather 'are fused on to the sound of this lead orchestra. I find the sound of lead in Kiefer's works incredibly fascinating. The strength captured in this material! It is flexible, malleable, but unbelievably heavy. I find this state exciting, and endeavour to make it audible.'

PRIAULX RAINIER

(1903–86)

Movement for strings (1950–51)
world premiere

PSM 3 • 10 AUGUST

Born in South Africa but resident in Britain since she arrived as a violin student, Priaulx Rainier struck out on a path all her own, her music precisely made, sometimes hard-edged, always finely poetic. She was alive to European modernism, Bartók especially, before many of her British-born contemporaries. Some of them, like Tippett, learnt new ways from her. But she also kept a hold on an older heritage: the rhythms and incantatory patterns of Africa.

In 1949 she formed a friendship with the sculptor Barbara Hepworth, another contemporary, and she wrote this piece for strings while staying with Hepworth in St Ives in the winter of 1950–51. When Tippett and Hepworth hit on the idea of a festival in the Cornish resort to coincide with the coronation, in June 1953, Rainier was roped in to organise it. Her *Movement for strings* was an obvious choice and was duly programmed, but not performed, probably because it was too difficult for the ensemble. Sixty years later it will at last be heard, at Cadogan Hall.

Growing from searching melodies, characteristically soft but stark, the piece begins to feel the vitality of dance and moves forward with increasing vigour to an ending in brilliant C major.

FREDERIC RZEWSKI

(BORN 1938)

Piano Concerto (2012–13)
BBC commission: world premiere

PROM 50 • 19 AUGUST

Frederic Rzewski's multiple endeavours – as a pianist, pioneer of live electronic music and improvisation, and consistently inquisitive composer – have all been steered by a search not only for fresh possibilities but also for ways of reinterpreting the past. His music may even be retrospective and experimental at the same time, reviewing aspects of the great tradition from a position outside.

That is the way of things here, in a concerto that suggests 19th-century models while introducing, as a matter of course, unusual piano sounds (the work starts with the soloist tapping on a string in the extreme bass, quietly echoing the bass drum), rapidly changing textures and swerves of direction.

'It's for a "Classical" orchestra,' Rzewski remarks, 'maybe half of what you might call a "full" one. I can't say why. I never really liked large masses.' This 'Classical' orchestra includes, however, an important part for ass's jaw (a Latin American rattle) in the first movement, just as the work's tonality is off-centre. 'There are four movements that play continuously: the second is a scherzo and in the third the conductor beats very slowly in a continuous curve, the players entering as they feel (not together) and holding each note, again, as they feel. The fourth movement could be described as a sort of fugue.'

CHARLOTTE SEITHER

(BORN 1965)

Language of Leaving (2013)
BBC commission: world premiere

PROM 61 • 28 AUGUST

Distance and nearness seem to coexist in Charlotte Seither's music, where, into a context faint and intangible, can come something sudden and immediate: a sound as raw as an animal call, perhaps, or a chord from the luxurious past. She has written a lot for orchestra and a lot also for choir. Her new piece brings voices and instruments together, as she explains: 'In this piece the voices are integrated into the orchestra and act as a kind of "inner shadow", emanating from instrumental sounds and introducing selected spots of "human colour" into the orchestra. While the sound is moving from the instruments to the voices and back, echoes of echoes are built up, creating an imaginary landscape that is always moving on towards an imaginary horizon.

'The text is taken from the Italian poet Francesco de Lemene (1634–1704), who describes his existence between hope and despair. In this text I was not so much interested in the difference between the two sides, more in the tendency for the gap between to be lost. His text is not used as a poem, but as a kind of tableau for the "spaces in between".

'The form of the piece gives an imaginary landscape, without time and place. It is a music of inner pictures, always moving on, always remaining "in between".'

SEAN SHEPHERD

(BORN 1979)

Magiya (2013)
BBC co-commission with Carnegie Hall: European premiere

PROM 13 • 21 JULY

Commissioned by the New York Philharmonic in 2009 when he was a doctoral student at Cornell University, Sean Shepherd has fast-tracked to prominence, thanks to his music's confident buoyancy and brilliance. He is Composer Fellow with the Cleveland Orchestra and has also composed for the National Symphony Orchestra. Now comes a piece for the National Youth Orchestra of the USA.

'Writing a piece to precede two pillars of the Russian repertoire,' he says, 'and to be performed in Russia, I immediately thought of music that I adore in the great tradition of the Russian overture – from Glinka's *Ruslan and Lyudmila*, Tchaikovsky's *Romeo and Juliet* and overtures by Mussorgsky and Rimsky-Korsakov, to many of the 20th century, including Shostakovich's *Festive Overture*. I find myself drawn also to a specifically "Russian" sense of magic, or *magiya*, in the stories, folklore and literature of the place – a kind that often gets no explanation or justification; a "normal", everyday magic. When these tales find their way to the stage, as in *The Golden Cockerel* or *Petrushka*, some of the most colourful and most exotic (and some of my favourite) music of the age is the result.

'*Magiya* is a celebration of a wonderful new orchestra and exciting tour and a humble nod to a brilliant musical tradition.'

NARESH SOHAL

(BORN 1939)

The Cosmic Dance (2012–13)
BBC commission: world premiere

PROM 27 • 2 AUGUST

It is almost a fairy story: a young man from Punjab, trained as a scientist, hears a recording of Beethoven's 'Eroica' Symphony, decides he must become a composer, takes himself to London and through determination and hard study achieves his dream. Nearly half a century later, Naresh Sohal has an impressive output of works behind him, all for Western resources, but all with a musical poetry that comes from his Indian home. This new work is characteristic in how it binds together what Sohal has learnt from Sanskrit writings and from modern astrophysics, the latter 'sometimes coming very close to the insights of the ancient scriptures, sometimes veering away from them again'. *The Cosmic Dance* also connects the experienced composer, long resident in Britain, to the small boy who lay on the rooftop of his family home, 'gazing at the stars in the clear night sky, struck by the vastness of the universe and feeling a sense of belonging'.

The piece, he goes on, 'is my musical account of the phenomenon of Creation. It has seven sections: Unmanifest, Big Bang and Aftermath, Galaxies Disperse, Milky Way, Sun, Moon, and Earth, the last mostly devoted to human aspirations, and failings. The theme of the Unmanifest ties the whole piece together and returns as a coda to indicate that Creation continues forever.'

KARLHEINZ STOCKHAUSEN

(1928–2007)

Mittwoch aus 'Licht' – Welt-Parlament (1995)
London premiere

PROM 11 • 19 JULY

Stockhausen's music was first performed at the Proms in 1967, when Pierre Boulez brought *Gruppen* to the Royal Albert Hall – a work repeated during the 2008 Stockhausen Day.

The absence thus far of the seven-opera cycle *Light*, however, is remedied by the startling, jubilant, serio-comic choral piece he devised as the opening scene of its *Wednesday* opera, presented by Ex Cathedra, who took part in the opera's world premiere in Birmingham last year. In the composer's own words: 'The world parliament is in session. The president announces the debate: "Wohorld [*sic*] parliament: love is our issue here." In unknown languages, the world parliamentarians sing in 12 groups, all with different rhythms. Every now and then, individual parliamentarians step forward, walk to the empty space between the two halves of the choir and – in the local language – intelligibly sing their declarations about love to the choir singers and for short moments also to the public. Each time, the president comments and the choir of parliamentarians reacts to this with characteristic leaps in the dynamic level and envelopes.'

Like most parliamentary debates, this one becomes heated at times. Unike most, it is joyously exuberant and wonderfully strange and full of tangled life.

MARK-ANTHONY TURNAGE

(BORN 1960)

Frieze (2013) *BBC co-commission with the Royal Philharmonic Society and the New York Philharmonic: world premiere*

PROM 38 • 11 AUGUST

Mark-Anthony Turnage's music has featured regularly at the Proms since 1990, when his *Three Screaming Popes* was introduced by Sir Simon Rattle and the City of Birmingham Symphony Orchestra. In 2008, *Chicago Remains* was brought over by the Chicago Symphony under Bernard Haitink and one of Turnage's *Three Asteroids* zoomed into the Doctor Who Prom. Last year he wrote a fanfare for brass and percussion, *Canon Fever*, to get the season going. Now comes a piece to celebrate the bicentenary of the Royal Philharmonic Society.

Previous commissions by the RPS include, most famously, Beethoven's Ninth Symphony and Turnage was invited to write something that could be programmed with that work. 'I've been obsessed with Beethoven from the age of 8,' he says. 'What a joy, therefore, to be asked by the RPS to write a piece inspired by Beethoven's great symphony.' Inspiration came also from the work of another artist who wanted to pay homage to the same Beethoven composition: Gustav Klimt, who, in 1902, created a frieze of human and mythological figures in a procession of rising enlightenment. Hence the title Turnage chose for his piece. Beethoven, however, is the focus of his endeavour. 'Beethoven,' he concludes, 'is a towering figure, but I find him more inspiring than intimidating.'

VAUGHAN WILLIAMS (1872–1958), ORCH. ANTHONY PAYNE

(BORN 1936)

Four Last Songs (1954–8, orch. 2013) *BBC commission: world premiere*

PROM 71 • 4 SEPTEMBER

Composer Anthony Payne is known for his own fine and atmospheric music, as in his *Visions and Journeys*, commissioned for the 2002 Proms, but he has also proved in recent years astonishingly able to adopt the voices of other composers. His completion of Elgar's Third Symphony is now part of the repertoire and in 2006 he gave the Proms a sixth *Pomp and Circumstance* March by the same composer. This year he turns to songs dating from Vaughan William's last year. Vaughan Williams may have intended them for two different cycles, since the first and last of them are on Greek mythological subjects ('Procris' and 'Menelaus') while the middle two are affectionate celebrations of marital love. However that may be, Payne finds that 'they combine rather intriguingly, the hauntingly uneasy harmony of Vaughan Williams's late style in the outer songs surrounding something near the early manner of 'Linden Lea' in the middle pair'. All four suit the mezzo-soprano voice and set words by the composer's wife, Ursula Vaughan Williams. 'There is something about their provenance that rather touched me,' Payne adds, 'as they appear to have been composed without Ursula's prior knowledge, perhaps as a love-present.'

PARAM VIR

(BORN 1952)

Cave of Luminous Mind (2012–13) *BBC commission: world premiere*

PROM 52 • 21 AUGUST

Born in Delhi, Param Vir began studying Western-style composition at 14 and moved to Britain in 1984 to complete his training with Oliver Knussen; Sir Peter Maxwell Davies was another early mentor. East and West inevitably fuse in his work, but in its unseen colours and glistening stillness his music also gives an intimation of another world, beyond geography. 'Eighteen years after I wrote my first orchestral work, *Horse Tooth White Rock* [performed at the BBC Proms in 2005], Tibetan Buddhism is once again a source of inspiration,' the composer explains. '*Cave of Luminous Mind* is inspired by the meditational journey towards enlightenment of the Tibetan saint Milarepa. In the mountains of Tibet, Milarepa moved from cave to cave, giving his abodes beautiful names, from which my piece adapts one. The meditation technique of following the in-breath and the out-breath with mindfulness has generated within me a musical response, with luminosity naturally at the forefront of my mind. Radiant textures are embedded within shimmering harmonic fields of varying density that generate surprising climaxes against slow rhythmic pulses.

'My composition is dedicated to the late Jonathan Harvey, whose life and musical expression embodied qualities of luminosity in such an astonishing proliferation of works.'

PROMS PLUS PORTRAITS

This year's Proms Plus Portraits at the Royal College of Music offer the chance to hear chamber music by Edward Cowie, Charlotte Seither, Naresh Sohal and Param Vir prior to the premieres of their new works at the Royal Albert Hall the same evening. In each event the composer talks about his or her music with BBC Radio 3 presenter Andrew McGregor.

EDWARD COWIE
5 AUGUST, 5.45PM
Blues Blues *world premiere*; **Two-Part Inventions** *world premiere*; **Badlands Gold**; **String Quartet No. 6** *world premiere*
Musicians from the Royal Northern College of Music

CHARLOTTE SEITHER
28 AUGUST, 5.15PM
Water, Earth and Air I; **Minzmeissel**; **Seul avec des ombres**
Musicians from the Royal Conservatoire of Scotland

NARESH SOHAL
2 AUGUST, 5.45PM
Chiaroscuro II; **String Quartet No. 3**; **Three Songs from Gitanjali**
Musicians from the Royal College of Music

PARAM VIR
21 AUGUST, 5.45PM
Constellations; **Beyond the Reach of the World**; **Intimations of Luminous Clarity** *world premiere*
Musicians from the Royal Academy of Music

RCM

LONDON

EXTRAORDINARILY TALENTED PEOPLE

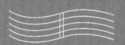

ROYAL COLLEGE OF MUSIC, LONDON

020 7591 4300

www.rcm.ac.uk

The National Art Pass. Free entry to over 200 galleries and museums across the UK and half-price entry to the major exhibitions.

Buy yours today at artfund.org

Aristocratic   **Democratic**

ArtFund

PLOUM sofa. Design: Ronan & Erwan Bouroullec.

Is it Gravity or attraction that keeps me here?

ligne roset

Ligne Roset Westend 23/25 Mortimer Street London W1T 3JE • www.ligne-roset-westend.co.uk
Ligne Roset City 37/39 Commercial Rd London E1 1LF • www.ligne-roset-city.co.uk

English National Ballet

Ecstasy & Death
18–21 April 2013.

A Tribute to Rudolf Nureyev
25–27 July 2013.

London Coliseum.
Call 020 7845 9300 for tickets from £10.

Registered charity 214005

www.ballet.org.uk

LOTTERY FUNDED | Supported using public funding by ARTS COUNCIL ENGLAND

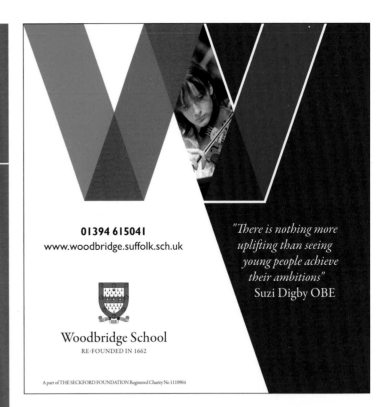

LAST BUT
NOT LEAST

From bobbing Promenaders to cutting-edge music, and from audience participation to the conductor's speech, **PETROC TRELAWNY** waves a flag for the history, customs and traditions of the Last Night of the Proms, the world's most famous musical party

The Last Night came unexpectedly early during the 1940 Proms. The onset of the Blitz forced planners to abandon the season after the concert on 7 September, a month ahead of schedule. Despite the obvious dangers, Promenaders had still arrived early to take their places in the queue. Benno Moiseiwitsch playing Rachmaninov's Piano Concerto No. 2 and the premiere of Elisabeth Lutyens's *Three Pieces* were among the evening's highlights. This was also the last ever Prom at the Queen's Hall. The following May, the much-loved Regent Street venue, where the festival had begun in 1895, was destroyed by an incendiary bomb. A bronze bust of Sir Henry Wood was one of the few items salvaged from the wreckage.

That same bust now presides over the musicians on the Royal Albert Hall stage during the Proms. At every Last Night, two Promenaders crown it with a laurel chaplet. This is just one of many traditions in an evening abundant in ritual: the fancy dress and flags, the conductor's speech, the

inevitable encore of 'Land of Hope and Glory', the unbilled singing of 'Auld Lang Syne'.

When Henry Wood conducted the first Last Night in 1895, he might have been relieved simply to have survived the season: he had planned, rehearsed and conducted every one of its 49 concerts. On that occasion, selections from Grieg's *Peer Gynt* and Verdi's *Aida* sat alongside the songs 'The Green Isle

> A bronze bust of Sir Henry Wood was one of the few items salvaged from the Queen's Hall wreckage. That same bust now presides over the musicians on the stage during the Proms.

of Erin' and 'The Death of Nelson'. The 'descriptive overture' *The Battle of the Flowers*, by T. H. Frewin, a first violinist in Wood's orchestra, had its third performance of the season; in the programme notes patrons were informed that one of its movements depicted 'the heat of the midday sun' with 'hints that siesta time is not unfavourable to love-making'.

Did that 1895 audience reach for handkerchiefs to wipe away an imagined bead of midday sweat, or pretend to yawn as siesta time began that overture? Ham dramatics from Prommers in the Arena are nothing new on the Last Night; it was in 1908 that patrons first had the opportunity to bob up and down and shed mock tears to Wood's *Fantasia on British Sea-Songs*. It didn't gain a Last Night

foothold until 1922, and its inclusion has never been guaranteed. But when it was excised for a year in 1953, Promenaders organised a protest committee; Proms posters were daubed with the slogan 'WE WANT SEA SONGS'.

It was Wood himself who encouraged audience participation in the Hornpipe of the *Sea-Songs*, relishing the opportunity to 'whip the orchestra into a fierce accelerando which ➤

Malcolm Sargent, addressing the crowd at the end of the Last Night, 1967, which he was unable to conduct owing to illness

leaves behind all those [Prommers] whose stamping is not of the very first quality'.

But after his death, one of those who took to campaigning against the *Sea-Songs* was his redoubtable former partner Lady Jessie, who lamented that the work's inclusion 'turned the season into a music hall rabble'.

She was not the last to raise concerns about the ebullient behaviour of Last Night audiences. In the 1990s, Proms director John Drummond enjoyed only limited success when he tried to ban balloons and party poppers. In his autobiography, *Tainted by Experience*, he talked of his attitude changing from 'tolerant enjoyment to almost physical revulsion as the audience inexorably took over from the music'. Drummond also recalled how his predecessor, Robert Ponsonby, would leave at the interval so as to avoid the undignified spectacle of the second half.

The sense of exuberant celebration at the Last Night has always divided Proms audiences. For some it is a party that provides an opportunity to celebrate after weeks of intense, concentrated musical appreciation. For others the Last Night represents a slightly vulgar musical fairground, filled with awkward reminders of a more patriotic age.

'I Prommed all through my teens, but I never went to the Last Night,' says Sir Andrew Davis, who has conducted more of them than anyone except Wood and Sir Malcolm Sargent. 'I suppose I was a bit snooty at 14 – I wanted to hear Schoenberg not "Rule, Britannia!". My first Last Night was the one I conducted in 1988.'

Schoenberg's music has never featured in a Last Night, but new works have long been part of the mix. In 1904 England and Italy were evoked in pieces by Henry Balfour Gardiner and Karl Goldmark. A waltz sequence from

THE LAST NIGHT SPEECH

'Throughout every Last Night the terrifying spectre on the horizon was the speech,' recalls Sir Andrew Davis.

The conductor's speech is a curious combination of best man's address and parish notices, with business to be set out, people to thank, jokes to be made and a rowdy audience to control. 'Will nanny please take those toys away' was typical of the put-downs in which Malcolm Sargent specialised.

Sometimes the speech is overtaken by global events. Leonard Slatkin found fitting words in the wake of the September 11 attacks of 2001; four years earlier Sir Andrew Davis had to choose his tone carefully as he paid tribute to Princess Diana, whose death had recently shocked the nation, as well as to Mother Teresa and Georg Solti, who had also recently passed away. Occasionally the speech provides the opportunity to make a point. In 2006 Sir Mark Elder

criticised airport security measures which had prevented violinists from taking their instruments on flights as hand luggage. Some have used the speech as an opportunity for light comedy, but Sir Roger Norrington turned to poetry in 2008: his own. 'Music brings us joy and love/Music deepens feeling/Music feeds our hearts and minds/Music brings us healing.' But it was Sir Andrew Davis who pioneered the use of rhyme a decade earlier when he sang his speech, to the tune of the Major-General's breathless patter aria in Gilbert & Sullivan's *The Pirates of Penzance*. 'With Adams, Bach and Berlioz, what music could be fruitier/ With Carter, Caskin, Delius and not forgetting Dutilleux … This is the very model of a modern music festival.'

This year's Last Night conductor, Marin Alsop, relishes speaking to audiences and she will make history by becoming the first female conductor of the Last Night. Any anxiety could be forgiven. 'The whole world is watching you, you're addressing the biggest audience of your career,' she says. 'It's the nearest a classical musician gets to an acceptance speech at the Oscars.'

Conductor-orator: Sir Andrew Davis giving his speech at the Last Night of the Proms, 1999

Richard Strauss's *Der Rosenkavalier* had its Proms premiere just months after the first London performance of the opera in 1913. Two arias from Roberto Gerhard's *The Duenna* were included in 1961, an opera the concert programme reported had never been staged and 'by an unhappy combination of mishaps, remains unpublished'.

In 1971, the audience itself was expected to take part in the premiere of a new mini-opera by Malcolm Williamson, *The Stone Wall*. Your seating position within the hall determined whether you were English, Scottish or a Viking. The concert-goers, it was assumed, would be able to read music, since the score was printed in the programme. There was a rehearsal immediately before the concert. 'Each group should learn (its songs) … well enough to be able to act, mime and sing,' wrote the composer. In a line that seems to have been taken as a mantra by subsequent generations of Promenaders, Williamson continued, 'The only remedy against shyness is that everyone should take part, and there be no passive audience.'

The new works have tended to be placed in the more formal, first half of the concert, broadcast on BBC Two (whereas coverage shifts to BBC One for the second half). Not in 1995. That year's Proms Guide noted that asking Sir Harrison Birtwistle to write a saxophone concerto was a 'bold choice. He is not a lightweight composer and he is not likely to modify his bold, rugged style for the sake of easy appeal.' *Panic*, the 18-minute work he produced, was indeed uncompromising. A complicated stage move meant it could only be scheduled immediately after the interval, and so would be seen by millions of BBC One viewers. Proms director John Drummond boasted that 'the BBC switchboard was

Balloon or bust? The Last Night combines playful irreverence with respectful tradition

swamped with several thousand protesting calls'.

This year, too, the Last Night opens with a premiere. London-born Anna Clyne's *Masquerade* recalls the pleasure-garden promenade concerts from which the Proms takes its name. Later the Londonderry Air and 'Over the Rainbow' sit alongside repertoire by Wagner and Britten. The *Sea-Songs* are absent this year, but their maritime flavour is reflected in works by George Lloyd and Granville Bantock, in a programme that maintains the Last Night tradition of placing major works alongside enjoyable obscurities.

The Last Night of the Proms has an ever broader range of audiences to please. TV viewers in Germany and the USA who regard

it as a highly pleasurable illustration of English eccentricity; audiences seeking musical entertainment to accompany picnics in parks around the UK; the Prommers in the front row for whom this is the 75th concert of the season.

'I looked forward to it with a sense of eager anticipation and dread,' recalls Sir Andrew Davis, who has so far conducted 11 Last Nights. 'But somehow the variations of tone and mood would get us through. Look,' he concludes, 'take it for what it is: a wonderful celebration at the end of what is the world's greatest music festival.' ●

Petroc Trelawny presents BBC Radio 3's *Breakfast* and *Live in Concert* and broadcasts on BBC Four. This is the 16th consecutive year he has introduced the BBC's live Proms coverage.

Talented Dancer or Musician?

Yes, TALENT is ALL you need for a place at a Music and Dance School.

All our schools are dedicated to encouraging talented young people from all financial and cultural backgrounds... we can offer up to 100% Government funding for places.

Music and Dance Schools are committed to the highest teaching standards in music and dance, as well as an excellent academic education.

If you are interested in one of the Music and Dance Schools just visit our website for contact details.

www.musicanddanceschools.com

There are nine Music and Dance Schools throughout the UK

• Chetham's School of Music, Manchester
• Elmhurst School for Dance, Birmingham
• St Mary's Music School, Edinburgh
• The Hammond, Chester
• The Purcell School for Young Musicians, Herts
• The Royal Ballet School, London
• Tring Park School for the Performing Arts, Herts
• Wells Cathedral School, Somerset
• Yehudi Menuhin School, Surrey

MUSIC & DANCE SCHOOLS
ACCESS TO EXCELLENCE

Last night
every night

A Pure radio is designed to move you every time you turn it on. Choose to fly the flag with our special edition Evoke Mio Union Jack, or our multi-award-winning Evoke 2S designed with classical music in mind. For the connoisseur it's the best way to enjoy all types of classical music as it is tuned to deliver rich, controlled brass, pitch-perfect piano, lush strings and rhythmic percussion. To make your choice, visit www.pure.com

PURE

NEW
ADVENTURES

ALEXANDRA COGHLAN introduces the myriad ways in which, no matter what your age or experience, you can join in the Proms and discover more about this summer's offerings

With almost two months of music, and over 90 concerts, the BBC Proms offers the most comprehensive range of opportunities to immerse yourself in classical music, whether in the Royal Albert Hall itself, or by watching performances on television or listening to Radio 3. But the concerts are just one part of the biggest classical music festival in the world. Every year there's also a wide array of events in which you can get involved – to be a performer as well as an audience member, to create as well

concert-goers. The low cost for Promming (standing) tickets and the annual Free Prom (see Listings, Prom 38) mean there's no excuse not to try something new or bring someone for the first time.

Younger first-timers can also enjoy the new Proms Plus Storytime events aimed especially at 3- to 7-year-olds. Presenter Hannah Conway will join her audience in the Royal College of Music to lead two interactive musical journeys based on Jon Klassen's

The whole family so enjoyed the experience and we already want to book our places for next year!

as consume the huge range of music and ideas. So whether you're interested in Wagner, world music or Doctor Who, whether you want to play in an orchestra, learn more about one or hear one for the very first time, the Proms has it covered.

Regular Proms-goers will recognise the particular energy and curiosity that characterise a Proms audience, something which has so much to do with first-time

I Want My Hat Back and Oliver Jeffers's *Lost and Found*. A chamber orchestra will be on hand to bring the stories to life through music, listeners will get up close to the action as well as getting the opportunity to join in and sing along. No prior musical experience is necessary – if you love stories, you'll love the concerts.

Children might also like to join their parents for the ever popular Family Prom (see Prom 66). This year, writer, broadcaster and former ►

New ways to play: Proms Plus Family Orchestra and Chorus

Inspire

Budding composers conspire: Proms Inspire, 2012

Children's Laureate Michael Rosen introduces new bear-hunt adventures inspired by his book *We're Going on a Bear Hunt*, along with live illustrations by Tony Ross. But don't get too comfortable in your seats, because the Royal Liverpool Philharmonic Orchestra will need a little help from the audience in what is always an exhilarating and collaborative concert. For families looking to delve deeper into the repertoire, the Proms Plus Family events offer free, one-hour workshop introductions to selected, family-friendly concerts. So come along and learn more about how Ravel's *Boléro* gets your feet tapping, or why Shostakovich's Fifth Symphony might just make you cry.

If you're feeling creative, the Proms Family Orchestra and Chorus offers a more practical opportunity for musicians of all ages and levels

> A wonderful, unique workshop: a hugely enjoyable and utterly memorable afternoon.

to participate. Sign up online to take part in workshops that will place you centre stage. Whatever your instrument or ability, get inside the music of Beethoven, Ravel and Vaughan Williams by playing alongside professionals, who'll also be working with the Brent and London Tri-borough music services in the run-up to the Proms to involve many local musicians in the project. If singing is more your thing, however, Proms Plus Sing lets you join professional singers to explore some of the big choral works by Proms anniversary composers including Britten, Verdi and Wagner, as well as music that will feature at the Last Night of the Proms. There's no better way to understand a musical work than to perform it yourself, so why not sign up to sing parts of Brahms's *A German Requiem* or even Wagner's *Parsifal*?

Further challenges come in the form of this year's Proms competitions, offering both adults and children a variety of ways to get involved creatively. The Proms Poetry competition – open to all – returns, encouraging listeners once again to turn author and write a poem inspired by any of the music performed at the 2013 Proms: the winners are announced at the final Proms Plus Literary event of the festival. Budding composers aged 11 to 16 can have the chance to hear their own music performed in the Royal Albert Hall. After the success of last year's Wallace & Gromit Soundtrack competition, this year

Learning the score: composer Stephen Montague leads a workshop at last year's Proms Inspire Day

musicians from schools across the UK are asked to compose an electronic soundtrack for scenes from *Doctor Who*. Short films explaining how to go about creating your own electronic soundscape will be available to schools and the two category winners get to work with experts from the world of electronic music, putting the final, professional touches to their soundtracks before they are performed as part of the Doctor Who Prom, which marks the 50th anniversary of the popular TV series (see Listings, Proms 2 & 3). Young composers will find another platform in the annual Proms Inspire Young Composers' Competition – returning in 2013 for its 15th year.

The Proms' support for creating new music extends beyond the main concerts: there's a chance to encounter and understand the music of established composers in the Proms Plus Portraits. Four composers featured at this year's Proms – Edward Cowie, Charlotte Seither, Naresh Sohal and Param Vir – appear in conversation, discussing their careers and approaches to composition, and presenting some of their chamber works, performed by students from UK music colleges. It's a chance to encounter and assimilate unfamiliar sound-worlds before hearing these composers' new works in the more formal setting of the concert hall. ▶

BBC PROMS YOUTH CHOIR

A decision to bring together youth choirs from across the UK to perform Handel's *Messiah* at the Proms in 2009 was the start of what has become a much larger and more ambitious project: the creation of the BBC Proms Youth Choir.

The choir, whose members are aged between 16 and 21, made its debut last summer in a performance of Tippett's *A Child of Our Time* with the BBC Symphony Orchestra under David Robertson, and will return to the Proms annually until at least 2015, each season presenting a major choral work in collaboration with a different orchestra and conductor. The choir's membership will also change each year, drawing on different regional and national youth choirs, youth choruses, prize-winning choirs and occasionally university ensembles – reaching as many young musicians from as many different regions and backgrounds as possible.

But with so many excellent youth choirs already around the UK, why create another? Simon Halsey, veteran choral conductor and director of the project, explains. 'It's one thing to hire in ensembles, but quite another to create one yourself. It's a commitment, a statement that these kinds of opportunities for young singers are vital to the future of music in this country.'

This year the BBC Proms Youth Choir opens the festival with Vaughan Williams's *A Sea Symphony*, combining its 300-strong forces with the 150 voices of the BBC Symphony Chorus to create a choir that matches the scale of this mighty work. 'I don't think there's any other nation which would be mad enough to open its greatest festival with 300 teenagers and young adults,' says Halsey, 'but there's a reason that our choral tradition is admired around the world. The idea of passing the musical baton to the next generation is an extremely important part of the Proms.'

PROMS PLUS EVENTS FOR ALL THE FAMILY

PROMS PLUS FAMILY*

Royal College of Music (see page 172)

Interactive workshop-introductions to the music of the evening's Prom. Bring an instrument, or just sit back and take it all in.

Thursday 18 July • 5.00pm–6.00pm
Thursday 25 July • 5.30pm–6.30pm
Tuesday 6 August • 5.30pm–6.30pm
Tuesday 13 August • 5.30pm–6.30pm
Saturday 24 August • 5.30pm–6.30pm
Friday 30 August • 5.30pm–6.30pm

PROMS PLUS FAMILY ORCHESTRA AND CHORUS†

Royal College of Music (see page 172)

Play or sing alongside professional musicians, whatever your age or ability.

Sunday 14 July • 2.00pm–3.30pm
Saturday 20 July • 11.00am–1.00pm
Sunday 18 August • 1.00pm–3.00pm
Sunday 1 September • 1.00pm–3.00pm

PROMS PLUS SING

Royal College of Music (see page 172)

Sing through some of the choral music of the day's Prom.
Suitable for ages 16-plus, except 26 August and 7 September (suitable for ages 7-plus)

Saturday 20 July • 5.00pm–6.30pm†
Sunday 4 August • 2.00pm–4.00pm†
Saturday 10 August • 11.30pm–1.00pm†
Saturday 17 August • 11.00am–1.00pm†
Monday 26 August • 2.30pm–4.00pm†
Saturday 7 September • 5.00pm–5.45pm*

All events are free and suitable for family members aged 7-plus, unless otherwise indicated.

*No ticket required; entry is on a first-come first-served basis (doors open 30 minutes before the event begins; capacity is limited)
†Places must be booked in advance: sign up at bbc.co.uk/ proms, or call 020 7765 0557*

Bowing or scraping, hitting or shaking: all are welcome to join the Proms Plus Family Orchestra and Chorus

Core classical repertoire, of course, can also benefit from an introduction, with fresh context, historical detail or explanation allowing you to hear it in more depth. Proms Plus Intro events bring experts and enthusiasts together to offer insights into the evening concerts, and you'll be able to hear Radio 3 presenter James Jolly discuss Mozart's life in Vienna (30 July) or pianist and musicologist Kenneth Hamilton explore the Romantic piano concerto (19 August). But with seven of his operas being performed at the Proms, marking the bicentenary of his birth, Wagner deserves more introduction than most. On 21 July a whole day is devoted to exploring his four-opera *Ring* cycle, allowing you to learn more about the story and characters, as well as gathering insights into the unique challenges of staging this epic: a perfect introduction for first-time *Ring*-goers.

'Can't believe you got my father singing.'

Of all cross-arts interactions, music and literature have an especially long and closely linked history, a fact reflected in a series of Proms Plus Literary talks and events intended to supplement and amplify the concert programme. So, if you need a contrast to this year's Wagner anniversary, look no further than events shining the spotlight on British Light Music, with writers Simon Heffer and Andrew O'Hagan exploring the history of the toe-tapping genre and the BBC's own role in shaping it (31 July). Alternatively, join Dame Monica Mason, former Director of the Royal Ballet, to celebrate the legacy

PROMS PLUS POETRY COMPETITION

Ian McMillan of BBC Radio 3's *The Verb* presents the winners of this year's Proms Poetry competition in a Proms Plus Literary event on 6 September. You can enter by writing a poem about a piece of music in this year's Proms.

For full details, visit bbc.co.uk/proms.

of Rudolf Nureyev on the 75th anniversary of his birth (15 August), or swap *sauts de chat* for spycraft and hear John le Carré talk about his iconic novel *The Spy Who Came in from the Cold*, written 50 years ago (29 July). Anniversaries are a recurring theme, with 2013 also marking 50 years since the publication of Sylvia Plath's *The Bell Jar*, celebrated by writer Lavinia Greenlaw and professor of American literature Sarah Churchwell (8 August).

Western classical music may be at the core of Proms programming, but gospel, world and urban music all have dedicated concerts this season, expanding a festival repertoire that is growing each year. While young classical artists gain support and invaluable career development through BBC Radio 3's New Generation Artists scheme, the World Routes Academy offers similar support to their world music counterparts. This year's protégée is British-Azeri singer Fidan Hajiyeva. At just 17 years old, this self-taught singer is the ▶

Dame Monica Mason, former Director of the Royal Ballet, celebrates Rudolf Nureyev

John le Carré reflects on *The Spy Who Came in from the Cold*, 50 years after its first publication

RCM SPARKS

The Royal College of Music's Learning and Participation programme provides opportunities for young people and families to engage in inspiring musical activities this summer.

RCM Sparks Family Discovery – workshops for families (ages 5-plus)
20, 30 July; 1, 6, 10, 12, 13, 16, 18 August 10.00am/10.30am–11.00am/11.30am (£3.50)
Hands-on interactive workshops, including storytelling, samba drumming and exclusive tours of the Royal Albert Hall.

Igniting Sparks – workshops for ages 6 to 12 **25, 31 July; 6, 13 August • 1.15pm–5.00pm (£12)**
Fun workshops packed with live music-making. Learn more about music featured in the Proms, create some masterpieces of your own and hear the music come alive with a special £5 Prom ticket offer.

RCM Sparks Explorers – course for ages 10 to 12 **13–15 August (£75)**
Join RCM musicians and Rachel Leach for a course inspired by Mussorgsky's *Pictures at an Exhibition*.

RCM Sparks Springboard – course for ages 13 to 18 **6–10 August (£125)**
Join an exciting new ensemble with RCM musicians and composer Fraser Trainer to create and perform a new piece. Join the Proms Inspire Day workshops and attend a Prom.

All RCM Sparks events must be booked in advance through the RCM Box Office (020 7591 4314). Free ticket scheme available for all events, subject to eligibility. For more information, please see www.rcm.ac.uk/summermusic.

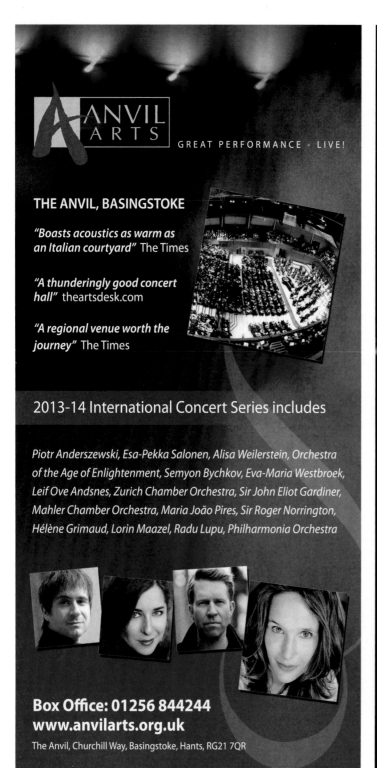

Having a blast at the Proms Inspire Day, 2012

youngest ever to be chosen for the scheme, and will perform at the Late Night World Routes Prom with her mentor, mugham singing pioneer Gochaq Askarov. The New Generation Artists will also be showcased, with singers Ruby Hughes and Jennifer Johnston appearing as soloists with the BBC Symphony Orchestra, and pianist Christian Ihle Hadland performing Beethoven's Piano Concerto No. 2 (as well as with the Signum Quartet in the Proms Chamber Music series). More young musicians, and poets, also feature this year in the informal Proms Plus Lates. Hosted in the Elgar Room, these seven post-concert events allow you to continue socialising and listening after the day's concerts

DISCOVER THE RING

Join Sara Mohr-Pietsch to explore the world of Wagner's *Ring* cycle. Familiarise yourself with the story and the characters, and learn about the production and performance challenges with behind-the-scenes insights.

21 July, 11.00am–4.00am
Free. For full details, visit bbc.co.uk/proms.

PROMS PLUS STORYTIME

Royal College of Music (see page 172)

A new initiative aimed at families with children aged 3 to 7, in which Hannah Conway presents stories based on popular children's books, with music performed by a chamber orchestra, and specially written songs (with audience participation).

Saturday 13 July • 11.30am–12.45pm
Based on Oliver Jeffers's *Lost and Found*, with the City of London Sinfonia

Sunday 4 August • 11.30am–12.45pm
Based on Jon Klassen's *I Want My Hat Back*, with the Britten Sinfonia

Admission is free but ticketed (unreserved seating). Tickets available from Friday 28 June at bbc.co.uk/ proms, by telephone on 0845 401 5040* (see page 167 for call-cost information) or in person at the Royal Albert Hall. On the day, 50 tickets will be available at the Royal College of Music foyer from 10.30am. Please note: each ticket guarantees entry only up to 10 minutes before the start of the concert.

> The whole family so enjoyed the experience and we already want to book our places for next year!

are done, with the chance to enjoy a drink while listening to sets of jazz or world music.

A festival in the truest sense, the BBC Proms is much more than just its concerts. Work in schools and music colleges, with individuals and ensembles, professional musicians and amateurs, continues throughout the year – the disparate strands coming together with spectacular impact and diversity during the eight weeks of the Proms. This season is no exception, so get involved and turn up the volume on your Proms experience. •

Alexandra Coghlan is the classical music critic for *The New Statesman* and formerly Performing Arts Editor at *Time Out*, Sydney. She has written on the arts for *The Times*, *The Guardian*, *Prospect* and *Gramophone*.

Every instrument has a place in the Proms Plus Family Orchestra and Chorus

PEREGRINE'S PIANOS

Piano Dealer • Concert & Domestic Hire • Music Rehearsal Rooms

We supply **quality instruments** for the professional pianist. Although selling pianos is not our sole 'raison d'être' we are committed to it and are proud of the pianos we present. Our stock includes both new and nearly new upright and grand pianos, all of which are guaranteed and sold with our comprehensive after-care assurances.

For customers looking to rent an instrument, our **piano hire service** covers both long-term home use, and concert and event hire. Small uprights through to full size concert grands are available.

We provide **spacious rehearsal rooms** for the working musician. To quote International Piano Magazine, "The practice rooms [Peregrine's Pianos] are some of the quietest and best stocked in the city, and attract musicians from all over the globe."

For further details, and information about our piano **tuning and servicing**, please see: www.peregrines-pianos.com

SCHIMMEL
PIANOS
Exclusive dealer in London

Peregrine's Pianos, 137A Grays Inn Road, London WC1X 8TU   Tel: 020 7242 9865

RIGGED AND
READY

GRAEME KAY goes behind the scenes to talk to the BBC and Royal Albert Hall staff whose skills and planning ensure that the Proms look and sound just right – for listeners and viewers as well as the live audience – from the First Night to the Last

The Proms concerts are such a fantastic experience in the Royal Albert Hall, I want them to sound as vivid, clear and exciting as possible on air,' declares Edward Blakeman, Radio 3's Editor for the Proms. 'If I'm listening at home, I want my sitting room to sound bigger, my kitchen to sound bigger, to feel that I'm connected to a really large event!'

There isn't a day of Blakeman's working life when he's not thinking about the Proms, such is the intricate web of arrangements – both immediate and stretching way into the future – which demands his attention. Translating his vision of providing the best possible musical experience for the Proms audience – now as broad is it is numerous because of TV, radio, mobile devices and the internet – requires technical and production teams across the BBC, and at the Royal Albert Hall, to come together in a giant logistical collaboration.

Jeremy Turner, Engineering Manager of SIS LIVE, the BBC's outside broadcast partner, is a veteran of assignments as diverse as the most recent Royal Wedding, Glastonbury Festival and the Enthronement of the new Archbishop of Canterbury; but the Proms are special and he looks forward to the season every year: 'The Proms office co-ordinates the pre-production meetings, which begin in February, and all of the planning culminates on the

Broadcast vehicles outside the Royal Albert Hall

Monday of Proms Week 1 (four days before the First Night), when we bring all the cables we need for sound and cameras into the Hall from our production 'village' opposite the former Royal College of Organists.

'From Tuesday onwards we bring in and position the rest of our trucks: the 'scanner' (TV production wagon), the Digital Sound Vehicle for Radio 3, technical support trucks and the security caravan; on occasion we also have to make way for a satellite truck. It's the technical hub of the operation and a familiar sight for the Prommers as they queue for the Arena and the Gallery.' On a human level SIS provides the men and women behind the cameras – and the specialised nature of the Proms demands experienced technicians. 'The Proms camera teams take their work very seriously and it's a top engagement for them.'

On the receiving end at the Royal Albert Hall is James Hirst, Technical Show Manager for the Proms. As the BBC's riggers arrive and start swarming all over the stage and up into the cavernous roof spaces, running cables and hanging the lights which give concerts the famous Proms 'look', does it feel like facing

an invading army? 'No, we're always pleased to see everyone back: the Proms is an exciting time for us. It's a large part of what the Hall is known for. Apart from welcoming our technical colleagues, when it comes to the public, we see a lot of different characters coming to the Proms – if we're in at seven in the morning, we love to see people already queuing and knowing we'll be opening the doors to them in the evening.'

Before that first Monday of the technical week, the Hall usually takes the opportunity to do some pre-Proms maintenance to make sure that everything looks spruce when the first Prommers arrive. 'When the Proms rig is in we remove a lot of our equipment for maintenance,' says Hirst. 'This actually helps us to maintain our event technical capacity for the rest of the year. And it's a "big rig", a festival rig rather than a single concert rig, because you can't move things around too much during the season; so what's there has to be able to cope with constantly changing stage settings and personnel. But once it's in, at the Hall we at least can relax a bit and look forward to the stability of running eight consecutive weeks of nightly concerts.'

One of the best-known names around the Proms is the near-legendary figure of Bernie Davis – his name comes up so often as 'Lighting Director' on the TV end-roller credits that you might wonder how he can cover so many nationally significant outside broadcasts – spanning the Royal Wedding, opera and ballet from Covent Garden, the BAFTAs, Carols from King's or BBC Young Musician. Davis's contribution to the look and feel of the Proms – both for TV viewers and the live audience – cannot be underestimated. 'The Proms just look so good in the Royal Albert Hall, as well as sounding good,' says ▶

EDWARD BLAKEMAN
Editor, BBC Radio 3 and Proms, looks ahead to the 2013 festival

I've always felt that first and foremost, we want to give the Radio 3 audience a sense of place, to take them not just to any concert venue, but to the Royal Albert Hall itself. I'd like listeners to feel that whenever they switch on their radios or listen online, or via mobile devices, they are in the ideal seat. That's a matter not just of capturing the sound and the atmosphere of the concert – every bit as important for us is the presentation and the context we can put around it. What we say about the music and the insights we hope to bring by talking to the artists is really integral to what we feel Radio 3 is there for. Of course: it's there to capture the music, so that afterwards you have a great record of what the performance sounded like, but it's also about making good radio: good radio tells you stories and offers you insights – it takes you behind the scenes.

I think the big challenge this year is that we have more operas than ever before, with a large Wagner component in the season. The operas will be semi-staged to various degrees, and for our sound balancers that can be a really big challenge as the singers are moving around and we only have a fraction of the rehearsal time you would have in an opera house. But we have very skilful people who are very good at doing it – in fact, with all the various production teams, the Proms brings together more trained ears than at any other time. If we get it right, it adds up to a great radio experience.

OLIVER MACFARLANE

Series Editor, BBC TV Proms, reveals what's new in 2013

This year, as well as the First and Last Nights on BBC One and BBC Two, we're going to broadcast three concerts a week – Thursday, Friday and Sunday – on BBC Four. The programmes will run in strands: Thursdays feature 'Orchestras of the World', Friday Proms will have a popular feel with especially well-known works (that's where you'll find the John Wilson Orchestra, for example); and Sundays will bring a feel of 'curated' concerts, focusing on 20th-century and new music programmes – that's also where Wagner's *Tristan and Isolde* will appear. As you'd expect, this year's key anniversaries will bring flavours of Wagner, Verdi and Britten. The significant thing is that, apart from the First and Last Nights – and two special events, a Proms broadcast for BBC Three (the Urban Classic Prom) and the Doctor Who Prom on BBC One – the concerts will be on BBC Four. So for the audience there's a regular appointment to view. Of course, in the 26 TV broadcasts we try to reflect that great balancing act which is the broad range of the Proms programme – BBC orchestras and singers, visiting orchestras, youth orchestras, and some of the great soloists and conductors – as much as we possibly can. And in our production and direction we try to make the concerts as vivid and informative as possible.

Edward Blakeman. Certainly, the audience in the Hall can't help but sense the excitement of an event about to happen when, with a blaze of electrical energy, Davis and his team bring up the TV lighting as the concert is about to start. 'What makes the job so absorbing,' says Davis, 'is that I'm lighting for many different requirements: the orchestras need to read their music easily and not be dazzled, Radio 3 wants a silent lighting rig, TV wants some visual excitement, the audience wants something reflecting a "classical" nature and the Hall wants to showcase the building.'

In addition to colour washes which can create or change the atmosphere or mood of a concert, and which Davis likes to control 'on the fly' in direct response to the music, during the Proms a great deal of work is done by a display of LED panels which work in the same way as big screens at outdoor venues, and which run along the back of the platform. Davis sources the imagery and controls these displays from his lighting desk, in collaboration with the Proms team and the TV directors. 'Last year I really needed a whole evening of theatre sets for *My Fair Lady*,' he says, 'so I went round parts of Victorian and Edwardian London taking pictures, which I then photoshopped and put into the graphics store.'

While every TV Prom will usually find Davis driving the desk, he really can't be at all the concerts, and so a system of categorisation helps to manage the workload: events are flagged as 'Simple' (an orchestral concert with straightforward lighting states and graphics), 'Moderate' (maybe a late-night session with a more tightly focused pool of light, requiring special attention), and 'Complex', such as *My Fair Lady*, or one of the operas.

But before any of this can happen, the Radio 3 balance engineers in particular will be waiting for the installation of the 'truss' – this is the giant lighting gantry suspended above the stage, which also carries the burgundy-coloured acoustic panels, public-address loudspeakers and the pelmet, with its BBC Proms and Royal Albert Hall branding, which dresses the truss and makes the Proms 'set' look complete. Its exact position used to be calculated by eye – now it's so critical for the acoustics, it has to be done by laser.

'We have the truss and all the cabling rigged by Tuesday lunchtime,' says Davis. Once it's all in place, Radio 3's sound engineers (who usually also provide the sound for TV) can really get to work, hanging some of the 40 to 50 microphones in the permanent rig, from wire slings above the stage. 'It might seem like a lot of mics,' says Radio 3 studio manager Paul Waton, one of the team responsible for locating the microphones and balancing the Radio 3 sound, 'but between concerts, especially on a double-Prom evening, we only have limited time to re-rig. So from one day to the next, the installation has to cope with any combination of instruments, genres and different stage positions – from symphony orchestra and chorus to Baroque or chamber ensemble; from solo instruments and singers, to a world music group; the organ alone has four "flown" mikes.'

For the live audience, the eye will always help the ear to locate a sound such as a woodwind or violin solo; but radio listeners need slightly more help – this is provided by onstage microphones, and the sound balancer's art is to point up those solos in the mix. One of the stiffest challenges for the sound team is capturing operas and musicals at the Proms when performers are mobile on stage. 'I worked on *My Fair Lady* last year, and it was like producing a complete West End show in only one evening!' In that case, radio microphones helped the sound to stay balanced, but those are out of the question for operas, of which a good number are planned

Vision on: inside the TV truck

for the 2013 season. 'It's a matter of getting as much as you can out of limited rehearsal time,' says Waton, 'and having someone to score-read and call the moves while the balancer keeps an eye on the TV monitor, making sure the performers are captured seamlessly wherever they are. Anyone coming into the truck on an opera night would be amazed at how much noise there is!'

By the Thursday of the technical week, the BBC Symphony Orchestra will be in the Hall, rehearsing for the following evening's First Night. All ears will be on the sound, all eyes on the pictures. As the TV and radio presenters open their microphones and launch the new season on Friday 12 July, all of the technicians will be on high alert. 'We'll be exhausted, because we've done the rig beforehand,' says Waton. 'But we usually hit the airwaves with a fantastic all-singing, all-dancing first weekend – it's a great thing to be involved in.' ●

Graeme Kay is an interactive producer for BBC Radio 3 and BBC Classical Music TV.

STEVE BOWBRICK

Interactive Editor, Radio 3, Proms and Performing Groups, describes the many ways of enjoying the Proms

For the Proms online, 2013 is all about expanding access. Since the very first season in 1895, the Proms has always been about taking the most engaging and vivid of musical experiences to the largest possible audience. Online, we've inherited that same obligation. We want users of the Proms on mobile phones, tablets and computers to be as close to the music, the composers and the artists as we can possibly get them.

As in recent years, every Prom will be streamed online in hi-fi-quality HD Sound (plug your computer into your stereo or use a pair of good headphones and hear the difference). The televised concerts will also be streamed online, and we'll be providing a selection of important and popular works on the website, for 30 days after broadcast – it's like a boxed-set of the most amazing Proms performances; look for the link on the Proms homepage.

Last season, over 40% of visits to the Proms website were from mobile phones and tablets. That number will certainly be higher this year. These days, mobile networking in its broadest sense makes us want to get all our music and information wherever we are, on whichever device we're using. So, more Proms content than ever will be available on your mobile phone or tablet. And the free BBC iPlayer Radio mobile app makes the concerts even easier to listen to.

THE PROMS ON BBC RADIO 3

- Every Prom broadcast live on BBC Radio 3 (available on digital radio, via TV, mobile, laptop and tablet as well as on 90–93 FM)
- Many Proms repeated during *Afternoon on 3* (weekdays, 2.00pm) and in *Sunday Concert* (Sundays, 2.00pm) plus a series of repeats over the Christmas period
- Listen Again for seven days after broadcast via bbc.co.uk/proms
- Proms-related programmes during the season, including *Breakfast* (daily, 6.30am), *In Tune* (weekdays, 4.00pm) and *Composer of the Week* (weekdays, 12.00pm and 6.30pm)

THE PROMS ON BBC TELEVISION

- 26 Proms broadcast across BBC One, BBC Two, BBC Three and BBC Four
- Regular Thursday-, Friday- and Sunday-evening broadcasts on BBC Four
- The Last Night of the Proms – first half on BBC Two and second half on BBC One – plus Proms in the Park events around the country via the red button

THE PROMS ONLINE

- Visit bbc.co.uk/proms for your definitive guide to the 2013 BBC Proms season
- Listen to every Prom live in HD Sound and on-demand for seven days after broadcast and watch every televised Prom via the BBC iPlayer. Visit the individual listings pages to discover how you can experience every Prom
- Keep up to date with the latest news and behind-the-scenes insights on the Proms blog, by joining the email newsletter, finding us on Facebook (facebook.com/theproms) or following us on Twitter (@bbcproms; #bbcproms)
- Access the Proms on the move via the Proms mobile site
- Search the Proms by artist, composer or repertoire in the Proms Archive, which details every Proms concert since they began in 1895

LATE NIGHT
TONIC

From Bach to the newest contemporary scores, and from solo piano to breathtaking beatboxing, this year's Late Night Proms have something for every enquiring ear, as **IGOR TORONYI-LALIC** discovers

For the composer and pianist Franz Liszt, night was a time 'when the soul … retreats into itself and soars aloft to secret regions of star and sky'. It's the same at the BBC Proms. The sun sets and the musical explorations begin. Only at the Late Night Proms will you be able to witness Frank Zappa's singing New World pig, Greggery Peccary, or get a glimpse of Karlheinz Stockhausen's transcendental operatic show-stopper, *Mittwoch aus 'Licht'*. Only at dusk do The Stranglers, the majesty of Bach, the cacophony of Edgard Varèse and the music of the Caucasus all jostle for our attention.

The dream logic of the Late Night Proms is almost into its fourth decade. And for many, the series offers some of the best bedtime stories London has to share. It's where the Royal Albert Hall undergoes the biggest metamorphoses, travelling far from comfort zones and deep into unfamiliar musical lands. This year it's no different. Africa, the

Caribbean and the Deep South are the first ports of call, as professionals and amateurs guide us, in the opening concert of the series, through the rich history of gospel music (16 July). Later we journey to Azerbaijan and Mali for the BBC Radio 3 World Routes Prom (22 August) and on the way welcome young string players from Palestine and Israel (8 August) and jazzers from Sweden (28 August).

The second late-nighter goes one step further, bringing representatives from all four corners of the globe. Following a long-awaited and universally acclaimed world premiere in Birmingham last year, Stockhausen's six-hour opera *Mittwoch aus 'Licht'* lands one of its epic, otherworldly acts in the Royal Albert Hall, Jeffrey Skidmore's Ex Cathedra reconvening the awe-inspiring 'World Parliament' (19 July). Dancing around the ceiling before this will be Stockhausen's seminal tape piece *Gesang der Jünglinge* – the work that won him a coveted place on the

album cover of The Beatles' *Sgt. Pepper's Lonely Hearts Club Band*.

There are generous helpings of new classical music, including the UK premieres of Philip Glass's 10th Symphony (31 July) and *No other people.* by Irish maverick Gerald Barry (19 August) and a world-premiere piano concerto from the feisty American experimentalist Frederic Rzewski (19 August), who is also the soloist. One of the joys of recent years has been exploring the Anglo-American experimentalist tradition with Ilan Volkov and the BBC Scottish Symphony Orchestra. This year, alongside the Rzewski and Barry, they present a rare outing for the music of the great English eccentric John White and the legendary American Morton Feldman.

The 6 Music Prom offers a microcosm of the Late Night ethos with an ambitious mash-up as Cerys Matthews, Laura Marling, The Stranglers and the London Sinfonietta come together for a celebration of

After-hours revellers: Django Bates (Prom 62), Sir John Eliot Gardiner (Prom 36) and Naturally 7 (Prom 22)

contemporary music in all its incarnations (12 August). Meanwhile, the Aurora Orchestra pays tribute to mash-up pioneer Frank Zappa and his surreal mock rock opera, *The Adventures of Greggery Peccary* (31 July).

From traditional African praise to Baroque oratorios, from Renaissance motets to Caribbean hymns, from Azerbaijani mugham to American gospel, from British 20th-century pastoralism to *a cappella* hip hop, the singing traditions of every continent and virtually every age are sampled across the two-month festival. The fertile contemporary African-American traditions get their own late-nighter, R&B and hip hop coming centre stage with Naturally 7, a virtuoso *a cappella* ensemble (29 July).

One night is devoted to the sacred works of two of the shadowier Renaissance masters, John Taverner and Carlo Gesualdo, performed by the Tallis Scholars under the direction of Peter Phillips (14 August). Baroque music is represented by Sir John Eliot Gardiner and his Monteverdi Choir, in whose expert hands we hear J. S. Bach's joyous *Easter* and *Ascension* Oratorios (9 August). Two British birthday boys are commemorated by David Hill and the BBC Singers: Benjamin Britten's centenary is honoured with a performance of *A Boy was Born*, while the 100th anniversary

of the birth of the perennially overlooked English Romantic George Lloyd is saluted with the London premiere of his *Requiem* (3 September).

Some of the greatest rewards of the Late Night Proms can be found in the smaller-scale music, when the cave-like Royal Albert Hall shrinks to become a sitting room. But it takes a special kind of performer to make the hall intimate enough for these smaller works to resonate and touch. Happily, the Late Night Proms aren't short of special performers.

Nigel Kennedy returns to revive Vivaldi's *The Four Seasons* with the help of the young Palestine Strings, and with his own band of musicians (8 August). The charismatic Django Bates and his trio – in league with the Swedish Norrbotten Big Band – rearrange several Charlie Parker classics (28 August). And, to end the season, there are two unadulterated classics – Schubert's disturbing Piano Sonata in C minor, D958, and barnstorming 'Grand Duo' Sonata, D812 – from two of the UK's most celebrated Schubertians, Imogen Cooper and Paul Lewis.

If this lot doesn't help your soul to soar 'to secret regions of star and sky', nothing will. ●

Igor Toronyi-Lalic is a music writer and curator, and co-founder and classical music and opera editor of theartsdesk.com.

LATE NIGHT PROMS

Gospel Prom
PROM 7 • 16 JULY

Stockhausen's 'Welt-Parlament'
PROM 11 • 19 JULY

Naturally 7
PROM 22 • 29 JULY

Zappa, Glass and Nancarrow
PROM 25 • 31 JULY

Nigel Kennedy plays Vivaldi's
The Four Seasons
PROM 34 • 8 AUGUST

Sir John Eliot Gardiner conducts Bach
PROM 36 • 9 AUGUST

6 Music Prom
PROM 40 • 12 AUGUST

Taverner and Gesualdo
PROM 43 • 14 AUGUST

Gerald Barry, Morton Feldman,
Frederic Rzewski and John White
PROM 50 • 19 AUGUST

World Routes Prom
PROM 54 • 22 AUGUST

A Celebration of
Charlie Parker
PROM 62 • 28 AUGUST

Britten and George Lloyd
PROM 70 • 3 SEPTEMBER

Imogen Cooper and Paul Lewis
play Schubert
PROM 73 • 5 SEPTEMBER

SMALL IS BEAUTIFUL

The series of Monday-lunchtime and Saturday-afternoon Proms at Cadogan Hall not only act as a microcosm of the Royal Albert Hall concerts – reflecting featured anniversaries and artists – but also offer a distinctiveness and intimacy all of their own, says **HELEN WALLACE**

'We're enlarging and varying the palette each year,' says Edward Blakeman, the BBC Radio 3 and Proms editor who oversees the two series of concerts which take place at Cadogan Hall as part of the BBC Proms. 'We try to think of the broadest definition of chamber music and keep pushing the envelope.'

Indeed, no-one could accuse this year's Monday-lunchtime Proms Chamber Music series of being predictable: there's not a straight string quartet concert or piano recital in sight.

Key to the series, according to Blakeman, is the Hall itself, which creates a special atmosphere and identity. 'These are not Proms in miniature,' he says. 'They offer an entirely different, more intimate experience.'

Most intimate of all, perhaps, is the Dowland recital (2 September), marking the 450th anniversary of the composer's birth, sung by Proms featured artist **Ian Bostridge** with **Fretwork** and lutenist **Elizabeth Kenny**. Contemporary dance rhythms in these heartfelt songs lend vitality to the composer's keening, expressive melodies. Another significant anniversary marked in this year's Proms is the centenary of Witold Lutosławski's birth. Norwegian violinist **Vilde Frang** (15 July) performs his *Partita* in her recital with **Michail Lifits**. This spirited young artist also plays Bruch's Violin Concerto No. 1 at the Royal Albert Hall (Prom 31).

Another young Norwegian making her Proms debut is star trumpeter **Tine Thing Helseth**, who brings her all-female ensemble **tenThing** for a selection of dazzling arrangements (5 August) and a new commission by Diana Burrell.

British women composers form a thread running through the Cadogan Hall concerts this year (Imogen Holst and Priaulx Rainier are among those featured) and the accomplished young German **Signum Quartet** gives a rare performance of Elizabeth Maconchy's richly expressive String Quartet No. 3 (26 August). This tightly argued, visceral work forms a brilliant preface to Brahms's monumental Piano Quintet, for which the quartet is joined by fellow BBC Radio 3 New Generation Artist **Christian Ihle Hadland** (who returns to play Beethoven's Piano Concerto No. 2 in Prom 69).

Rarely heard repertoire of a very different kind is sung by the **Huelgas Ensemble** in its programme of Polish Renaissance music (22 July). Conductor **Paul Van Nevel**'s research in Warsaw has thrown up a treasure-trove of works, revealing how culturally cosmopolitan the 15th-century Polish kings were. 'I first heard the Huelgas Ensemble live in Blythburgh Church in Suffolk and thought they were jaw-droppingly good,' comments Blakeman.

Renaissance music, this time from England, also graces the second choral chamber concert (12 August), sung by the **BBC Singers**. The UK premiere of Sir Harrison Birtwistle's *The Moth Requiem* is interleaved with pieces from the Eton Choirbook. 'Birtwistle said early English polyphony would set off his piece particularly well,' explains Blakeman. The text of this *Requiem* lists extraordinary moth names – *Scopula immorata*, *Depressaria discipunctella* – and also includes a poem by Robin Blaser, inspired by the eerie sound of a moth caught under the lid of a piano. Holst's *Choral Hymns from the Rig Veda* make an illuminating counterpoint.

Holst's contemporary Peter Warlock wrote the central work in the **London Conchord Ensemble**'s concert (19 August), *The Curlew*. Tenor **Robin Tritschler** sings these passionately elegiac settings of W. B. Yeats's poems of unrequited love. Imogen Holst also features, with her prizewinning *Phantasy Quartet*, written while she was still a student; and the concert is framed by Poulenc's glittering Sextet and Thomas Adès's imaginative reworking of Couperin's *Les baricades mistérieuses*.

Not surprisingly, the centenary of Benjamin Britten's birth finds its way into the Cadogan Hall concerts: pianist **Imogen Cooper** and guitarist **Christoph Denoth** are joined by singers **Christianne Stotijn** and **James Gilchrist** for an enchanting programme of song and reflective music (29 July). And there's more Britten in the Proms Saturday Matinee concerts, with a very particular focus: 'We wanted to set Britten's music for chamber orchestra in the context of his contemporaries,' explains Blakeman. The **English Chamber Orchestra** takes on the Variations on 'Sellinger's Round' (24 August), which gives a neat snapshot of British music in 1952: Arthur Oldham, Michael Tippett, Lennox Berkeley, Britten Humphrey Searle and William Walton each contributing a variation. Two new variations, by John Woolrich and Tansy Davies, are being written for this concert, which will also feature Britten's *Serenade for tenor, horn and strings* and Lutosławski's *Paroles tissées* sung by **Ben Johnson**. The **Britten Sinfonia** contrasts Britten's *Prelude*

VILDE FRANG   IAN BOSTRIDGE
(PCM 1)   (PCM 8)

and Fugue with works by Holst, Tippett and Lennox Berkeley on 3 August): 'There are some fascinating counterpoints to be heard here,' says Blakeman. 'Britten's absolute mastery is clear, but the same can be said of Tippett's *Fantasia*; and Berkeley's *Four Poems*, for example, are works of great originality, as is his *Serenade for strings*, which the **Camerata Ireland** performs.' **Barry Douglas** directs this concert (10 August), in which he is also the soloist in Britten's radiant early *Young Apollo* and in Shostakovich's Piano Concerto No. 1, with trumpeter **Alison Balsom**. He also conducts an intriguing world premiere by South African-English composer Priaulx Rainier: *Movement for strings*, completed in 1951 but never performed. Making its Proms debut is Swedish-based **Camerata Nordica**, bringing another unexpected premiere, the 14-year-old Britten's *Elegy for strings*, alongside Walton and Tippett (31 August). Last but not least, the **Academy of Ancient Music** celebrates Handel's 1707 visit to Rome, where he met Corelli (who died 300 years ago), in the first of the Proms Saturday Matinees (20 July). ●

Helen Wallace is Consultant Editor of *BBC Music Magazine* and former Editor of *The Strad*. She has written histories of the music publisher Boosey & Hakwes and of the Orchestra of the Age of Enlightenment, and is a regular critic for BBC Radio 4's *Front Row*.

PROMS CHAMBER MUSIC
Mondays, 1.00pm

PROMS CHAMBER MUSIC 1
Vilde Frang *violin*, Michail Lifits *piano* • 15 July

PROMS CHAMBER MUSIC 2
Huelgas Ensemble/Paul Van Nevel • 22 July

PROMS CHAMBER MUSIC 3
Christianne Stotijn *mezzo-soprano*,
James Gilchrist *tenor*, Christoph Denoth *guitar*,
Imogen Cooper *piano* • 29 July

PROMS CHAMBER MUSIC 4
tenThing • 5 August

PROMS CHAMBER MUSIC 5
BBC Singers, Nash Ensemble/Nicholas Kok
12 August

PROMS CHAMBER MUSIC 6
Robin Tritschler *tenor*, London Conchord
Ensemble • 19 August

PROMS CHAMBER MUSIC 7
Signum Quartet, Christian Ihle Hadland *piano*
26 August

PROMS CHAMBER MUSIC 8
Ian Bostridge *tenor*, Elizabeth Kenny *lute*,
Fretwork • 2 September

• • •

PROMS SATURDAY MATINEES
Saturdays, 3.00pm

PROMS SATURDAY MATINEE 1
Sophie Bevan *soprano*,
Academy of Ancient Music/Richard Egarr
(harpsichord/director) • 20 July

PROMS SATURDAY MATINEE 2
Sarah Connolly *mezzo-soprano*,
Britten Sinfonia/Sian Edwards • 3 August

PROMS SATURDAY MATINEE 3
Alison Balsom *trumpet*, Camerata Ireland/
Barry Douglas *piano/director* • 10 August

PROMS SATURDAY MATINEE 4
Ben Johnson *tenor*, Richard Watkins *horn*,
English Chamber Orchestra/Paul Watkins
24 August

PROMS SATURDAY MATINEE 5
Catherine Bullock *viola*, Camerata Nordica,
Terje Tønnesen *violin/director* • 31 August

Proms Chamber Music and Proms Saturday Matinee concerts are broadcast live on BBC Radio 3; Proms Chamber Music concerts are also repeated the following Saturday at 2.00pm.

FROM THE STREETS
TO THE STAGE

Three boundary-crossing Proms this summer bring the raw energy of urban pop, the vocal dexterity of beatboxing and the warm glow of gospel under the Royal Albert Hall spotlights. **ANDY MORGAN** finds their contrasting grooves share a power to shake the soul

I can picture conductor Jules Buckley playing matchmaker, sitting between a classical music fan and an urban pop lover. To Mr Classical: 'I love and respect classical music, but that doesn't mean an orchestra can't explore other styles, other musical worlds.' Then, to Ms Urban Pop: 'Look, an orchestra can produce the richest, subtlest sounds imaginable and they'll go with anything … hip hop, samba, tango, grime … Believe me!'

If you don't rate Buckley's chances of getting these two to tie the knot, you might need to think again. Buckley, who formed the multi-purpose Heritage Orchestra in his final year at the Guildhall School of Music & Drama back in 2004, has already married the lush intricacies of a full-blown orchestra with contemporary artists as diverse as Basement Jaxx, Amon Tobin, Arctic Monkeys, Airto Moreira and Professor Green, and he's also backed Jamie Cullum and Australian comic genius Tim Minchin at the Proms.

By dint of his talent, affability and daring, Buckley has managed to work with some of Europe's greatest orchestral ensembles and expand the frontiers of rock, pop, jazz and urban music at the same time.

On 10 August Buckley conducts the BBC Symphony Orchestra in a night of orchestral mash-ups called 'Urban Classic'. His job is to create the intricate sonic landscapes through which the rhymes and voices of a host of urban music stars will be free to roam, prominent among whom are rapper, DJ and producer Fazer from hip hop group N-Dubz.

'To perform a mash-up project like this in a classical music festival might attract some scepticism,' Buckley recognises. 'The challenge with this Prom is to bring these two worlds together and unify them in one strong musical message.' What does Buckley aim to achieve?

'To get the Albert Hall banging from the rafters, of course!'

The essence of the Urban Classic Prom is to prove that the raw emotional energy of pop and the trumping graces of classical music and jazz – intricacy, rigour, precision and a kind of heightened sonic curiosity – aren't mutually exclusive. Quite the opposite.

A similar credo has elevated Naturally 7 from what they might have been – a reliable *a cappella* septet from New York singing

> The essence of the Urban Classic Prom is to prove that the raw emotional energy of pop and the trumping graces of classical music and jazz aren't mutually exclusive. Quite the opposite.

text-book gospel and pop – into one of the most extraordinary vocal groups in the world.

Roger Thomas and his brother Warren formed Naturally 7 back in 1999 but they soon hit a musical identity crisis. Were they going to remain a vocal group in the great African

Seven voices, an orchestra of sounds: Naturally 7 (Prom 22)

American tradition that winds its way back through doo-wop to gospel and beyond? Or were they going to become a band with drums, bass, keyboards and all the rest? The eureka moment came when Roger Thomas realised that they could do both – but without the need for physical instruments.

The seven vocal crusaders set about inventing a whole new genre, which they called 'vocal play'. Those tempted to define it as *a cappella* with a bit of beatboxing (emulating bass, drums and turntable 'scratching' sounds with the voice alone) are wide of the mark. Even the best beatboxers don't have more than a handful of sounds in their box of tricks.

Naturally 7 have an entire big band in theirs, including bass, drums, keyboards, brass section and several varieties of guitar. Oh, and all their 'regular' singing voices as well. I mean real, soaring, soul-melting voices.

The result is an orchestra without instruments, an *a cappella* group that's also a band, a virtuoso vocal combo that has expanded the boundaries of the term 'vocal ensemble' almost beyond the imagination. If you're not that impressed by the fact that they've supported Coldplay and vocal superstar Michael Bublé or duetted with hip-hop giant Ludacris at Quincy Jones's request and appeared on Jay Leno's late-night

US TV show, perhaps the simple claim that Naturally 7 give 'one of the must-see performances of all time', made by none other than Brian Eno, will sound convincing.

Their fresh and fearless reinterpretations of Simon and Garfunkel and Herbie Hancock classics, their skyscraping version of Phil Collins's 'In the Air Tonight' (a spontaneous version of which, on the Paris Métro, has scored nearly 5.5 million hits on YouTube), their skilful union of vocal precision and heart-grasping emotion make their Late Night Prom on 29 July an unmissable event.

And finally, we go back to where it all began, to a group of men and women ▶

WNO
WELSH
NATIONAL
OPERA
CENEDLAETHOL
CYMRU

2013/2014

The Tudors
Autumn 2013

Anna Bolena
Maria Stuarda
Robert Devereux
Donizetti

Tosca
Puccini

Fallen Women
Spring 2014

Manon Lescaut
Puccini
Boulevard Solitude
Henze
La traviata
Verdi

Faith/British Firsts
Summer 2014

Moses und Aron
Schoenberg
Nabucco
Verdi
**The Fall of the
House of Usher**
(Double bill)
Getty/Debussy

Across Wales and England
Book now **wno.org.uk**

Supported by
The National Lottery®
through the Arts Council of Wales

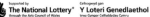
Cefnogwyd gan
Y Loteri Genedlaethol
trwy Gyngor Celfyddydau Cymru

Cyngor Celfyddydau Cymru
Arts Council of Wales

Noddir gan
Lywodraeth Cymru
Sponsored by
Welsh Government

Supported using public funding by
**ARTS COUNCIL
ENGLAND**

Registered Charity No 221538

An urban classic: Fazer (Prom 37)

Harmony with soul: London Community Gospel Choir (Prom 7)

standing in a hallowed place and pouring out their hearts and souls in praise of God. Gospel is the granddaddy of the most uplifting soul, urban and pop music. Those massed voices, reaching higher, delving deeper, in complete, goose-pimpling harmony, produce one of the most rousing sounds that humanity has ever invented.

On 16 July that sound will pour forth as the best choirs and soloists in the UK – including Muyiwa & Riversongz and the London Community Gospel Choir – take you on a journey through the history of British gospel. From Wesleyan hymns that were sung in the churches of Jamaica, Barbados, Saint Kitts and Trinidad in the 18th century, via the spirituals that gave

succour to African men and women in the days of slavery, to traditional American gospel and the pride of African praise songs, the whole epic of African spiritual music in exile bursts into the Royal Albert Hall in its fullest glory.

Which of these three unforgettable deviations from the classical core of the BBC Proms most effectively blows the rafters remains to be seen. What's certain is that, looking up, as well as seeing grand arches and the Hall's handsome dome, you'll be glimpsing the stars. ●

Andy Morgan writes about music, culture, society and politics for *The Independent*, *fRoots*, *Songlines* and other publications. He is currently writing a book about the band Tinariwen, and researching and editing a book about the singer Manu Chao.

GOSPEL PROM

Pastor David Daniel *host*,
London Adventist Chorale,
London Community Gospel Choir,
Muyiwa & Riversongz,
People's Christian Fellowship Choir

PROM 7 • 16 JULY

NATURALLY 7
PROM 22 • 29 JULY

URBAN CLASSIC PROM

Fazer, Laura Mvula,
Maverick Sabre, BBC Symphony
Orchestra/Jules Buckley

PROM 37 • 10 AUGUST

PASSING THE
BATON

Conductors Sakari Oramo and Marin Alsop respectively take the helm at the First and Last Nights of this year's BBC Proms – **JAMES JOLLY** talks to them about how they are preparing

The First Night and the Last Night: the Alpha and Omega of the British musical summer season. Only this year it's not A&O but O&A – Oramo and Alsop! The two concerts that bookend this greatest of classical musical festivals hold their own special significance.

When the Finnish conductor Sakari Oramo takes to the podium on Friday 12 July, he'll be making his first official appearance as the Chief Conductor of the BBC Symphony Orchestra. 'I'm so excited by our partnership,' he explains, with barely controlled anticipation. 'The orchestra offers endless possibilities and there's more: the choruses, the exuberance of the Proms and all the other special projects such as the Total Immersion days. It's the whole package that attracts me.'

The First Night has gone through various incarnations down the years: sometimes a head-spinning potpourri of different composers, sometimes a huge work such as Mahler's 'Symphony of a Thousand', Handel's *Messiah* or Schoenberg's *Gurrelieder*, or sometimes a kind of 'taster menu' of the concerts to follow. Sakari Oramo's programme is broad, with a nod in the direction of two of this year's great anniversary composers, Benjamin Britten and Witold Lutosławski. The first music we'll hear is a fanfare – a world premiere – by Julian Anderson, a composer Oramo came to know in the early 2000s during his tenure at the City

The theme of communal sharing, growth and celebration epitomises the spirit of the Last Night.

Sakari Oramo takes up the baton as Chief Conductor of the BBC Symphony Orchestra at the First Night

Marin Alsop pairs Britten and Bernstein in her first Last Night

of Birmingham Symphony Orchestra. Reflecting on the two anniversaries, Oramo suggests that the stars must have been in some very special alignment in 1913. 'I recently conducted an all-Lutosławski programme in Stockholm and the wisdom, humanity and sheer beauty of his music makes me feel very close to him. I also love Britten, a powerful and humane voice – just listen to the incredible and unprecedented "brightissimo" colours in the Sea Interludes.'

The 'big work', however, is Vaughan Williams's *A Sea Symphony*, his first foray into symphony writing. 'It certainly is a most intriguing piece and a very bold first symphonic statement indeed. I'm sure it will be one of my favourites once I get past the huge amount of brainwork that goes into understanding a piece on this scale.' That scale has been enlarged by the enormous chorus that will be assembled for the First Night: some 450 voices in all, drawing on singers from across the UK who have formed the Proms Youth Choir and will be joining forces with the BBC Symphony Chorus. At the heart of the programme is a reunion with the pianist Stephen Hough, with whom Oramo recorded all of Saint-Saëns's piano concertos – a set that won them *Gramophone*'s Recording of the Year. 'Stephen is a complete treasure to work with. Although we are temperamentally

fairly different, his combination of depth, mercurial reaction and profound clarity of musical thought never fails to excite me.' So expect a performance of Rachmaninov's *Rhapsody on a Theme of Paganini* that sets some sparks flying – and if you crave more of that catchy Paganini theme, Lutosławski's *Variations* on the same tune close the first part of the concert.

The Last Night is another beast entirely. Marin Alsop, it hardly needs stating, is the first woman to take charge and she, too, is champing at the bit. The exuberance of the occasion holds few fears for her, especially after last year's rapturous response to her visit with the São Paulo Symphony Orchestra: 'To be the first Brazilian orchestra to perform at the Proms and to feel the overwhelming warmth and support from the public and press was thrilling. For me the real joy came from watching my musicians embracing and relishing every moment of the experience.' She is very fond of British music and music-making too. 'I adore working with British musicians; they are passionate, funny, hard-working and brutally honest. Perhaps it is my own personal mix of deep emotionality behind a controlled exterior that enables me to relate so profoundly to so many works by British composers, past and present.'

She plans to link Britten and Bernstein (who in real life held each other in slightly wary regard) by fusing the former's *The Building of the House* with Bernstein's 'Make our Garden Grow' from *Candide*. 'This theme of communal sharing, growth and celebration epitomises the spirit of the Last Night for me.' The festive close also contains a new work by Anna Clyne, a composer of whom Alsop has become a passionate champion: 'Anna's a unique and compelling voice in today's new music, with depth and relevance to our current world. She's a fascinating and compassionate human being also, which makes performing her music all the more fulfilling.'

Finally, no Last Night would be complete without some star-soloist appeal: the mezzo of the moment, Joyce DiDonato, takes vocal charge and Nigel Kennedy, a contemporary of Marin's at New York's Juilliard School, will lend his unique charisma to the occasion. 'We've known each other peripherally for a long time!' Marin recalls, 'I love jazz and had a swing band for 20 years called String Fever. I used to go hear Nigel jam with Stéphane Grappelli in New York City and so admire his wealth of talent.' ●

James Jolly is Editor-in-Chief of *Gramophone* and a regular voice on BBC Radio 3 as co-presenter of *Sunday Morning*.

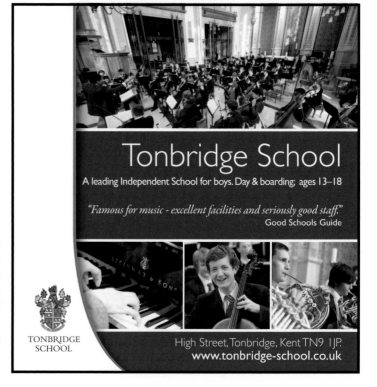

Music Scholarships

Music scholarships and exhibitions available for girls and boys 13+ and 16+

Bursaries up to full sponsorship (means tested)

Visiting consultants include Remus Azoitei, Roderick Williams, David Whitson, Paul Cosh and the Maggini Quartet

Specialist Music Scheme

Concerto opportunities, recording studio, international tours

You are very welcome to visit our excellent facilities and meet the Director of Music, Simon Williamson, to discuss how Wellington can help to shape your child's future in music.

WELLINGTON COLLEGE

WELLINGTONCOLLEGE.ORG.UK
MUSIC@WELLINGTONCOLLEGE.ORG.UK
+44 (0)1344 444201 | @ WELLY_MUSIC 🐦
WELLINGTON COLLEGE, CROWTHORNE, BERKSHIRE RG45 7PU

The Pilgrims' School, Winchester

Be a Chorister Day
12th October
Assessment Day
9th November
Choristers' Assessments and Auditions
16th November

Nestled in the historic heart of Winchester, less than one hour from London, the cathedral school offers a rounded education for boys aged 4-13, with boarding available for boys aged 8 and above.

Incorporating the Winchester Cathedral Choristers and the Winchester College Quiristers, the school offers free instrumental tuition to the boys of both professional choirs, with scholarships and bursaries available worth up to 100% of the full fees. Potential choristers are warmly invited to come for an informal audition at any time throughout the year.

www.thepilgrims-school.co.uk
admissions@pilgrims-school.co.uk |01962 854189

SEAFORD
COLLEGE

Founded in 1884 and set in a 400 acre park at the foot of the South Downs, Seaford College is an independent HMC co-educational day and boarding school for pupils aged 7-18.

The Chapel Choir has performed at Cathedrals around the country, including Chichester, Winchester and York Minster. Tuition is available in all standard and popular instruments and the College has a number of thriving rock and jazz bands.

Magnificent music department with recital room, computer room, ten sound-proofed practice rooms, separate class and keyboard rooms & music technology suite.

The Johnson Trust. Registered Charity No. 277439

Music Awards - Annual organ scholarship.

Further details from the admissions secretary Julie Mackay Smith
email: JMackay@seaford.org
Telephone: 01798 867456 Fax: 01798 867606

www.seaford.org

THE LONDON ORATORY SCHOOL
Junior House

"standards of singing throughout the school are exceptional"

Ofsted Music Inspection - 2010

A free first class specialist musical education for Roman Catholic boys aged 7-18

Places for instrumentalists and choristers

A free chorister education within the State system with guaranteed admission to the Senior School at 11

A first-rate education at one of the country's premier state schools

Continued annual success with Oxbridge choral/organ scholarships and conservatoire places

"a super start in life for your musical, Catholic motivated little boy." The Good Schools Guide 2010

The London Oratory School's Junior House provides a unique opportunity for potential choristers and instrumentalists.

The school's leading choir, the Schola Cantorum, sings at the London Oratory Church frequently and records for television and film including *Harry Potter* and *Lord of the Rings* and performances at The Royal Opera House.

Further information may be obtained from the school t: 020-7385-0102 or visit our website www.london-oratory.org

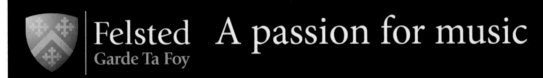

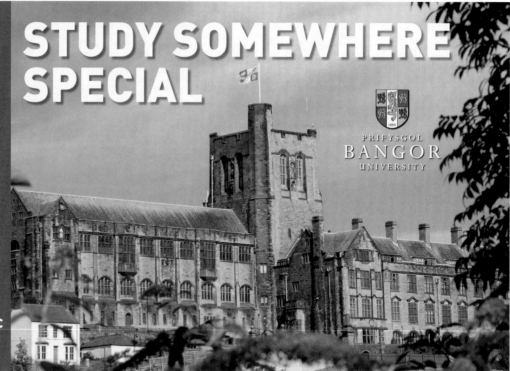

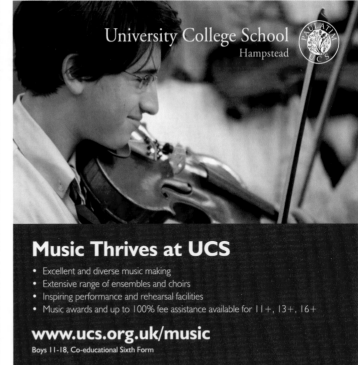

UNIVERSITY OF
WEST LONDON
London College of **Music**

Connect**Ed.**

London College of Music

s one of the largest specialist music and performing arts
nstitutions in the UK, offering an impressive range of
traditional, innovative and creative courses, delivered with
passion and flair. We also offer many of our courses on a
part-time basis to fit around your current commitments.

Located among the UK's leading music and media
businesses, we will ensure that your experience is real and
relevant in preparing you to pursue your own musical
interests.

Undergraduate portfolio:
- Music Technology
- Performance
- Composition
- Musical Theatre
- Music Management

Postgraduate portfolio:
- Performance
- Composition
- Music Technology
- Music Management

uwl.ac.uk/
lcm

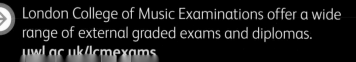

London College of Music Examinations offer a wide
range of external graded exams and diplomas.
uwl.ac.uk/lcmexams

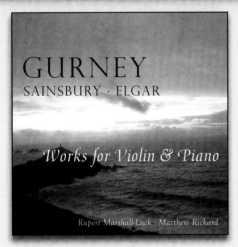

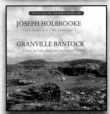

   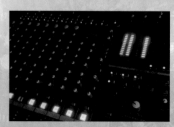

CONCERT LISTINGS

BOOKING

Tickets will go on sale at 9.00am on Saturday 11 May – online, by telephone and in person. Tickets may also be requested by post.

Plan your Proms concert-going online, before tickets go on sale, by using the Proms Planner at bbc.co.uk/proms from 2.00pm on Thursday 18 April until midnight on Friday 10 May.

ONLINE bbc.co.uk/proms

TELEPHONE 0845 401 5040*

For full booking information, see pages 162–72

*see page 167 for call-cost information

PRICE CODES

Each concert at the Royal Albert Hall falls into one of eight price bands, colour-coded for ease of reference. For a full list of prices, see page 164. For special offers, see page 168.

Please note: *concert start-times vary across the season – check before you book*

The BBC: bringing the Proms to you – in concert, on radio, television and online

FRIDAY 12 JULY

PROM 1
7.30pm–c10.20pm • Royal Albert Hall

PRICE BAND Ⓑ *Seats £9.50 to £46*

Julian Anderson
Harmony   *c4'*
BBC commission: world premiere

Britten
Four Sea Interludes from 'Peter Grimes'   *17'*

Rachmaninov
Rhapsody on a Theme of Paganini   *23'*

Lutosławski
Variations on a Theme by Paganini   *8'*

INTERVAL

Vaughan Williams
A Sea Symphony   *66'*

Sally Matthews soprano
Roderick Williams baritone
Stephen Hough piano

BBC Proms Youth Choir
BBC Symphony Chorus
BBC Symphony Orchestra
Sakari Oramo conductor

The 2013 BBC Proms begins with a surge of natural energy in sea-inspired works by Britten and Vaughan Williams (the latter combining the 300-strong Proms Youth Choir and the BBC Symphony Chorus). A world premiere from Julian Anderson and two sets of Paganini variations by Rachmaninov and featured composer Lutosławski add pianistic stardust. *See 'A Polish Awakening', pages 30–35; 'Revealing Britten', pages 38–43; 'New Music', pages 62–69; 'Passing the Baton', pages 102–103.*

BROADCAST
RADIO *Live on Radio 3*
ONLINE *Live and 'listen again' options at bbc.co.uk/proms*
TV *Broadcast on BBC Two later this evening*

PROMS PLUS IN TUNE
4.30pm • Royal College of Music Suzy Klein presents a live Proms edition of BBC Radio 3's *In Tune*, featuring artists from the season. *Broadcast live on BBC Radio 3. Tickets available from BBC Studio audiences, bbc.co.uk/tickets*

SPOTLIGHT ON...
Stephen Hough • Prom 1

Stephen Hough opens this year's festival with a Proms first: the back-to-back performance of two responses to Paganini's famous theme. 'I've played Rachmaninov's *Rhapsody* many times but the Lutosławski is new to me. I think the pieces work really well as a pair – the latter is almost like an encore really. Besides the Slavic roots of both composers, there's a glitter of pianism and colour of orchestration that they both share.' Paganini's 24th *Caprice* has inspired composers from Liszt to Andrew Lloyd Webber, but what makes it so irresistible? 'It's clean and simple; its harmonic outline is clear enough to allow for plenty of twists and turns, and it has a circle of fifths in the second half that allows for emotional poignancy. The Rachmaninov is a work of genius, a fully composed piece using the variation form as a launching pad, whereas the Lutosławski is more lightweight, taking the Paganini as a template.'

Having given concerts all over the world, how does Hough think the Proms attracts such a diverse audience? 'It's partly pricing, partly the summer – warm days and the chance perhaps to take in the green grass of Hyde Park beforehand. But it's also the result of years of innovative programming. It's like a great feast where you can enter, eat and leave day after day.'

SATURDAY 13 JULY

PROM 2
7.30pm–c9.45pm • Royal Albert Hall

PRICE BAND Ⓒ *Seats £14 to £57*

DOCTOR WHO PROM

Programme to include:

Murray Gold
Music from the *Doctor Who* series

and other music from the series, including the Habanera from Bizet's Carmen Suite No. 2, Debussy's 'La fille aux cheveux de lin' and Bach's Toccata and Fugue in D minor

London Philharmonic Choir
BBC National Orchestra of Wales
Ben Foster conductor

There will be one interval

Doctor Who returns to the Proms to celebrate the 50th anniversary of the popular BBC series. As well as showcasing Murray Gold's music from the past eight years, the concert also journeys back to the early days of *Doctor Who* and the groundbreaking work of the BBC Radiophonic Workshop. Featuring special guests from the series, big screens and a host of monsters ready to invade the Royal Albert Hall, this is not the year to be exterminated! *See 'New Adventures', pages 80–87.*

BROADCAST
RADIO *Live on Radio 3*
ONLINE *Live and 'listen again' options at bbc.co.uk/proms*
TV *Recorded for broadcast on BBC One*

PROMS PLUS STORYTIME
11.30am • Royal College of Music Hannah Conway presents stories and music based on Oliver Jeffers's *Lost and Found*. For details, see page 87.
Recorded for broadcast on BBC Radio 3 and Radio 4 Extra

PROMS PLUS INTRO
5.45pm • Royal College of Music *Doctor Who* enthusiast Matthew Sweet looks back over 50 years of the BBC series.
Edited version broadcast on BBC Radio 3 during tonight's interval

SUNDAY 14 JULY

PROM 3
10.30am–c12.45pm • Royal Albert Hall

PRICE BAND *Seats £6/£12*

DOCTOR WHO PROM

London Philharmonic Choir
BBC National Orchestra of Wales
Ben Foster *conductor*

For programme details, see Prom 2

DOCTOR WHO PROM, 2010

PROMS PLUS FAMILY ORCHESTRA & CHORUS
2.00pm • Royal College of Music Join the Proms Family
Orchestra and Chorus in creating its own *Doctor Who*
soundtrack. See pages 80–87 for details of how to sign up.

SUNDAY 14 JULY

PROM 4
7.30pm–c9.45pm • Royal Albert Hall

PRICE BAND **B** *Seats £9.50 to £46*

Lully
Le bourgeois gentilhomme – overture
and dances   *11'*

Rameau
Les Indes galantes – dances   *16'*

Delibes
Coppélia – excerpts   *15'*

Massenet
Le Cid – ballet music (excerpts)   *13'*

INTERVAL

Stravinsky
The Rite of Spring   *35'*

Les Siècles
François-Xavier Roth *conductor*

An evening of riot and revolution in dance music
from the court of Louis XIV to the Ballets Russes.
François-Xavier Roth directs Les Siècles in the
first period-instrument performance at the Proms
of Stravinsky's *The Rite of Spring*, marking the work's
centenary. Suites from Lully's piquant social comedy
Le bourgeois gentilhomme, Rameau's *Les Indes
galantes*, Delibes's *Coppélia* and Massenet's
Moorish romance *Le Cid* provide more than
two centuries of historical context for the
work that scandalised and galvanised Paris
at its 1913 premiere.

SAME-
DAY SAVER
Proms 3 & 4
(see page 168)

BROADCAST
RADIO *Live on Radio 3*
ONLINE *Live and 'listen again' options at bbc.co.uk/proms*
TV *Recorded for broadcast on BBC Four on 21 July*

PROMS PLUS INTRO
5.45pm • Royal College of Music A discussion on the
history of French ballet from Lully to Stravinsky and an
examination of *The Rite of Spring*, 100 years after its
premiere, with Jane Pritchard, Dance Historian at the
Victoria & Albert Museum.
Edited version broadcast on BBC Radio 3 during tonight's interval

---

SPOTLIGHT ON...

François-Xavier Roth • Prom 4

'We will be bringing so many instruments
along for this concert, you wouldn't believe it!'
Conductor François-Xavier Roth is not
exaggerating. His orchestra Les Siècles takes
the ideal of using period instruments to its
logical conclusion – by applying it to all
repertoire. His programme follows the theme
of the ballet in French culture from Lully and
Rameau, to Delibes and Massenet,
culminating in Stravinsky's *The Rite of Spring*.
'We have researched the first performance of
this great work in Paris in 1913 and we will be
recreating the exact orchestra used at the Paris
Opéra, from the specific French harps and
pianos to the brass and fascinating French
wind instruments of the period.' The concert
starts with just 20 to 30 instruments for
Lully's *Le bourgeois gentilhomme*, growing
to over 100 for *The Rite*.

Roth is particularly keen to present the
music of Delibes and Massenet, sometimes
neglected outside France: 'These are beautiful
scores, which combine colour and rhythmical
dexterity in such a sophisticated way. It's vital
to find a balance between the articulation and
the dancing rhythms: they must never be
pushed, or too loud. I would say the same
equilibrium is needed for Lully, too – I hope
we will be able to trace these links in dance
music down the centuries.'

MONDAY 15 JULY

PROMS CHAMBER MUSIC 1
1.00pm–c2.00pm • Cadogan Hall

Seats £10 / £12

Ravel
Violin Sonata   17'

Mozart
Violin Sonata in G major, K379   20'

Lutosławski
Partita   15'

Vilde Frang *violin*
Michail Lifits *piano*

There will be no interval

Ahead of her Proms concerto debut with the
BBC Philharmonic and John Storgårds (Prom 31),
Norwegian violinist Vilde Frang explores the cool
contours and tart syncopations of Ravel's
jazz-influenced Violin Sonata with German pianist
Michail Lifits. An expressive Partita from centenary
composer Lutosławski and the lyrical dialogue of
Mozart's 1781 Sonata in G, K379, complete the first
programme of the Proms Chamber Music series at
Cadogan Hall. See 'A Polish Awakening', pages 30–35;
'Small is Beautiful', pages 96–97.

BROADCAST
RADIO *Live on Radio 3*
ONLINE *Live and 'listen again' options at bbc.co.uk/proms*

MICHAIL LIFITS

SPOTLIGHT ON...
Vilde Frang • PCM 1

The young Norwegian violinist may be making
her debut this year, but the Proms has already
played an important part in Vilde Frang's
musical life. 'I've never attended the concerts
live, but some of my greatest musical
experiences have come through Proms
broadcasts. I shall never forget hearing
Sir Roger Norrington conduct Schubert's
Ninth Symphony on the radio in 2001 with
the Stuttgart Radio Symphony Orchestra.
Listening to it, I felt as if I was on a train seeing
a landscape fly by; it was amazing. The next
day I asked the radio station for a tape – it's
still one of my top three recordings!'

   As well as Bruch's Violin Concerto No. 1
(Prom 31) Frang gives a Proms Chamber Music
recital with Michail Lifits, which includes
Lutosławksi's *Partita*. 'It's right up there with
the great sonatas,' she enthuses. 'I feel very
emotional about it, it really matters. Certainly,
it was a challenge to learn, I enjoyed digging
into it. I find the small movements without
bar lines between the main ones a refreshing
element.' The daughter of an artist and double
bassist, Frang thinks of programming like
the grouping of paintings. The Lutosławksi
is contrasted with Mozart and with Ravel's
Sonata, a particular favourite: 'It's light,
lyrical and I'm very attracted to its
wonderful, elegant Blues.'

MONDAY 15 JULY

PROM 5
7.30pm–c9.55pm • Royal Albert Hall

PRICE BAND (A) *Seats £7.50 to £36*

Helmut Lachenmann
Tanzsuite mit Deutschlandlied   c36'
UK premiere

INTERVAL

Mahler
Symphony No. 5 in C sharp minor   73'

Arditti Quartet

Bamberg Symphony Orchestra
Jonathan Nott *conductor*

The brilliantly virtuosic Arditti Quartet and a
conductor and orchestra acclaimed for their
interpretations of Mahler join forces in the
UK premiere of Helmut Lachenmann's *Tanzsuite
mit Deutschlandlied*. Previously unheard at the
Proms, the blistered, metallic timbres and subtle
textures of Lachenmann's 'musique concrète
instrumentale' unsettle and transfix, creating an
abrasive yet alluring sound-world ideally suited to
the Ardittis and the Bamberg Symphony Orchestra.
Written over the summers of 1901 and 1902,
Mahler's Fifth Symphony concludes the programme,
its famous Adagietto
a love-letter to the
composer's wife, Alma.
See 'New Music' pages
62–69.

JONATHAN NOTT

BROADCAST
RADIO *Live on Radio 3*
ONLINE *Live and 'listen
again' options at bbc.co.uk/
proms*
TV *Recorded for broadcast
on BBC Four on 18 July
(Mahler only)*

PROMS PLUS LITERARY
5.45pm • Royal College of Music Conductor Kenneth
Woods introduces a selection of readings about Gustav
Mahler, including the composer's letters, reviews and
biographies. Rana Mitter presents.
Edited version broadcast on BBC Radio 3 during tonight's interval

SPOTLIGHT ON...

Nobuyuki Tsujii • Prom 6

Young Japanese pianist Nobuyuki Tsujii came to international attention when he became joint winner of the Van Cliburn International Piano Competition in 2009. Blind since birth, he not only has an international performing career but is in demand as a film composer. He admires composer-pianists from Rachmaninov to Fazil Say and says, 'It's one of my wildest dreams to compose a sonata or concerto that will survive and remain in the repertoire.'

He first encountered Rachmaninov's Second Piano Concerto when he was 10, and is 'fascinated by its romantic and deep emotion'. He may be making his Proms debut this year, but he and the BBC Philharmonic are old friends. Indeed, he was touring Japan with that very orchestra in March 2011 when the earthquakes struck: 'The tour was immediately terminated. It was heartbreaking such a huge number of people were lost or injured. The experience led me to think about what music can do for those who suffer. It may not help directly in reconstructing a town, but I believe music has the power to heal the souls of those who have given up hope.' This April, the BBC Philharmonic returns to Japan with Nobuyuki. 'I respect these musicians so much: they had a scary experience but they have decided to come back. Their message to the Japanese people is "You will never walk alone."'

TUESDAY 16 JULY

PROM 6
7.00pm–c9.15pm • Royal Albert Hall

PRICE BAND **A** *Seats £7.50 to £36*

David Matthews
A Vision of the Sea   c20'
BBC commission: world premiere

Rachmaninov
Piano Concerto No. 2 in C minor   35'

INTERVAL

Nielsen
Symphony No. 4, 'Inextinguishable'   36'

Nobuyuki Tsujii *piano*

BBC Philharmonic
Juanjo Mena *conductor*

Herring gulls loop and wheel overhead as Juanjo Mena conducts the BBC Philharmonic in the world premiere of David Matthews's *A Vision of the Sea*, inspired by Shelley's poetry, the pull of the tide on the Kent coast and an evocation of the sound of sunrise as recorded by scientists from Sheffield University. Nobuyuki Tsujii – a regular collaborator with the orchestra and a winner of the Van Cliburn International Piano Competition – makes his Proms debut in Rachmaninov's Second Piano Concerto before Mena and his players tackle Nielsen's irrepressible 'Inextinguishable' Fourth Symphony. *See 'Craving the Keyboard' pages 56–59; 'New Music', pages 62–69.*

JUANJO MENA

BROADCAST
RADIO *Live on Radio 3*
ONLINE *Live and 'listen again' options at bbc.co.uk/proms*
TV *Recorded for broadcast on BBC Four on 19 July*

PROMS PLUS INTRO
5.15pm • **Royal College of Music** Louise Fryer speaks to David Matthews about his new commission and Daniel Grimley gives an introduction to Nielsen and his 'Inextinguishable' Symphony No. 4.
Edited version broadcast on BBC Radio 3 during tonight's interval

---

TUESDAY 16 JULY

PROM 7
10.15pm–c11.30pm • Royal Albert Hall

PRICE BAND **E** *Seats £12/£16*

GOSPEL PROM

Pastor David Daniel *host*

Muyiwa & Riversongz

London Adventist Chorale
Ken Burton *conductor*

London Community Gospel Choir
Rebecca Thomas *conductor*

People's Christian Fellowship Choir
Ruth Waldron *conductor*

There will be no interval

SAME-DAY SAVER
Proms 6 & 7
(see page 168)

What does gospel music mean today? The Proms explores this emotive and richly varied world – the meeting and mixing of musical styles of four continents. Leading vocal ensembles combine with community choirs and soloists to create a thrilling massed wall of sound for favourites such as 'How Great Thou Art', 'Swing Low, Sweet Chariot' and 'O Happy Day', interspersed with individual contributions. The British-Caribbean People's Christian Fellowship Choir juxtaposes popular hymns with calypso choruses, while the London Adventist Chorale reminds us how African Americans turned to spirituals in their fight for freedom. Muyiwa & Riversongz bring West African highlife praise to another level, while the London Community Gospel Choir merges Caribbean and African traditions with new songs inspired by funk and rock. *See 'Late Night Tonic', pages 94–95; 'From the Streets to the Stage', pages 98–101.*

MUYIWA

BROADCAST
RADIO *Live on Radio 3*
ONLINE *Live and 'listen again' options at bbc.co.uk/proms*

WEDNESDAY 17 JULY

PROM 8
7.30pm–c9.55pm • Royal Albert Hall

PRICE BAND (A) Seats £7.50 to £36

Britten
Sinfonia da Requiem   20'

Lutosławski
Cello Concerto   24'

INTERVAL

Thomas Adès
Totentanz   c45'
world premiere

Paul Watkins cello
Christianne Stotijn mezzo-soprano
Simon Keenlyside baritone

BBC Symphony Orchestra
Thomas Adès conductor

Britten's *Sinfonia da Requiem* opens
a programme of testimony and
remembrance. Paul Watkins is
the soloist in Lutosławski's bleak
and beautiful Cello Concerto,
composed for and dedicated to
Mstislav Rostropovich in a period of
violent protest and political repression in Poland.
Thomas Adès conducts the BBC Symphony
Orchestra and soloists Christianne Stotijn and
Simon Keenlyside in the world premiere of his
Totentanz, a commission in memory of Lutosławski,
which sets an anonymous 15th-century text that
accompanied a frieze destroyed when Lübeck's
Marienkirche was bombed in the Second World
War. See 'A Polish Awakening', pages 30–35; 'New
Music', pages 62–69.

CHRISTIANNE
STOTIJN

BROADCAST
RADIO Live on Radio 3
ONLINE Live and 'listen again' options at bbc.co.uk/proms
TV Recorded for broadcast on BBC Four on 28 July

PROMS PLUS LITERARY
5.45pm • Royal College of Music Writer Eva Hoffman talks
to Rana Mitter about the proliferation of contemporary
literature and visual arts created by Polish artists.
Edited version broadcast on BBC Radio 3 during tonight's interval

SPOTLIGHT ON...
Paul Watkins • Prom 8

Cellist Paul Watkins observes that both pieces
in the first half of this concert start with the
note D: 'The D minor of Britten's *Sinfonia da
Requiem* spells the height of tragedy, but
Lutosławski asks the soloist to play the repeated
Ds that open his concerto 'indifferently': you
spend your entire life training to emote and here
you're asked to do nothing at all! They exist in
a sort of vacuum.'

We have Rostropovich to thank for
Lutosławski's Cello Concerto – many have seen
it as dramatising his suppressed conflict with the
Soviet state. Watkins is keen to steer away from
specific narratives: 'Lutosławski strongly resisted
attempts to put programmes on to his music and
I approach this as an essentially musical drama.
The soloist is engaged in a heroic struggle against
groups from the orchestra, who become more
and more assertive, until a battery of irascible
trumpets threatens to overwhelm me. There's
a point near the end when the cello makes
weeping sounds like an exhausted child, but it
eventually escapes into its own space.' Aleatoric
or chance elements written into optional
passages are tightly controlled, as Watkins
explains: 'These need to be discussed and agreed
on. It's a huge challenge, rather like a relay race
where the soloist is unexpectedly passing on a
baton to the conductor. I'm so glad Tom Adès
is conducting as this is child's play for him!'

THURSDAY 18 JULY

PROM 9
7.00pm–c9.05pm • Royal Albert Hall

PRICE BAND (A) Seats £7.50 to £36

Stenhammar
Excelsior!   13'

Szymanowski
Symphony No. 3, 'The Song of the Night'   25'

INTERVAL

R. Strauss
An Alpine Symphony   50'

Michael Weinius tenor

BBC National Chorus of Wales
BBC Symphony Chorus
BBC National Orchestra of Wales
Thomas Søndergård conductor

Evocations of Nordic forests, Persian gardens and
snow-capped mountains feature in Thomas
Søndergård's first Prom as Principal Conductor
of tonight's orchestra. Wilhelm Stenhammar's 1896
symphonic overture *Excelsior!* leads into the opulent
sound-world of Karol Syzmanowski's Symphony
No. 3, 'The Song of the Night'. A journey from
just before dawn and into the
following night, Richard Strauss's
Alpine Symphony is as much a
statement of the composer's
personal philosophy as a
description of the natural world at
its most dramatic. See 'A Polish
Awakening', pages 30–35.

THOMAS
SØNDERGÅRD

BROADCAST
RADIO Live on Radio 3
ONLINE Live and 'listen again' options at bbc.co.uk/proms

PROMS PLUS FAMILY
5.00pm • Royal College of Music Join Rachel Leach on an
epic climb up an Alpine mountain, from twilight to nightfall
with every tiny detail described along the way.

PROMS PLUS LATE
Elgar Room, Royal Albert Hall Informal post-Prom music
and poetry. For details see bbc.co.uk/proms

FRIDAY 19 JULY

PROM 10
6.30pm–c9.10pm • Royal Albert Hall

PRICE BAND **C** *Seats £14 to £57*

Mozart
Symphony No. 35
in D major, K385, 'Haffner'   20'

Schumann
Piano Concerto in A minor   30'

INTERVAL

Rachmaninov
Symphony No. 2 in E minor   60'

Jan Lisiecki *piano*

**Orchestra of the Academy
of Santa Cecilia, Rome**
Sir Antonio Pappano *conductor*

Sir Antonio Pappano and the Orchestra of
the Academy of Santa Cecilia, Rome, take a
musical journey that begins with the ceremonial fizz
and pomp of Mozart's 'Haffner' Symphony and ends
in the burnished melancholy and high drama of
Rachmaninov's Symphony No. 2. Jan Lisiecki makes
his Proms debut in Schumann's Piano Concerto, a
work that eschews empty technical display and calls
instead for a detailed and intimate dialogue between
pianist and orchestra: chamber music on a grand
scale. See 'Craving the
Keyboard', pages 56–59.

BROADCAST
RADIO *Live on Radio 3*
ONLINE *Live and 'listen
again' options at bbc.co.uk/
proms*

JAN LISIECKI

PROMS PLUS INTRO
4.45pm • Royal College of Music Louise Fryer is joined by
composer and musicologist William Mival to discuss
Rachmaninov and his Symphony No. 2.
Edited version broadcast on BBC Radio 3 during tonight's interval

FRIDAY 19 JULY

PROM 11
10.15pm–c11.30pm • Royal Albert Hall

PRICE BAND **E** *Seats £12/£16*

Stockhausen
Gesang der Jünglinge   14'

Mittwoch aus 'Licht' – Welt-Parlament   40'
(concert performance)
London premiere

Kathinka Pasveer *sound projection*

Ex Cathedra
Jeffrey Skidmore *director*

There will be no interval

SAME-
DAY SAVER
Proms 10 & 11
(see page 168)

Last summer Graham Vick's Birmingham Opera
Company transformed a disused factory in
Digbeth, Birmingham, into the fantastical
world of Karlheinz Stockhausen's epic opera
Mittwoch aus 'Licht' with two bactrian camels,
four helicopters and a wash of yellow light.
Tonight Ex Cathedra and Jeffrey Skidmore revisit
the Babel tower of the opera's most dazzling
section, *Welt-Parlament* ('World Parliament'):
a multilingual *a cappella* tour de force of extended
vocal techniques. Written 30 years earlier, *Gesang
der Jünglinge* has been hailed as Stockhausen's first
electronic masterpiece, a mind-popping sonic
translation of the biblical story of Shadrach, Meshach
and Abednego. See 'New Music', pages 62–69;
'Late Night Tonic', pages 94–95.

BROADCAST
RADIO *Live on Radio 3*
ONLINE *Live and 'listen again' options at bbc.co.uk/proms*

SPOTLIGHT ON...

Jeffrey Skidmore • Prom 11

One of the cultural highlights of 2012 was the
premiere of Stockhausen's *Mittwoch aus 'Licht'*
in Birmingham. This vast and ambitious opera,
which at one point features a string quartet
playing in four helicopters, includes *Welt-
Parlament*, a remarkable choral work that
receives its London premiere at the Proms,
given by Ex Cathedra under the ensemble's
director, Jeffrey Skidmore. 'Stockhausen always
intended it to stand alone as a concert work as
well as being a theatre piece,' explains Skidmore.
'It's an absolutely sensational piece of choral
writing for 37 singers, who form a futuristic
world parliament discussing the theme of love.'

So what is it like for a renowned early music
choir to turn to one of the 20th century's most
provocative, revolutionary composers? 'We
took it on last year with trepidation as it was
way beyond our comfort zone. The score is
enormously complex, pretty terrifying when
you first look at it,' says Skidmore. 'But we all
grew to love it. We wanted to make it sound
beautiful. And in a way it's like tackling the
fiddly stylistic language of an early music
piece – in fact in Stockhausen's foreword
there's a chapter called performance practice,
like a Baroque treatise. Stockhausen's notation
is so prescribed that at first you think, is there
anything beyond that? But there is. There's
an incredible spiritual feeling.'

PROMS SATURDAY MATINEE 1
3.00pm–c4.30pm • Cadogan Hall

Seats £10 / £12

Corelli
Concerto grosso in D major, Op. 6 No. 1   12'

Handel
Cantata 'Pensieri notturni di Filli'   7'

Valentini
Concerto grosso in A major
for four violins, Op. 7 No. 1   20'

Handel
Cantata 'Tra le fiamme'   17'

Corelli
Concerto grosso in F major, Op. 6 No. 12   11'

Sophie Bevan soprano

Academy of Ancient Music
Richard Egarr director/harpsichord

There will be no interval

The year is 1707 and a young composer from
Saxony, George Frideric Handel, has come to Rome
to hear the music of the great violinist and innovator
Arcangelo Corelli. In the first of the five Proms
Saturday Matinees, Richard Egarr, Sophie Bevan
and the Academy of Ancient Music examine
Handel's vivacious Italian cantatas in the context
of virtuosic *concerti grossi* by Corelli and his younger
contemporary Giuseppe Valentini, linked by duo
keyboard interludes by Prince Giambattista
Borghese's court harpsichordist, Bernardo Pasquini.
See 'Small is Beautiful', pages 96–97.

BROADCAST
RADIO *Live on Radio 3*
ONLINE *Live and
'listen again' options at
bbc.co.uk/proms*

SOPHIE BEVAN

PROM 12
7.30pm–c9.30pm • Royal Albert Hall

PRICE BAND **C** Seats £14 to £57

Verdi, arr. C. Hermann
String Quartet (version for orchestra)   23'

Verdi
Ave Maria (1880)   5'
Requiem – Libera me (original version)   12'

INTERVAL

Verdi
Four Sacred Pieces   40'

Maria Agresta soprano

**Orchestra and Chorus of the
Academy of Santa Cecilia, Rome**
Sir Antonio Pappano conductor

Giuseppe Verdi's antipathy towards the church is
vividly demonstrated in his operas, yet the *Four
Sacred Pieces*, the original version of the 'Libera me'
from his dramatic *Requiem* and his setting of the
'Ave Maria' for soprano and string orchestra are
works of great fervour and beauty. The orchestral
version of his 1873 String Quartet opens a
programme in which conductor Sir Antonio
Pappano, soprano Maria Agresta and the Orchestra
and Chorus of the Academy of Santa Cecilia, Rome,
bring an authentically Italian bite to the music of the
man who, with Wagner, shaped the development
of 19th-century opera.

BROADCAST
RADIO *Live on Radio 3*
ONLINE *Live and 'listen again' options at bbc.co.uk/proms*
TV *Recorded for broadcast on BBC Four on 25 July*

PROMS PLUS FAMILY ORCHESTRA & CHORUS
11.00am • Royal College of Music Join the Proms Family
Orchestra and Chorus. See pages 80–87 for details of
how to sign up.

PROMS PLUS SING
5.00pm • Royal College of Music Experience some of the
vocal writing of Verdi's *Four Sacred Pieces* with Mary King.
See pages 80–87 for details of how to sign up.

SPOTLIGHT ON...
Maria Agresta • Prom 12

Verdi's *Requiem* began life as a response to the
death of Rossini in 1868, when the composer
supplied the 'Libera me' for a collaboration
with 13 Italian composers. In the event, that
piece had to wait 120 years for its premiere
and Verdi went on to use his 'Libera me' in his
famous *Requiem* for the writer Alessandro
Manzoni. In a Prom with the Academy of Santa
Cecilia under Sir Antonio Pappano, Italian
soprano Maria Agresta sings the 'Libera me'
in its first incarnation, as she explains: 'The
differences are slight and concern the musical
part as a whole. In the earlier version the
soprano sings more, in fact: the part doesn't
have the long tacet of the later version. In the
final part there isn't the declaimed solo on the
words "Libera me, Domine, de morte aeterna,
in die illa tremenda."'

Verdi's roles are core to Agresta's singing
life, and include Violetta, Leonora and
Desdemona, but there's one she treasures above
all: 'Verdi is a great composer because his women
are always special and strong, even if fragile.
I'm particularly bound to Elena [*I vespri
siciliani*] because this was the role that launched
my international career and I think in that
part a soprano can express herself completely.
One aria needs pure lyricism, another force
and great technique and agility and throughout
you need the right dramatic spirit.'

SUNDAY 21 JULY

PROM 13
7.30pm–c9.45pm • Royal Albert Hall

PRICE BAND Ⓐ *Seats £7.50 to £36*

Sean Shepherd
Magiya   *c10'*
BBC co-commission with Carnegie Hall:
European premiere

Tchaikovsky
Violin Concerto   *33'*

INTERVAL

Shostakovich
Symphony No. 10 in E minor   *45'*

Joshua Bell *violin*

**National Youth Orchestra of the
United States of America**
Valery Gergiev *conductor*

The UK debut of the newly
formed National Youth
Orchestra of the United
States of America opens
with the European
premiere of a work by
American rising star Sean
Shepherd. Joshua Bell joins
Valery Gergiev and the
orchestra for Tchaikovsky's
Violin Concerto in a bravura
programme that concludes with Shostakovich's
monumental 10th Symphony. See 'Tchaikovsky and
the Russian Symphony', pages 22–27; 'New Music',
pages 62–69.

JOSHUA BELL

BROADCAST
RADIO *Live on Radio 3*
ONLINE *Live and 'listen again' options at bbc.co.uk/proms*
TV *Recorded for broadcast on BBC Four on 26 July*

PROMS PLUS INTRO
5.45pm • Royal College of Music Sean Shepherd talks
about his new commission and working with the
NYO-USA. Gerard McBurney introduces Shostakovich's
Symphony No. 10.
Edited version broadcast on BBC Radio 3 during tonight's interval

---

MONDAY 22 JULY

PROMS CHAMBER MUSIC 2
1.00pm–c2.00pm • Cadogan Hall

Seats £10 / £12

Anon.
Chwała tobie, Gospodzinie   *3'*
Cracovia civitas   *5'*

Wanning
Dixit angelus ad Petrum   *5'*
Et valde mane   *5'*

Zieleński
Mihi autem nimis   *4'*

Demantius
Neue liebliche Intraden und frölichen
Polnischen Täntzen – Intrada; Chorea
polonica; Gaillarde   *10'*

Marenzio
Lamentabatur Jacob   *4'*
Solo e pensoso i più deserti campi   *5'*

Klabon
Tryumfuj, wierny poddany   *4'*

Huelgas Ensemble
Paul Van Nevel *conductor*

There will be no interval

Continuing the exploration of Polish music in this
year's Proms, Paul Van Nevel and the Flemish
singers and instrumentalists of the Huelgas
Ensemble explore the little-known choral music
of 15th- and 16th-century Poland. Motets by Polish
composers Mikołaj Zieleński and Krzysztof Klabon
are contrasted with works by Christoph Demantius
and Johannes Wanning in a programme of intriguing
polyphonic discoveries from the archives of
the University Library of Warsaw that includes
the earliest surviving setting of a Polish text:
'Chwała tobie, Gospodzinie' (Praise to Thee,
O Lord). See 'A Polish Awakening', pages 30–35;
'Small is Beautiful', pages 96–97.

BROADCAST
RADIO *Live on Radio 3*
ONLINE *Live and 'listen again' options at bbc.co.uk/proms*

MONDAY 22 JULY

PROM 14
7.00pm–c9.55pm • Royal Albert Hall

PRICE BAND Ⓓ *Seats £18 to £68*

Wagner
Das Rheingold   *160'*
(concert performance; sung in German)

Cast to include:
Stephan Rügamer *Loge*
Jan Buchwald *Donner*
Marius Vlad *Froh*
Ekaterina Gubanova *Fricka*
Anna Samuil *Freia*
Anna Larsson *Erda*
Johannes Martin Kränzle *Alberich*
Peter Bronder *Mime*
Iain Paterson *Fasolt*
Eric Halfvarson *Fafner*
Aga Mikolaj *Woglinde*
Maria Gortsevskaya *Wellgunde*
Anna Lapkovskaja *Flosshilde*

Staatskapelle Berlin
Daniel Barenboim
conductor

There will be no interval

Stolen gold, slave labour and
a world order on the edge of
collapse. Daniel Barenboim
launches his Proms *Ring* cycle
(and conducts his first Wagner opera in the UK),
following his Beethoven symphony cycle last year.
The Staatskapelle Berlin explores the corrupting
influence of the all-powerful ring with a cast mined
from Barenboim's recent Berlin and Milan *Ring*
cycles. See 'All Around the Ring', pages 14–19.

DANIEL BARENBOIM

BROADCAST
RADIO *Live on Radio 3*
ONLINE *Live and 'listen again' options at bbc.co.uk/proms*

PROMS PLUS INTRO
5.15pm • Royal College of Music Sara Mohr-Pietsch
is joined by Barbara Eichner for an introduction to
Das Rheingold.
Edited version broadcast on BBC Radio 3 before tonight's Prom

TUESDAY 23 JULY

PROM 15
5.00pm–c10.05pm • Royal Albert Hall

PRICE BAND D *Seats £18 to £68*

Wagner

Die Walküre   225'

(concert performance; sung in German)

Cast to include:
Simon O'Neill *Siegmund*
Anja Kampe *Sieglinde*
Eric Halfvarson *Hunding*
Nina Stemme *Brünnhilde*
Ekaterina Gubanova *Fricka*
Danielle Halbwachs *Gerhilde*
Carola Höhn *Ortlinde*
Ivonne Fuchs *Waltraute*
Anaïk Morel *Schwertleite*
Susan Foster *Helmwige*
Leann Sandel-Pantaleo *Siegrune*
Anna Lapkovskaja *Grimgerde*
Simone Schröder *Rossweisse*

Staatskapelle Berlin
Daniel Barenboim
conductor

*There will be two intervals
of 30 minutes*

NINA STEMME

Daniel Barenboim's
Proms *Ring* cycle with
the Staatskapelle Berlin
continues with the razored
strings and yelping brass of
a violent storm, the
cloudburst of incestuous love, a bitter marital
dispute and the first appearance of Wotan's rebel
daughter, Brünnhilde, sung by a leading exponent
of the role, Nina Stemme. See 'All Around the Ring',
pages 14–19.

BROADCAST
RADIO *Live on Radio 3*
ONLINE *Live and 'listen again' options at bbc.co.uk/proms*

PROMS PLUS INTRO
3.15pm • Royal College of Music Sara Mohr-Pietsch is
joined by Elaine Padmore for an introduction to *Die Walküre*.
Edited version broadcast on BBC Radio 3 during tonight's first interval

WEDNESDAY 24 JULY

PROM 16
7.30pm–c9.50pm • Royal Albert Hall

PRICE BAND A *Seats £7.50 to £36*

Elgar

Falstaff   33'

Bantock

Sapphic Poem   15'

INTERVAL

Walton

Henry V – Touch her soft lips and part;
Death of Falstaff   5'

Tchaikovsky

Symphony No. 4 in F minor   42'

Raphael Wallfisch *cello*

BBC National Orchestra of Wales
Jac van Steen *conductor*

Jac van Steen and the BBC National Orchestra of
Wales launch the Proms cycle of Tchaikovsky
symphonies with the baleful fanfare of the Fourth.
Celebrating his 60th birthday this year, Raphael
Wallfisch is the soloist in the Proms premiere
of Granville Bantock's *Sapphic Poem*, launching
the Proms focus on the composer this summer.
Rich, lyrical and lushly orchestrated, it is framed
by two very different portraits of Sir John Falstaff,
by Edward Elgar and
William Walton. See
'Tchaikovsky and the
Russian Symphony',
pages 22–27; 'Bring
out the Bantock',
pages 50–51.

JAC VAN STEEN

BROADCAST
RADIO *Live on Radio 3*
ONLINE *Live and 'listen again' options at bbc.co.uk/proms*

PROMS PLUS LITERARY
5.45pm • Royal College of Music What makes Falstaff so
irresistible to writers and composers? Timothy West talks
about his experiences of playing one of Shakespeare's
greatest characters.
Edited version broadcast on BBC Radio 3 during tonight's interval

---

SPOTLIGHT ON...

Raphael Wallfisch • Prom 16

This year will be the first time Bantock's
Sapphic Poem for cello and orchestra has
been heard at the Proms. The soloist Raphael
Wallfisch, a passionate advocate of British
music, says we're in for a treat: 'It's basically
like an aria, with the cello singing ardently.
It's in Bantock's Tchaikovsky/Wagnerian-
influenced style and is an absolutely beautiful
romantic flow of melody.'

Composed around the same time as he was
writing a major work for mezzo-soprano and
orchestra setting nine fragments of Sappho's
poems, this piece was one of five Bantock
wrote for cello and orchestra: 'I think
composers love the vocal, rhetorical character
of the cello,' says Wallfisch. 'Think of works
such as Strauss's *Don Quixote* where the cello
is the protagonist, or Bloch's *Schelomo* where
it represents King Solomon.'

It will also be Wallfisch's first performance
of the *Sapphic Poem*. Now he's got to know it,
does it seem strange that it's been left in the
wings for so long? 'Bantock was quite radical
in a way for Edwardian times, far more
daring than Elgar. But, not long afterwards,
when people such as Schoenberg were going
in a completely different direction, he seemed
incredibly old-hat. More recently people are
realising that Bantock and others like him
wrote music of great beauty and unique style.'

THURSDAY 25 JULY

PROM 17
7.30pm–c9.55pm • Royal Albert Hall

PRICE BAND Ⓐ *Seats £7.50 to £36*

John McCabe
Joybox   c7'
BBC commission: world premiere

Beethoven
Symphony No. 7 in A major   40'

INTERVAL

Falla
The Three-Cornered Hat   35'

Ravel
Boléro   15'

Clara Mouriz *mezzo-soprano*

BBC Philharmonic
Juanjo Mena *conductor*

The world premiere of John McCabe's BBC
commission *Joybox* opens a concert of music
inspired by or written for dance, from the
Bohemian stamp and whirl of Beethoven's
Seventh Symphony to the slow-burning ostinato of
Ravel's *Boléro*. Mezzo-soprano Clara Mouriz joins
conductor Juanjo Mena and the BBC Philharmonic
in Falla's colourful Ballets Russes commission *The
Three-Cornered Hat*, a tale of intrigue and jealousy
shot through with the spirit of Spanish folk dances.
See 'New Music', pages 62–69.

BROADCAST
RADIO *Live on Radio 3*
ONLINE *Live and 'listen again' options at bbc.co.uk/proms*
TV *Recorded for broadcast on BBC Four on 2 August*

PROMS PLUS FAMILY
5.30pm • Royal College of Music Step into the heat of
Spain as Rachel Leach re-tells the story of Falla's most
popular ballet, featuring a beautiful lady, an angry husband
and a man with a three-cornered hat!

PROMS PLUS LATE
Elgar Room, Royal Albert Hall Informal post-Prom music
and poetry. For details see bbc.co.uk/proms

SPOTLIGHT ON...
Clara Mouriz • Prom 17

Spanish mezzo-soprano Clara Mouriz counts
her experiences with the BBC Philharmonic
as highlights of her time as a BBC Radio 3
New Generation Artist: 'I've sung Ravel,
Mahler, Turina, Montsalvatge and Falla with
this orchestra, gaining experience in recording,
thanks to their producers and engineers; and
every time, I've fallen in love with their sound
and energy, which is pure magic in the hands
of Juanjo Mena.'

In the ballet score of Falla's *The Three-
Cornered Hat* she'll need to employ the
cante jondo style of singing: 'Falla's music
is often inspired by Andalusian colours and
The Three-Cornered Hat takes a definite step
towards the old, pure style of the *cante jondo*.
The words of the poet Lorca, a friend of the
composer, come to my mind when singing this
music: *cante jondo* is like the trilling of birds,
the cry of the cockerel, and the natural music
of woods and streams. It is a rare specimen of
primitive song, the oldest in Europe, bearing
in its notes the naked shiver of emotion of the
oriental races.'

Mouriz is on a mission to bring a wider
Spanish repertoire to British ears: 'I've recorded
songs by Turina and Montsalvatge with Mena
and the BBC Philharmonic, so I feel that I'm
taking a step in the right direction. But there's
still so much Spanish music I would love to share!'

FRIDAY 26 JULY

PROM 18
5.00pm–c10.20pm • Royal Albert Hall

PRICE BAND Ⓓ *Seats £18 to £68*

Wagner
Siegfried   238'
(concert performance; sung in German)

Lance Ryan *Siegfried*
Nina Stemme *Brünnhilde*
Terje Stensvold *Wanderer*
Peter Bronder *Mime*
Johannes Martin Kränzle *Alberich*
Eric Halfvarson *Fafner*
Rinnat Moriah *Woodbird*
Anna Larsson *Erda*

Staatskapelle Berlin
Daniel Barenboim *conductor*

There will be two intervals of 30 minutes

Daniel Barenboim's survey of Wagner's epic
tetralogy reaches its third instalment, introducing
the naive hero Siegfried. Lance Ryan sings the role
of the dragon-slaying innocent who only learns
fear when he falls in love with Brünnhilde (Nina
Stemme). See 'All Around the Ring', pages 14–19.

BROADCAST
RADIO *Live on Radio 3*
ONLINE *Live and 'listen again' options at bbc.co.uk/proms*

LANCE RYAN   ANNA LARSSON

PROMS PLUS INTRO
3.15pm • Royal College of Music Sara Mohr-Pietsch is
joined by Mark Berry (Royal Holloway, University of
London) for an introduction to tonight's opera, *Siegfried*.
Edited version broadcast on BBC Radio 3 during tonight's first interval

SATURDAY 27 JULY

PROM 19

5.00pm–c11.00pm • Royal Albert Hall

PRICE BAND Ⓑ *Seats £9.50 to £46*

Wagner

Tristan and Isolde   284'
(concert performance; sung in German)

Peter Seiffert *Tristan*
Kwangchul Youn *King Mark*
Violeta Urmana *Isolde*
Boaz Daniel *Kurwenal*
David Wilson-Johnson *Melot*
Sophie Koch *Brangäne*
Andrew Staples *Shepherd/Young Sailor*

BBC Singers
BBC Symphony Chorus
BBC Symphony Orchestra
Semyon Bychkov *conductor*

There will be two intervals of 30 minutes

The Wagner bicentenary celebrations continue
with the composer's boldest fusion of legend and
harmonic innovation, *Tristan and Isolde*, which forced
him to break off work on his *Ring* cycle near this
very juncture in the Proms *Ring* – during the
composition of *Siegfried* and before the final
instalment, *Götterdämmerung*.
Semyon Bychkov conducts the
BBC Symphony Orchestra and
a cast led by Violeta Urmana
and Peter Seiffert in a drama
where love and death become
one. *See 'All Around the Ring',*
pages 14–19.

PETER SEIFFERT

BROADCAST
RADIO *Live on Radio 3*
ONLINE *Live and 'listen again' options at bbc.co.uk/proms*
TV *Recorded for broadcast on BBC Four on 1 September*

PROMS PLUS LITERARY

3.15pm • Royal College of Music Wagner's sets are
notoriously challenging: giant dragons, underwater singing,
storms, horses and destruction by raging fires. Designer
Peter Mumford talks to Anne McElvoy about staging
solutions in the 21st century.
Edited version broadcast on BBC Radio 3 during tonight's first interval

SPOTLIGHT ON...

Violeta Urmana • Prom 19

Isolde is one of Violeta Urmana's 'absolutely
favourite roles'. The Lithuanian soprano
made her stage debut in the part in an Opéra
de Paris production in Japan, conducted
by Semyon Bychkov, who takes up the baton
in this Proms performance. 'It was a huge
experience. When I performed it for the first
time on stage, I remember thinking, "Oh my
goodness, I've been singing for so long
already, and I've not even sung half of the
first act!" You have to manage to conserve
the voice until the end of the opera. Each act
is like singing a whole *Aida*.' She also sang
the role at the Proms in 2010, when Sir Simon
Rattle conducted the Orchestra of the Age
of Enlightenment in Act 2 of the opera.

    For Urmana, Isolde is a conflicted
character: 'She's in a bad situation in
that she must marry an old king. And, most
importantly, she's desperately in love with
Tristan, the man who killed her fiancé.
This is a major conflict in her that she needs
to resolve.' So is Isolde a tough role to
portray? 'There's already so much in Wagner's
score: the atmosphere, the music, the words.
If you read the text and the music in the right
way, it should not be difficult. Wagner was
such a genius – we just have to give the right
colour and emotion to the music, to pass
it on to the public.'

SUNDAY 28 JULY

PROM 20

4.30pm–c10.15pm • Royal Albert Hall

PRICE BAND Ⓓ *Seats £18 to £68*

Wagner

Götterdämmerung   259'
(concert performance; sung in German)

Nina Stemme *Brünnhilde*
Ian Storey *Siegfried*
Mikhail Petrenko *Hagen*
Gerd Grochowski *Gunther*
Anna Samuil *Gutrune/Third Norn*
Johannes Martin Kränzle *Alberich*
Waltraud Meier *Waltraute/Second Norn*
Margarita Nekrasova *First Norn*
Aga Mikolaj *Woglinde*
Maria Gortsevskaya *Wellgunde*
Anna Lapkovskaja *Flosshilde*

Chorus of the Royal Opera House
Staatskapelle Berlin
Daniel Barenboim *conductor*

There will be two intervals of 30 minutes

Daniel Barenboim and the
Staatskapelle Berlin conclude
the Proms *Ring* cycle with
Götterdämmerung –
unleashing the final chain
of betrayals that culminates in
the destruction of the gods.
Ian Storey is the tragic hero
Siegfried, Nina Stemme the
fallen valkyrie Brünnhilde,

IAN STOREY

while Mikhail Petrenko sings Hagen, born to hatred
and despair. *See 'All Around the Ring', pages 14–19.*

BROADCAST
RADIO *Live on Radio 3*
ONLINE *Live and 'listen again' options at bbc.co.uk/proms*

PROMS PLUS INTRO

2.45pm • Royal College of Music
Sara Mohr-Pietsch is joined by Sarah Lenton for
an introduction to *Götterdämmerung*.
Edited version broadcast on BBC Radio 3 during tonight's first interval

MONDAY 29 JULY

PROMS CHAMBER MUSIC 3
1.00pm–c2.00pm • Cadogan Hall

Seats £10 / £12

Britten
Canticle I 'My beloved is mine'	8'
A Charm of Lullabies	13'
Night Piece (Notturno)	5'
Songs from the Chinese	10'
Canticle II 'Abraham and Isaac'	16'
Master Kilby	2'

Christianne Stotijn *mezzo-soprano*
James Gilchrist *tenor*
Christoph Denoth *guitar*
Imogen Cooper *piano*

There will be no interval

A sequence of bittersweet works by Benjamin Britten for the third Proms Chamber Music concert. Pianist Imogen Cooper revisits music she first played as a student, *Night Piece (Notturno)*, and accompanies Christianne Stotijn and James Gilchrist in Britten's unnerving story of absolute faith, *Abraham and Isaac*. The sublimated eroticism of *My beloved is mine*, the gentle curves of *A Charm of Lullabies*, the brittle elegance of *Songs from the Chinese* (with guitarist Christoph Denoth) and the tart miniature *Master Kilby* give an intimate portrait of the composer. See 'Revealing Britten', pages 38–43; 'Small is Beautiful', pages 96–97.

BROADCAST
RADIO *Live on Radio 3*
ONLINE *Live and 'listen again' options at bbc.co.uk/proms*

JAMES GILCHRIST   CHRISTIANNE STOTIJN

MONDAY 29 JULY

PROM 21
7.00pm–c9.20pm • Royal Albert Hall

PRICE BAND Ⓐ *Seats £7.50 to £36*

Colin Matthews
Turning Point	18'
UK premiere	

Prokofiev
Violin Concerto No. 2 in G minor	27'

INTERVAL

Shostakovich
Symphony No. 11, 'The Year 1905'	55'

Daniel Hope *violin*

BBC National Orchestra of Wales
Thomas Søndergård *conductor*

Thomas Søndergård and the BBC National Orchestra of Wales return to give the UK premiere of Colin Matthews's mercurial *Turning Point* and Daniel Hope is the soloist in the first of two 20th-century Russian masterpieces. The flinty beauty of Prokofiev's Second Violin Concerto stands in sharp contrast to the granite heft of Shostakovich's Symphony No. 11, 'The Year 1905', written four years after the death of Joseph Stalin and studded through with revolutionary songs. See 'New Music', pages 62–69.

DANIEL HOPE

BROADCAST
RADIO *Live on Radio 3*
ONLINE *Live and 'listen again' options at bbc.co.uk/proms*
TV *Recorded for broadcast on BBC Four on 4 August*

PROMS PLUS LITERARY
5.15pm • Royal College of Music John le Carré, one of the greatest spy novelists, celebrates 50 years since the publication of his groundbreaking Cold War espionage novel, *The Spy Who Came in from the Cold*, with Anne McElvoy. *Edited version broadcast on BBC Radio 3 during tonight's interval*

MONDAY 29 JULY

PROM 22
10.15pm–c11.30pm • Royal Albert Hall

PRICE BAND Ⓔ *Seats £12/£16*

Naturally 7

There will be no interval

Who needs instruments when you have seven voices and seven bodies? The inimitable *a cappella* group Naturally 7 comes to the Proms fresh from performances at the O₂ supporting Michael Bublé. Building on the heritage of gospel with a style described as 'vocal play', the group performs its own original material as well as its inventive arrangements – including George Harrison's 'While My Guitar Gently Weeps' and Phil Collins's 'In the Air Tonight' – which incorporate scratching, drum kit, harmonica, brass, electric guitars and bass – all produced, naturally, with the human voice. See 'Late Night Tonic', pages 94–95; 'From the Streets to the Stage', pages 98–101.

BROADCAST
RADIO *Live on Radio 3*
ONLINE *Live and 'listen again' options at bbc.co.uk/proms*

SAME-
DAY SAVER
Proms 21 & 22
(see page 168)

NATURALLY 7

TUESDAY 30 JULY

PROM 23
7.30pm–c10.00pm • Royal Albert Hall

PRICE BAND Ⓑ *Seats £9.50 to £46*

Mozart
Masonic Funeral Music, K477   6'

Schumann
Symphony No. 2 in C major   38'

INTERVAL

Mozart
Piano Concerto No. 25
in C major, K503   33'

Sibelius
Symphony No. 7 in C major   23'

Paul Lewis *piano*

Mahler Chamber Orchestra
Daniel Harding *conductor*

Daniel Harding returns to the Proms after 10 years,
directing the Mahler Chamber Orchestra, with
which he has a long association, in a programme
exploring the subtly different properties of the keys
of C major and C minor. Paul Lewis is the soloist in
Mozart's Piano Concerto, K503, its urbane elegance
and delicate woodwind writing a
contrast to the austerity of the
1785 *Masonic Funeral Music*.
Two great symphonies acutely
expressive of light and shade,
Schumann's Second and Sibelius's
Seventh, complete an imaginative
and stimulating sequence of
works. See 'Craving the Keyboard',
pages 56–59.

PAUL LEWIS

BROADCAST
RADIO *Live on Radio 3*
ONLINE *Live and 'listen again' options at bbc.co.uk/proms*
TV *Recorded for broadcast on BBC Four on 1 August*

PROMS PLUS INTRO
5.45pm • Royal College of Music James Jolly explores
Mozart's life in Vienna and the city's influences on the
music in tonight's programme.
Edited version broadcast on BBC Radio 3 during tonight's interval

SPOTLIGHT ON...
Daniel Harding • Prom 23

'The great challenge with Sibelius's Seventh
Symphony is its long, gradual, almost
imperceptible *accelerando*,' says Daniel
Harding, who conducts it with the Mahler
Chamber Orchestra. 'I'm really looking
forward to doing it with these players. It can
be tricky with a very big group. Every single
musician needs to be able to hear each other
and to know exactly where the points of
change are – and then, of course, you bury
them. I sometimes think of my father's model
railway: each hill had struts, but they were
hidden and smoothed over. It's essential
you don't hear any gear shifts.'

Before the Sibelius comes the Second
Symphony by Schumann, a composer about
whom Harding is passionate: 'It drives me nuts
when people talk about the "problems" of
Schumann. It started right back with people like
Mahler saying he couldn't orchestrate, which is
preposterous. I do think that Schumann
requires patience, though, and intense rehearsal,
because there's no template – you can't play it as
if it's Brahms. His writing can be fragile and to
make it too muscular can obliterate it. But if I
could have only one composer with me on a
desert island, it would be Schumann. I've had
an almost obsessive relationship with his music.
He belongs in the exalted circle that includes
Beethoven, Schubert and Mozart.'

WEDNESDAY 31 JULY

PROM 24
7.00pm–c9.15pm • Royal Albert Hall

PRICE BAND Ⓐ *Seats £7.50 to £36*

Bantock
Pierrot of the Minute   12'

Elgar
Nursery Suite   22'

Arnold
Concerto for two pianos (three hands)   13'

INTERVAL

Walton
Crown Imperial   7'

Coates
The Three Elizabeths   20'

Arnold
English Dances, Set 1, Op. 27   13'

Gordon Langford
Medley 'Say it with Music'   7'

Noriko Ogawa *piano*
Kathryn Stott *piano*

BBC Concert Orchestra
Barry Wordsworth
conductor

SAME-
DAY SAVER
Proms 24 & 25
(see page 168)

A celebration of British light and occasional music,
including pieces written by Walton and Coates used
to celebrate the coronation of Queen Elizabeth II
60 years ago, and Elgar's *Nursery Suite*, dedicated in
1931 to the Princesses Margaret and Elizabeth and to
their mother Elizabeth, then Duchess of York. See
'Bring out the Bantock', pages 50–51; 'Orb and Sceptre',
pages 52–53; 'Craving the Keyboard', pages 56–59.

BROADCAST
RADIO *Live on Radio 3 and Radio 2*
ONLINE *Live and 'listen again' options at bbc.co.uk/proms*

PROMS PLUS LITERARY
5.15pm • Royal College of Music Writers Simon Heffer
and Andrew O'Hagan celebrate the halcyon days of
light music at the BBC with Matthew Sweet.
Edited version broadcast on BBC Radio 3 during tonight's interval

WEDNESDAY 31 JULY

PROM 25
10.15pm–c11.30pm • Royal Albert Hall

PRICE BAND **E** *Seats £12/£16*

Zappa
The Adventures of Greggery Peccary   25'
Nancarrow, arr. Y. E. Mikhashoff
Study for Player Piano No. 7   10'
Philip Glass
Symphony No. 10   27'
UK premiere

Aurora Orchestra
Nicholas Collon *conductor*

There will be no interval

Trend-mongers, philosophers and hunchmen.
A car-chase, a love-in and a replica mahogany desk.
A coughing mountain, a choir of stenographers and
an exceptional swine-pig called Greggery. Nicholas
Collon and the Aurora Orchestra give the first
Proms performance of Frank Zappa's high-energy
counter-culture satire *The Adventures of Greggery
Peccary*. An arrangement of a zany
Nancarrow study and the UK premiere
of Philip Glass's 10th Symphony
complete a far-out late-night
happening from one of Britain's most
vivacious young orchestras. See 'New Music',
pages 62–69; 'Late Night Tonic', pages 94–95.

SAME-
DAY SAVER
Proms 24 & 25
(see page 168)

BROADCAST
RADIO *Live on Radio 3*
ONLINE *Live and 'listen again' options at bbc.co.uk/proms*

FRANK ZAPPA

THURSDAY 1 AUGUST

PROM 26
7.30pm–c9.45pm • Royal Albert Hall

PRICE BAND **A** *Seats £7.50 to £36*

Henze
Barcarola   20'
Stravinsky
Concerto for piano and wind instruments   19'
INTERVAL
Stravinsky
Movements   10'
Tippett
Symphony No. 2   32'

Peter Serkin *piano*

BBC Symphony Orchestra
Oliver Knussen *conductor*

Composer-conductor Oliver
Knussen directs the BBC
Symphony Orchestra in Tippett's
Symphony No 2, inspired by the
rhythmic energy of a Vivaldi
bassline and the first in a series of
works by Tippett to be featured
in parallel with the Britten
centenary. The revered American pianist Peter
Serkin makes his Proms debut in Stravinsky's
neo-Classical Concerto for piano and winds
and compact serialist conceit *Movements*. Written
in memory of his friend Paul Dessau, the late
Hans Werner Henze's 1979 *Barcarola* opens
this programme of 20th-century masterpieces.
See 'A Composer of Our Time', pages 44–47;
'Craving the Keyboard', pages 56–59.

PETER SERKIN

BROADCAST
RADIO *Live on Radio 3*
ONLINE *Live and 'listen again' options at bbc.co.uk/proms*

PROMS PLUS LITERARY
5.45pm • Royal College of Music Rana Mitter introduces an
anthology of readings about Michael Tippett, including his
letters, autobiography, talks for Radio 3 and reviews.
Edited version broadcast on BBC Radio 3 during tonight's interval

---

FRIDAY 2 AUGUST

PROM 27
7.30pm–c10.45pm • Royal Albert Hall

PRICE BAND **A** *Seats £7.50 to £36*

Naresh Sohal
The Cosmic Dance   c45'
BBC commission: world premiere
INTERVAL
Rachmaninov
Piano Concerto No. 3 in D minor   41'
INTERVAL
Tchaikovsky
Symphony No. 5 in E minor   45'

Nikolai Lugansky *piano*

Royal Scottish National Orchestra
Peter Oundjian *conductor*

The Proms Tchaikovsky symphony cycle continues
with the musky melancholy of the Fifth as conductor
Peter Oundjian makes his Proms debut. Nikolai
Lugansky is the soloist in Rachmaninov's Third Piano
Concerto, notorious for its technical demands yet
based around melodic ideas of great simplicity.
Punjabi-born British composer Naresh Sohal's
second Proms commission, *The Cosmic Dance*,
examines the idea of creation as interpreted in
two very different disciplines: mathematical theory
and the ancient texts of the *Upanishads* and the
Rig Veda. See 'Tchaikovsky and the Russian Symphony',
pages 22–27; 'New Music', pages 62–69.

BROADCAST
RADIO *Live on Radio 3*
ONLINE *Live and 'listen again' options at bbc.co.uk/proms*

PROMS PLUS PORTRAIT
5.45pm • Royal College of Music Naresh Sohal, in
conversation with Andrew McGregor, discusses his
BBC commission and introduces his chamber works.
Edited version broadcast on BBC Radio 3 after tonight's Prom

PROMS PLUS LATE
Elgar Room, Royal Albert Hall Informal post-Prom music
and poetry. For details see bbc.co.uk/proms

SATURDAY 3 AUGUST

PROMS SATURDAY MATINEE 2
3.00pm–c4.30pm • Cadogan Hall

Seats £10/£12

Britten
Prelude and Fugue   10'

Holst
St Paul's Suite   13'

L. Berkeley
Four Poems of St Teresa of Avila   14'

Tippett
Fantasia concertante on a Theme
of Corelli   19'

Britten
Phaedra   15'

Sarah Connolly *mezzo-soprano*

Britten Sinfonia
Sian Edwards *conductor*

There will be no interval

Two great British works for voice and string
orchestra appear in the second Proms Saturday
Matinee, which focuses on Britten and his peers.
Sarah Connolly joins conductor Sian Edwards
and the Britten Sinfonia in Britten's searing final
vocal work, *Phaedra*, and a rare performance
of Lennox Berkeley's intensely felt *Four Poems of
St Teresa of Avila*, premiered by Kathleen Ferrier
in 1948. In addition to featuring classics of the
string orchestra repertoire in Holst's *St Paul's
Suite* and Tippett's *Fantasia
concertante on a Theme
of Corelli*, the programme
includes Britten's inventive
Prelude and Fugue for
18-part string orchestra.
*See 'Revealing Britten', pages
38–43; 'A Composer of Our
Time', pages 44–47; 'Small
is Beautiful', pages 96–97.*

SARAH CONNOLLY

BROADCAST
RADIO *Live on Radio 3*
ONLINE *Live and 'listen again' options at bbc.co.uk/proms*

SATURDAY 3 AUGUST

PROM 28
7.30pm–c9.30pm • Royal Albert Hall

PRICE BAND Ⓐ *Seats £7.50 to £36*

J. Strauss II
By the Beautiful Blue Danube – waltz   10'

James MacMillan
Violin Concerto   25'

INTERVAL

Beethoven
Overture 'Coriolan'   8'

Symphony No. 5 in C minor   33'

Vadim Repin *violin*

BBC Scottish Symphony Orchestra
Donald Runnicles *conductor*

Donald Runnicles conducts the BBC Scottish
Symphony Orchestra and Vadim Repin in James
MacMillan's Violin Concerto. Written for Repin's
big-boned Russian sound and premiered in 2010,
the concerto is threaded through with allusions
to the traditional fiddle music and Scottish laments
that MacMillan regards as the 'ancient modes of
expression and storytelling'. The concentrated
drama of Beethoven's 1807 'Coriolan' overture
acts as an up-beat to his Fifth Symphony, its opening
four-note motif as arresting today as it was in 1808.

BROADCAST
RADIO *Live on Radio 3*
ONLINE *Live and
'listen again' options at
bbc.co.uk/proms*
TV *Recorded for broadcast on
BBC Four on 9 August*

VADIM REPIN

PROMS PLUS LITERARY
5.45pm • Royal College of Music Robert Crawford and
Fiona Stafford discuss how the Romantic movement linked
Beethoven with the poetry of Scottish writers such as
Burns, James Macpherson and Walter Scott.
Edited version broadcast on BBC Radio 3 during tonight's interval

---

SUNDAY 4 AUGUST

PROM 29
6.00pm–c10.10pm • Royal Albert Hall

PRICE BAND Ⓑ *Seats £9.50 to £46*

Wagner
Tannhäuser   183'
(concert performance; sung in German)

Robert Dean Smith *Tannhäuser*
Heidi Melton *Elisabeth*
Daniela Sindram *Venus*
Ain Anger *Landgraf*
Christoph Pohl *Wolfram*
Thomas Blondelle *Walther*
Andrew Rees *Heinrich*
Brian Bannatyne-Scott *Reinmar*
Ashley Holland *Biterolf*
Hila Fahima *Shepherd Boy*

Chorus of the Deutsche Oper Berlin
BBC Scottish Symphony Orchestra
Donald Runnicles *conductor*

There will be two intervals of 30 minutes

In their second Proms appearance together,
Donald Runnicles and the BBC Scottish Symphony
Orchestra turn to *Tannhäuser*. Robert Dean Smith
sings the role of the troubadour who tires of Venus's
charms and yearns for spiritual redemption. Elisabeth
is the woman who loves him, Wolfram the man who
loves her. *See 'All Around the Ring', pages 14–19.*

BROADCAST
RADIO *Live on Radio 3*
ONLINE *Live and 'listen again' options at bbc.co.uk/proms*

PROMS PLUS STORYTIME
11.30am • Royal College of Music Hannah Conway presents
stories and music based on Jon Klassen's *I Want My Hat Back*.
For details, see page 87.
Recorded for broadcast on BBC Radio 3 and Radio 4 Extra

PROMS PLUS SING
2.00pm • Royal College of Music Sing extracts from
Tannhäuser with Mary King. See pages 80–87 for details
of how to sign up.

PROMS PLUS INTRO
4.15pm • Royal College of Music An introduction to
Wagner's *Tannhäuser*, with James Jolly.
Edited version broadcast on BBC Radio 3 during tonight's first interval

PROMS CHAMBER MUSIC 4
1.00pm–c2.00pm • Cadogan Hall

Seats £10 / £12

Grieg
Holberg Suite – Praeludium   3'

Lyric Pieces – Grandmother's Minuet,
Op. 68 No. 2   2'

19 Norwegian Folk Songs – Gjendine's
Lullaby, Op. 66 No. 19   2'

Lyric Pieces – March of the Dwarfs,
Op. 54 No. 3   4'

Diana Burrell
Blaze   c10'
BBC commission: world premiere

Weill
The Threepenny Opera – suite   18'

Piazzolla
Oblivion   3'

Bizet
Carmen – Suite No. 2   6'

tenThing

There will be no interval

Ahead of her Royal Albert Hall concerto debut (Prom 48), Norwegian trumpeter Tine Thing Helseth brings her all-female 10-piece brass ensemble tenThing to Cadogan Hall for this colourful Proms Chamber Music concert. A bold new work by the British composer Diana Burrell is the centrepiece of a virtuosic programme of tangos, seguidillas, habaneras and serenades from Grieg, Piazzolla and Bizet, arranged for tenThing by Jarle Storløkken.
See 'New Music', pages 62–69; 'Small is Beautiful', pages 96–97.

BROADCAST
RADIO *Live on Radio 3*
ONLINE *Live and 'listen again' options at bbc.co.uk/proms*

TENTHING

SPOTLIGHT ON...
Tine Thing Helseth • PCM 4

'It's been a dream of mine to be a part of the Proms,' says Norwegian trumpet star Tine Thing Helseth, who makes her debut this year, 'and to be able to play two concerts is amazing. Matthias Pintscher's double concerto (Prom 48) is fascinating and it's great he's conducting.'

Helseth's chamber Prom features her brass group tenThing, formed when she and three trumpeter friends were studying in Oslo. Listening to a string orchestra, 'we realised we wanted to make a brass ensemble that could perform that repertoire with the same level of joy and integrity. Since we were all girls, we thought that making it all-female would be extra fun. We asked some friends and players we knew and that was it – tenThing was born!'

She sees the Cadogan programme as representing the 'soul' of tenThing: 'I'm always looking for new, challenging repertoire and we almost solely play arrangements. I mostly come up with the ideas, some crazier than others, and Jarle Storløkken, our arranger, makes it work – he's a true magician! We mix in a bit of choreography and humour too. To include a premiere by Diana Burrell makes this programme extra special.'

The group meets up four times a year for projects: 'As a soloist, I really treasure these moments when I can travel with some of my best friends and perform great music.'

PROM 30
7.30pm–c9.55pm • Royal Albert Hall

PRICE BAND (A) *Seats £7.50 to £36*

Borodin
Prince Igor – overture; Polovtsian Dances   24'
Prokofiev
Piano Concerto No. 2 in G minor   34'
INTERVAL

Edward Cowie
Earth Music 1 – The Great Barrier Reef   c9'
BBC commission: world premiere

Tchaikovsky
Symphony No. 2 in C minor,
'Little Russian'   35'

Jean-Efflam Bavouzet *piano*

BBC Philharmonic
Gianandrea Noseda
conductor

GIANANDREA
NOSEDA

Borodin's overture to *Prince Igor* opens a programme celebrating the 70th birthday of composer Edward Cowie and the close musical relationship between the BBC Philharmonic, conductor Gianandrea Noseda and pianist Jean-Efflam Bavouzet. Bavouzet plays Prokofiev's brilliant Second Piano Concerto, its orchestral score destroyed in the Russian Revolution and revised by the composer in Paris in 1923. The fragile beauty of the Great Barrier Reef is the subject of Cowie's *Earth Music 1*, while the 'Little Russian' continues the season's Tchaikovsky symphony cycle. See 'Tchaikovsky and the Russian Symphony', pages 22–27; 'Craving the Keyboard', pages 56–59; 'New Music', pages 62–69.

BROADCAST
RADIO *Live on Radio 3*
ONLINE *Live and 'listen again' options at bbc.co.uk/proms*

PROMS PLUS PORTRAIT
5.45pm • Royal College of Music Edward Cowie discusses his BBC commission with Andrew McGregor prior to its world premiere and introduces performances of his chamber works. *Edited version broadcast on BBC Radio 3 after tonight's Prom*

TUESDAY 6 AUGUST

PROM 31
7.30pm–c9.50pm • Royal Albert Hall

PRICE BAND Ⓐ *Seats £7.50 to £36*

Walton
March 'Orb and Sceptre'   7'

Rubbra
Ode to the Queen   13'

Bruch
Violin Concerto No. 1 in G minor   24'

INTERVAL

Korngold
Symphony in F sharp minor   50'

Vilde Frang *violin*
Susan Bickley *mezzo-soprano*

BBC Philharmonic
John Storgårds *conductor*

SUSAN BICKLEY

The BBC Philharmonic and its Principal Guest Conductor return to the Royal Albert Hall for the first Proms performance of Erich Korngold's Symphony. Dedicated to the memory of Franklin D. Roosevelt, the symphony refers back to Korngold's score for the 1939 Errol Flynn and Bette Davis romance *The Private Lives of Elizabeth and Essex*. Rubbra's *Ode to the Queen* and Walton's *Orb and Sceptre* celebrate the 60th anniversary of the Queen's coronation, while Vilde Frang joins Storgårds and the orchestra for Bruch's ever-popular Violin Concerto. See 'Orb and Sceptre', pages 52–53.

BROADCAST
RADIO *Live on Radio 3*
ONLINE *Live and 'listen again' options at bbc.co.uk/proms*

PROMS PLUS FAMILY
5.30pm • Royal College of Music Create your own coronation music in the style of two British greats – Rubbra and Walton – with Rachel Leach and professional musicians.

SPOTLIGHT ON...

John Storgårds • Prom 31

'Korngold's only symphony had a difficult start in life,' says John Storgårds, Principal Guest Conductor of the BBC Philharmonic. 'When it was just composed in the 1950s Dimitri Mitropoulos was really excited about it and felt it was the perfect modern symphony that he'd been waiting for. But he died before he could conduct its premiere and, without that influential personal promotion, it somewhat languished, along with Korngold's other concert music, during a period when the composer was mainly associated with Hollywood film scores.' Storgårds describes the work as a 'big, serious, fantastic symphony', which makes huge demands on the orchestra: 'As with Mahler, it's very detailed: every dynamic and articulation mark is there. The effect is overwhelmingly moving.'

This concert marks the end of Storgårds's first year with the BBC Philharmonic, so what have been the highlights? 'We've done some great concerts and recordings and the Bridgewater Hall is a great venue to perform in,' he enthuses, 'but I think that the most memorable performance was at the LuostoClassic festival in Lapland, where I took the BBC Philharmonic to play Kalevi Aho's huge 12th Symphony outdoors with the Lapland Chamber Orchestra. Now *that's* a work I'd like to bring to the Proms!'

WEDNESDAY 7 AUGUST

PROM 32
7.30pm–c9.55pm • Royal Albert Hall

PRICE BAND Ⓐ *Seats £7.50 to £36*

Lutosławski
Symphonic Variations   9'

Holst
Egdon Heath   12'

Lutosławski
Piano Concerto   25'

INTERVAL

Holst
The Planets   50'

Louis Lortie *piano*

BBC Symphony Chorus
BBC Symphony Orchestra
Edward Gardner *conductor*

Leading champion of Lutosławski's music and Music Director of English National Opera, Edward Gardner conducts the BBC Symphony Orchestra in a programme contrasting one each of the Polish composer's earliest and latest works with music by the British composer Gustav Holst. Completed shortly before the occupation of Poland, Lutosławski's *Symphonic Variations* is juxtaposed with Holst's rarely heard tribute to Thomas Hardy, *Egdon Heath*. Louis Lortie is the soloist in Lutosławski's monumental 1988 Piano Concerto in a concert that closes with Holst's extraordinarily visionary *The Planets*. See 'A Polish Awakening', pages 30–35; 'Craving the Keyboard', pages 56–59.

BROADCAST
RADIO *Live on Radio 3*
ONLINE *Live and 'listen again' options at bbc.co.uk/proms*

PROMS PLUS INSPIRE
5.00pm • Royal College of Music The Aurora Orchestra, under Nicholas Collon, performs the winning entries in this year's BBC Proms Inspire Young Composers' Competition.
Edited version broadcast on BBC Radio 3 on 9 August

THURSDAY 8 AUGUST

PROM 33
7.00pm–c9.10pm • Royal Albert Hall

PRICE BAND C *Seats £14 to £57*

Beethoven
Piano Concerto No. 4 in G major   *35'*

INTERVAL

Berlioz
Symphonie fantastique   *50'*

Mitsuko Uchida *piano*

Bavarian Radio Symphony Orchestra
Mariss Jansons *conductor*

Mitsuko Uchida returns to the Proms after an absence of almost 20 years as the soloist in Beethoven's Piano Concerto No. 4, which overturned formal traditions by opening with a simple statement for solo piano. Musical ideas are tested to their limits in a conversation between keyboard and orchestra. The opium-fuelled obsessions, flower-like dancers, rural idyll, rolling tumbrel and danse macabre of Berlioz's 1830 gothic masterpiece *Symphonie fantastique* conclude the first of the Bavarian Radio Symphony Orchestra's two Proms (see also Prom 35) with Mariss Jansons, who celebrates his 70th birthday this year. See *'Craving the Keyboard'*, pages 56–59.

BROADCAST
RADIO *Live on Radio 3*
ONLINE *Live and 'listen again' options at bbc.co.uk/proms*
TV *Broadcast on BBC Four at 7.30pm*

MITSUKO UCHIDA

PROMS PLUS LITERARY
5.15pm • **Royal College of Music** To mark the 50th anniversary of the death of Sylvia Plath and the publication of her novel *The Bell Jar*, Lavinia Greenlaw and Sarah Churchwell look back on the legacy of a remarkable poet. *Edited version broadcast on BBC Radio 3 during tonight's interval*

THURSDAY 8 AUGUST

PROM 34
10.15pm–c11.30pm • Royal Albert Hall

PRICE BAND F *Seats £18/£24*

Vivaldi
The Four Seasons   *65'*

Nigel Kennedy *violin/director*
Palestine Strings
Members of the Orchestra of Life

There will be no interval

Following his two Proms appearances in 2008 and his more recent one in 2011 to play solo violin works by J. S. Bach, Nigel Kennedy returns with Vivaldi's *The Four Seasons* – with the Palestine Strings from the Edward Said National Conservatory of Music as well as members of his own Orchestra of Life. Revisiting a work he recorded to great acclaim nearly 25 years ago, he brings fresh insights to these visionary concertos, including the addition of his own improvised links between them. See *'Late Night Tonic'*, pages 94–95.

SAME-DAY SAVER
Proms 33 & 34
(see page 168)

BROADCAST
RADIO *Live on Radio 3*
ONLINE *Live and 'listen again' options at bbc.co.uk/proms*
TV *Recorded for broadcast on BBC Four on 23 August*

NIGEL KENNEDY

SPOTLIGHT ON...

Nigel Kennedy • Prom 34

When Nigel Kennedy tore into Vivaldi's *The Four Seasons* on his high-octane recording of 1989, it raised a few eyebrows. More than 20 years later his Proms performance of these four concertos comes with a different twist. He'll be directing the Palestine Strings – musicians from the Edward Said National Conservatory of Music – boosted by members of his Orchestra of Life.

'There's some fantastic talent in this orchestra,' he says of the young Palestinians, 'and a good number of them still play traditional Arabic music. In the Prom I'm going to call on the players' heritage, so between the Seasons there might be interludes of Arabic or improvised music, which will also act as a signpost for the one that's coming next.'

Kennedy is taken by the strong imagery in Vivaldi's score, which conveys shivering tremolos in Winter, the drunken peasants in Autumn and the barking shepherd's dog in Spring. 'You don't want beautiful legato notes for that,' Kennedy says of the barking effect. 'It's an intrusion and if it's played along those lines, it really makes it more three-dimensional.'

What attracted Kennedy to this particular string group? 'They value life more than we do in some ways, and there's a vitality in their performances which stems from that.'

FRIDAY 9 AUGUST

PRICE BAND **C** *Seats £14 to £57*

Mahler
Symphony No. 2 in C minor,
'Resurrection'   85'

Genia Kühmeier *soprano*
Anna Larsson *mezzo-soprano*

Bavarian Radio Symphony Choir
Bavarian Radio Symphony Orchestra
Mariss Jansons *conductor*

There will be no interval

In their second Proms appearance this summer,
Mariss Jansons and the Bavarian Radio Symphony
Orchestra are joined by the Bavarian Radio
Symphony Choir for Mahler's transcendent
'Resurrection' Symphony. Soprano Genia
Kühmeier and mezzo-soprano Anna Larsson
are the soloists in a work that begins with a
depiction of a funeral procession and opens out
into a vision of life after death. With allusions to
Beethoven's Ninth Symphony and klezmer melodies,
its off-stage brass and percussion, and a grand choral
climax, the symphony stands alone and unmissable.

BROADCAST
RADIO *Live on Radio 3*
ONLINE *Live and
'listen again' options at
bbc.co.uk/proms*
TV *Recorded for broadcast
on BBC Four on 15 August*

MARISS JANSONS

PROMS PLUS INTRO
5.15pm • Royal College of Music Norman Lebrecht and
Jeremy Barham discuss Mahler's conversion from Judaism
to Christianity, spirituality and the social context of the
'Resurrection' Symphony.
Edited version broadcast on BBC Radio 3 after tonight's Prom

FRIDAY 9 AUGUST

PRICE BAND **F** *Seats £18/£24*

J. S. Bach
Easter Oratorio   38'
Ascension Oratorio   32'

Hannah Morrison *soprano*
Meg Bragle *mezzo-soprano*
Nicholas Mulroy *tenor*
Peter Harvey *bass*

Monteverdi Choir
English Baroque Soloists
Sir John Eliot Gardiner *conductor*

There will be no interval

*SAME-
DAY SAVER
Proms 35 & 36
[see page 168]*

The ensembles that took Bach's cantatas to
14 countries in their Bach Pilgrimage of
2000 return to the Royal Albert Hall for
a Late Night Prom. The *Easter Oratorio* opens
with a Sinfonia that pitches a trio of trumpets
against consorts of woodwinds and strings, and a
poignant Adagio for solo oboe. Scored for similar
forces, the *Ascension Oratorio* features an alto aria
that mirrors the curves of the Agnus Dei from
Bach's Mass in B minor. Sir John Eliot Gardiner,
70 this year, directs the internationally renowned
Monteverdi Choir and English Baroque Soloists.
See 'Late Night Tonic', pages 94–95.

BROADCAST
RADIO *Live on Radio 3*
ONLINE *Live and 'listen again' options at bbc.co.uk/proms*
TV *Recorded for broadcast on BBC Four on 16 August*

SPOTLIGHT ON...
Sir John Eliot Gardiner • Prom 36

'The *Ascension Oratorio* is one of my very
favourite of Bach's pieces,' says Sir John Eliot
Gardiner. 'The trumpet writing – indeed, the
whole of the orchestral writing in the opening
and closing choruses – is so ebullient and
euphoric. The rhythms make you want to get
up and dance. It's Bach at his absolute best.'

Gardiner first learnt Bach's motets as a
young boy (and conducted four of them at
the Proms in 2009). Since then, the composer
has been a lifelong companion and in 2000
Gardiner conducted all of Bach's cantatas
over one year in an extraordinary pilgrimage.
His Late Night Prom this summer features the
Easter and *Ascension* Oratorios. And, while
Gardiner himself conducted the *Ascension
Oratorio*'s Proms premiere back in 1971,
the *Easter Oratorio* hasn't been heard at
the Proms since the 1950s.

'It's an elusive but wonderful piece.
It doesn't have the surface attraction of
Bach's Passions or the Mass in B minor,' says
Gardiner, 'it's a more subtle and understated
approach. It's somewhere between being
a contemplative and a dramatic piece but it
does have drama, as all Bach's music does.
After the appalling loss we hear in the
Passion music, here there's a sense of joy
and Resurrection. I think it's one of
the undiscovered jewels in Bach's output.'

SATURDAY 10 AUGUST

PROMS SATURDAY MATINEE 3
3.00pm–c4.30pm • Cadogan Hall

Seats £10 / £12

Britten
Young Apollo   8'
L. Berkeley
Serenade for strings   13'
Shostakovich
Concerto for piano, trumpet and strings
(Piano Concerto No. 1)   21'
Rainier
Movement for strings   c6'
world premiere
Britten
Variations on a Theme of Frank Bridge   27'

Alison Balsom *trumpet*

Camerata Ireland
Barry Douglas *piano/director*

There will be no interval

Pianist Barry Douglas directs
Camerata Ireland in its Proms debut
with a programme continuing the season's focus
on the music of Benjamin Britten and his
contemporaries. Withdrawn from performance
for 40 years after its 1939 premiere, Britten's
Young Apollo opens a sequence of works of brittle,
edgy beauty, including the world premiere of
Priaulx Rainier's 1951 *Movement for strings*. Lennox
Berkeley's *Serenade for strings* and Britten's *Variations
on a Theme of Frank Bridge* frame a performance
of Shostakovich's Piano Concerto No. 1, whose
witty trumpet part is played by Alison Balsom.
*See 'Revealing Britten', pages 38–43; 'New Music',
pages 62–69; 'Small is Beautiful', pages 96–97.*

ALISON BALSOM

BROADCAST
RADIO *Live on Radio 3*
ONLINE *Live and 'listen again' options at bbc.co.uk/proms*

PROMS PLUS SING
11.30am • Royal College of Music Mary King explores
Britten's mastery of word-setting in his vocal writing.
See pages 80–87 for details of how to sign up.

SATURDAY 10 AUGUST

PROM 37
8.00pm–c10.00pm • Royal Albert Hall

PRICE BAND Ⓐ Seats £7.50 to £36

URBAN CLASSIC PROM

Fazer *singer*
Laura Mvula *singer*
Maverick Sabre *singer*

BBC Symphony Orchestra
Jules Buckley *conductor*

There will be one interval

A dynamic meeting of musical cultures as conductor
Jules Buckley brings together the BBC Symphony
Orchestra with leading performers from the UK's
vibrant urban music scene. In Urban Classic's
experimental fusion of musical styles, high-octane
orchestral showpieces by Mosolov and Henze
rub shoulders with rap, R&B and soul. 'It's a culture
clash,' says Jules Buckley. 'We're taking artists from
different worlds and messing with their music,
putting it in an orchestral context and exploring
it in a new way.' See 'From the Streets to the Stage',
pages 98–101.

BROADCAST
RADIO *Live on Radio 3, Radio 1 and Radio 1Xtra*
ONLINE *Live and 'listen again' options at bbc.co.uk/proms*
TV *Recorded for broadcast on BBC Three on 10 August*

JULES BUCKLEY

PROMS PLUS INTRO
6.15pm • Royal College of Music An introduction to
tonight's Urban Classic Prom.
Edited version broadcast on BBC Radio 3 during tonight's interval

PROMS PLUS LATE
Elgar Room, Royal Albert Hall Informal post-Prom music
and poetry. For details see bbc.co.uk/proms

SUNDAY 11 AUGUST

PROM 38
7.30pm–c9.45pm • Royal Albert Hall

FREE PROM: tickets available from 28 June

Vaughan Williams
Toward the Unknown Region   11'
Mark-Anthony Turnage
Frieze   c15'
*BBC co-commission with the Royal
Philharmonic Society and the New York
Philharmonic: world premiere*

INTERVAL

Beethoven
Symphony No. 9 in D minor, 'Choral'   70'

Lisa Milne *soprano*
Jennifer Johnston *mezzo-soprano*
Andrew Kennedy *tenor*
Gerald Finley *baritone*

Codetta
Irish Youth Chamber Choir
National Youth Choir of Great Britain
**National Youth Orchestra of
Great Britain**
Vasily Petrenko *conductor*

The first ever free main-evening Prom celebrates
the bicentenary of the Royal Philharmonic Society
with a new work by Mark-Anthony Turnage and
a performance of the society's most famous
commission for choir and orchestra, Beethoven's
boundary-breaking 'Choral' Symphony, with youth
choirs from the UK and Ireland, including from
Derry-Londonderry, UK City of Culture 2013.
*See 'New Music', pages 62–69; 'New Adventures',
pages 80–87.*

BROADCAST
RADIO *Live on Radio 3*
ONLINE *Live and 'listen again' options at bbc.co.uk/proms*
TV *Recorded for broadcast on BBC Four on 6 September*

PROMS PLUS INTRO
5.45pm • Royal College of Music Helen Wallace and
Amanda Glauert discuss Beethoven's Symphony No. 9
and its link with the Royal Philharmonic Society.
Edited version broadcast on BBC Radio 3 during tonight's interval

PROMS CHAMBER MUSIC 5
1.00pm–c2.00pm • Cadogan Hall

Seats £10 / £12

Gustav Holst
Choral Hymns from the Rig Veda   14'

Imogen Holst
Hallo, my fancy, whither wilt thou go?   7'

Sir Harrison Birtwistle
The Moth Requiem   20'
*BBC co-commission with the Danish National
Vocal Ensemble: UK premiere*

*interspersed with a selection of motets from
The Eton Choirbook (15th century)*

BBC Singers
Nash Ensemble
Nicholas Kok *conductor*

There will be no interval

Nicholas Kok conducts the UK premiere of
Sir Harrison Birtwistle's *The Moth Requiem* for
women's voices, alto flute and three harps, a
dream-like incantation of the names of the dustier
cousins of the sun-loving butterfly. Pre-Reformation
motets preserved in the Eton Choirbook thread
through the BBC Singers' alluring programme of
works by Gustav Holst and his daughter Imogen,
including the third set of *Choral Hymns from the
Rig Veda* for female voices and harp, as a prelude
to tonight's performance of *Indra*. See 'New Music',
pages 62–69; 'Small is Beautiful', pages 96–97.

BROADCAST
RADIO *Live on Radio 3*
ONLINE *Live and
'listen again' options at
bbc.co.uk/proms*

NICHOLAS KOK

SPOTLIGHT ON...
Nishat Khan • Prom 39

Sitar virtuoso Nishat Khan is a Proms veteran,
having first played as a soloist in the festival
in 1989 and then again in 2008, when he
combined ragas with plainchant. This is the
first time one of his own compositions has
appeared at the Proms: 'I've been wanting to
do this concerto for many years, so it really is
a dream come true.' He's very clear about the
'core sound picture' he has created in his new
sitar concerto, but his own role will be fluid:
'I have a huge love and respect for the Western
classical tradition, and it's a daunting challenge
to find a way of combining the sitar with this
beautiful, gigantic orchestral sound. I've taken
a minimalist approach. There will be composed
music for myself and the orchestra, and parts
where I improvise alone; there will be dialogue,
development, rhythmic exploration, a lot of
interaction.' He says he won't be using specific
ragas, as the harmonies needed in Western
music interfere with the way ragas are
developed horizontally in the Indian tradition,
nor will he introduce other Indian instruments:
'I've found ways of using Western percussion
that will work. I think of Western classical
music as a huge ocean I'm swimming through,
with so many different fish, plants and
temperatures! I particularly love the sound
of the cello, and the oboe goes beautifully
with the sitar, it has a piercing nostalgia.'

PROM 39
7.00pm–c9.15pm • Royal Albert Hall

PRICE BAND Ⓐ *Seats £7.50 to £36*

Holst
Indra   12'

Nishat Khan
The Gate of the Moon
(Sitar Concerto No. 1)   c40'
BBC commission: world premiere

INTERVAL

Vaughan Williams
A London Symphony (Symphony No. 2)   45'

Nishat Khan *sitar*

**BBC National Orchestra
of Wales**
David Atherton *conductor*

SAME-
DAY SAVER
Proms 39 & 40
(see page 168)

Two visions of India and a portrait of
London. Gustav Holst's fascination with
Sanksrit literature found early expression in
the 1903 tone-poem *Indra*, composed before the
first set of his *Hymns from the Rig Veda* (see PCM 5).
David Atherton conducts the BBC National
Orchestra of Wales in this and the world premiere
of Nishat Khan's Sitar Concerto No. 1, with the
composer as soloist. First performed in 1914,
Vaughan Williams's *A London Symphony* evokes
the chimes of Westminster, a chill November
in Bloomsbury and the bright
lights of the Strand in a city that
would soon be scarred by war.
See 'New Music', pages 62–69.

BROADCAST
RADIO *Live on Radio 3
and the Asian Network*
ONLINE *Live and 'listen again'
options at bbc.co.uk/proms*

DAVID ATHERTON

PROMS PLUS INTRO
5.15pm • Royal College of Music Louise Fryer talks to
Stephen Johnson and musicologist Kate Kennedy about
Vaughan Williams and introduces *A London Symphony*.
Edited version broadcast on BBC Radio 3 during tonight's interval

12–13 AUGUST

142

BOOK ONLINE AT BBC.CO.UK/PROMS • BY TELEPHONE 0845 401 5040* • IN PERSON AT THE ROYAL ALBERT HALL • BOOKING OPENS 9.00AM ON 11 MAY

MONDAY 12 AUGUST

PROM 40
10.15pm–c11.30pm • Royal Albert Hall

PRICE BAND **E** *Seats £12/£16*

6 MUSIC PROM

Steve Lamacq *presenter*
Tom Service *presenter*
Laura Marling *singer*
Cerys Matthews *singer*
Anna Stéphany *mezzo-soprano*

The Stranglers
London Sinfonietta

There will be no interval

They may come from different ends of the radio dial but, for one night only, BBC Radio 6 Music's Steve Lamacq and Radio 3's Tom Service combine their passions for music to produce the first ever collaboration between these two diverse and distinctive radio stations. As well as featuring double Mercury Prize-nominated Laura Marling, 6 Music's own Cerys Matthews and original punk rock purveyors The Stranglers, the line-up includes the London Sinfonietta, playing works by Varèse, Berio, John Adams and Anna Meredith. *See 'Late Night Tonic', pages 94–95.*

SAME-DAY SAVER
Proms 39 & 40 (see page 168)

BROADCAST
RADIO *Live on Radio 3 and Radio 6 Music*
ONLINE *Live and 'listen again' options at bbc.co.uk/proms*

STEVE LAMACQ   TOM SERVICE

SPOTLIGHT ON...

Cerys Matthews • Prom 40

For Cerys Matthews, founder-member of Catatonia and now a BBC Radio 6 Music DJ, the idea of a Prom involving the radio station is a no-brainer. 'In line with Henry Wood's original intentions, the "new" must have its place and the public has always responded to that. This time the new is 6 Music, a station that defines itself as representing the cutting edge of music today.' Matthews grew up playing folk and classical music but made her career in the rock and folk worlds: 'I now often combine the two, with the orchestral parts integral to song-writing itself.' She hopes that the bands selected for this Prom will make the most of the added scope an orchestra offers: 'It's not just about the London Sinfonietta taking on what were once guitar or keyboard lines, it's using the huge palette of colours and the extreme dynamics of an orchestra to make new music,' she observes.

'I hope it will be a collision; that the things which might divide them bring them together. Radio 3's *Late Junction* is a treasure-trove of new music, 6 Music is the first entry point for 99% of today's new artists to perform live on air, and the Proms as a platform is the place for it to be happening. The Promenaders are the most dedicated music fans I've ever encountered.'

TUESDAY 13 AUGUST

PROM 41
7.30pm–c9.50pm • Royal Albert Hall

PRICE BAND **A** *Seats £7.50 to £36*

Borodin
Symphony No. 2 in B minor   28'

Glazunov
Piano Concerto No. 2 in B major   20'

INTERVAL

Sofia Gubaidulina
The Rider on the White Horse   13'
UK premiere

Mussorgsky, orch. Ravel
Pictures at an Exhibition   32'

Daniil Trifonov *piano*

London Symphony Orchestra
Valery Gergiev *conductor*

Valery Gergiev conducts the London Symphony Orchestra in a concert that justaposes the UK premiere of Sofia Gubaidulina's *The Rider on the White Horse* with Ravel's celebrated orchestration of Mussorgsky's *Pictures at an Exhibition*. Works by Mussorgsky's contemporary Alexander Borodin and by Alexander Glazunov, whose career as composer and conductor began in Tsarist Russia and ended in exile in Paris, add further colour to a programme steeped in history. Daniil Trifonov makes his Proms debut in Glazunov's rarely heard Piano Concerto No. 2, premiered in the first concert in Petrograd (St Petersburg) after the 1917 Revolution. *See 'Craving the Keyboard', pages 56–59; 'New Music', pages 62–69.*

VALERY GERGIEV

BROADCAST
RADIO *Live on Radio 3*
ONLINE *Live and 'listen again' options at bbc.co.uk/proms*

PROMS PLUS FAMILY
5.30pm • Royal College of Music Take an imaginary stroll through an art gallery with Rachel Leach and hear 15 pictures brought to life as music.

WEDNESDAY 14 AUGUST

PROM 42
7.00pm–c9.25pm • Royal Albert Hall

PRICE BAND **A** *Seats £7.50 to £36*

Janáček
Sinfonietta   *24'*

Beethoven
Piano Concerto No. 3 in C minor   *36'*

INTERVAL

Tchaikovsky
Symphony No. 3 in D major, 'Polish'   *46'*

Sunwook Kim *piano*

Bournemouth Symphony Orchestra
Kirill Karabits *conductor*

This summer's Tchaikovsky symphony cycle
continues as Kirill Karabits conducts the
Bournemouth Symphony Orchestra in the
dance-infused Third Symphony, written in the
summer of 1875 and dubbed the 'Polish'
following its 1899 London premiere in the
Crystal Palace. Leeds International Piano
Competition-winner Sunwook Kim makes his
Proms debut in Beethoven's dramatic Piano
Concerto No. 3 in a concert that begins with the
dazzling brass fanfares and bustling street-life of
Brno as translated into music in Janáček's 1926
*Sinfonietta. See 'Tchaikovsky
and the Russian Symphony',
pages 22–27; 'Craving the
Keyboard', pages 56–59.*

BROADCAST
RADIO *Live on Radio 3*
ONLINE *Live and 'listen again'
options at bbc.co.uk/proms*

SUNWOOK KIM

PROMS PLUS INTRO
5.15pm • **Royal College of Music** Ian Skelly talks to Marina
Frolova-Walker and Rosamund Bartlett about Tchaikovsky
and his world, looking at the influences in his life at the time
of writing his Third Symphony.
Edited version broadcast on BBC Radio 3 during tonight's interval

WEDNESDAY 14 AUGUST

PROM 43
10.15pm–c11.30pm • Royal Albert Hall

PRICE BAND **E** *Seats £12/£16*

Taverner
Kyrie 'Leroy'   *4'*

Gesualdo
Ave, dulcissima Maria   *4'*

Ave, regina caelorum   *4'*

Maria, mater gratiae   *4'*

interspersed with:

Taverner
Missa Gloria tibi Trinitas   *42'*

Tallis Scholars
Peter Phillips *conductor*

There will be no interval

SAME-
DAY SAVER
Proms 42 & 43
(see page 168)

Peter Phillips directs the Tallis Scholars, as the
group celebrates its 40th anniversary, in a
Late Night Prom contrasting the music of
John Taverner and of Carlo Gesualdo, who
died 400 years ago. Taverner was the first
organist and choirmaster of what is now Christ
Church, Oxford, falling from favour a year after his
master, Cardinal Wolsey, and into professional
obscurity. Aristocrat and harmonic adventurer
Carlo Gesualdo is best known for the boldness of
his madrigals. *See 'Late Night Tonic', pages 94–95.*

BROADCAST
RADIO *Live on Radio 3*
ONLINE *Live and 'listen again' options at bbc.co.uk/proms*

TALLIS SCHOLARS

SPOTLIGHT ON...
Peter Phillips • Prom 43

Peter Phillips has much to celebrate in the Tallis
Scholars' 40th-birthday year, including the
400th anniversary of Gesualdo's death. 'I'm not
sure this juxtaposition of Taverner and
Gesualdo has ever been tried before, which
makes it very exciting. We've chosen Taverner's
wonderful *Missa Gloria tibi Trinitas* as the
work to represent our anniversary. It has such
a rich legacy in British music, with composers
from Byrd to Purcell to Sir Peter Maxwell Davies
basing works on its "In nomine". In this Prom,
we'll interleave each part of the Mass with
motets by Gesualdo. Both composers belong
to the Renaissance but each explores opposite
ends of the artistic spectrum. With Taverner
you have these lovely long melodies and
extended sections proceeding from them, which
gives a sense of seamless flow. Gesualdo is all
gesture and passionate chromaticism; he cuts
up rhythms and makes them jump around. Like
the Mannerist painters, he deliberately goes too
far in the interests of extreme expression.'

Phillips has remained single-minded in his
sound ideal for the Tallis Scholars. 'I've always
had just one sound in my mind: I wanted it to
be bright, agile and beautiful, to draw the
listener in. The singers have found a technique
to sound more muscular over time. We've
never strayed from the Renaissance: I think
of us as artisans perfecting our craft.'

THURSDAY 15 AUGUST

PROM 44
7.30pm–c9.30pm • Royal Albert Hall

PRICE BAND **A** *Seats £7.50 to £36*

Stravinsky
Fireworks   4'

Krzysztof Penderecki
Concerto grosso   37'

INTERVAL

Debussy
La mer   24'

Ravel
Daphnis and Chloe – Suite No. 2   17'

Leonard Elschenbroich *cello*
Daniel Müller-Schott *cello*
Arto Noras *cello*

Royal Philharmonic Orchestra
Charles Dutoit *conductor*

Brilliance and brevity as Stravinsky's *Fireworks* opens
a concert in which Charles Dutoit and the RPO
explore the sensuous orchestrations of Debussy's
La mer and the second suite from Ravel's *Daphnis
and Chloe*. The Proms focus on Polish music
continues as Leonard Elschenbroich, Daniel
Müller-Schott and Arto Noras are the soloists
in the *Concerto grosso* by Krzysztof Penderecki,
80 this year. Written in 2000 and championed
by Dutoit in Tokyo, Philadelphia and Chicago,
the concerto plays with Baroque forms, pitting
the trio of cellists against choirs of woodwind.
See 'A Polish Awakening', pages 30–35 .

BROADCAST
RADIO *Live on Radio 3*
ONLINE *Live and 'listen again' options at bbc.co.uk/proms*

PROMS PLUS LITERARY
5.45pm • Royal College of Music Dame Monica Mason,
former director of the Royal Ballet, who partnered Rudolf
Nureyev in *Hamlet*, celebrates his life and legacy.
Edited version broadcast on BBC Radio 3 during tonight's interval

PROMS PLUS LATE
Elgar Room, Royal Albert Hall Informal post-Prom music
and poetry. For details see bbc.co.uk/proms

FRIDAY 16 AUGUST

PROM 45
6.30pm–c10.10pm • Royal Albert Hall

PRICE BAND **B** *Seats £9.50 to £46*

Tippett
The Midsummer Marriage   160'
(concert performance)

Paul Groves *Mark*
Erin Wall *Jenifer*
Peter Sidhom *King Fisher*
Ailish Tynan *Bella*
Allan Clayton *Jack*
Catherine Wyn-Rogers *Sosostris*
David Soar *He-Ancient*
Madeleine Shaw *She-Ancient*

BBC Singers
BBC Symphony Chorus
BBC Symphony Orchestra
Sir Andrew Davis *conductor*

There will be two intervals of 20 minutes

Last heard at the Proms in 1977, *The Midsummer
Marriage* is Tippett's answer to Mozart's *The Magic
Flute*, an opera rich in symbolism and psychology,
trials and transformations. Paul Groves and Erin
Wall are Mark and Jenifer, Ailish Tynan and Allan
Clayton, Bella and Jack, two couples tested by a
series of supernatural interventions on the shortest
night of the year. One of today's leading Tippett
exponents, Sir Andrew
Davis conducts the
centrepiece of this summer's
Proms focus on Tippett's
music alongside Britten's
centenary. *See 'A Composer
of Our Time', pages 44–47.*

ERIN WALL

BROADCAST
RADIO *Live on Radio 3*
ONLINE *Live and 'listen again'
options at bbc.co.uk/proms*

PROMS PLUS INTRO
4.45pm • Royal College of Music Louise Fryer talks to Oliver
Soden about Tippett's own libretto for *The Midsummer
Marriage* and the influence on the opera of poet T. S. Eliot.
Edited version broadcast on BBC Radio 3 during tonight's first interval

---

SPOTLIGHT ON...
Sir Andrew Davis • Prom 45

Sir Andrew Davis first fell in love with
Tippett's *The Midsummer Marriage* as a
young boy, so he is, he says, thrilled to be
conducting it at this year's Proms. 'The BBC
Symphony Orchestra did a studio recording
of it, conducted by Norman Del Mar, in
Maida Vale Studio 1 in 1963,' says Davis.
'I found out about it by accident and I went
to some of the sessions – I remember being
absolutely spellbound. A young Janet Baker
was singing Sosostris the soothsayer and I
was just bowled over.'

When Tippett's opera was first performed
back in 1955, it met with mixed reactions:
'One of the problems is that Tippett wrote
his own librettos. There are real flashes of
genius there, but other times you wince a
little bit. It's a bit like Mozart's *The Magic
Flute* and Strauss's *Die Frau ohne Schatten*
as seen through the eyes of a devotee of
Carl Jung,' says Davis.

'The music is ravishingly beautiful and
full of energy, the culmination of Tippett's
first period, characterised by luxuriant
textures, melismatic lines and colourful
orchestration. It's also a great chorus opera,
with some fantastic virtuosic writing –
the great finale to the first act, for instance.
This to me is one of his most wonderful,
perfect pieces.'

SATURDAY 17 AUGUST

PROM 46
3.00pm–c.5.00pm • Royal Albert Hall

PRICE BAND Ⓐ *Seats £7.50 to £36*

Dvořák
Symphony No. 8 in G major — *38'*

INTERVAL

Verdi
Otello – Willow Song; Ave Maria — *14'*

Tchaikovsky
Eugene Onegin – Polonaise; Letter Scene — *17'*

J. Strauss II
Emperor Waltz — *11'*
Thunder and Lightning – polka — *3'*

Kristīne Opolais *soprano*

City of Birmingham Symphony Orchestra
Andris Nelsons *conductor*

Andris Nelsons conducts the City of Birmingham Symphony Orchestra and soprano Kristīne Opolais in Desdemona's poignant Willow Song and Ave Maria from Act 3 of Verdi's 1887 opera *Otello* and Tatyana's touching Letter Scene from Tchaikovsky's 1879 opera *Eugene Onegin*. Shot through with birdsong and Bohemian dance rhythms, Dvořák's Eighth Symphony was the last to be completed in the Old World before he left for New York in 1892. A pair of popular Johann Strauss favourites concludes this matinee Prom with Viennese sparkle. See *'Tchaikovsky and the Russian Symphony'*, pages 22–27.

KRISTĪNE OPOLAIS

BROADCAST
RADIO *Live on Radio 3*
ONLINE *Live and 'listen again' options at bbc.co.uk/proms*

PROMS PLUS SING
11.00am • Royal College of Music Explore the vocal writing in Brahms's *A German Requiem* with Mary King. Suitable for singers familiar with the work who want to get some vocal tips! See pages 80–87 for details of how to sign up.

SATURDAY 17 AUGUST

PROM 47
7.30pm–c.9.55pm • Royal Albert Hall

PRICE BAND Ⓑ *Seats £9.50 to £46*

Brahms
Tragic Overture — *14'*

Schumann
Symphony No. 4 in D minor — *28'*

INTERVAL

Brahms
A German Requiem — *68'*

Rachel Harnisch *soprano*
Henk Neven *baritone*

Orchestra and Choir of the Age of Enlightenment
Marin Alsop *conductor*

SAME-DAY SAVER Proms 46 & 47 (see page 168)

Sacred but non-liturgical, *A German Requiem* is one of the most powerful works for choir and orchestra. Twenty-one years after Sir Roger Norrington directed the first British performance on period instruments, American conductor Marin Alsop, the Orchestra of the Age of Enlightenment and an 80-strong chorus explore Brahms's 1868 masterpiece in the context of his relationship with Robert Schumann and Schumann's widow, Clara. Schumann's Fourth Symphony and Brahms's *Tragic Overture* act as preludes to a work of great seriousness and humanity.

BROADCAST
RADIO *Live on Radio 3*
ONLINE *Live and 'listen again' options at bbc.co.uk/proms*

MARIN ALSOP

PROMS PLUS INTRO
5.45pm • Royal College of Music Laura Tunbridge looks at Brahms and the works performed in tonight's concert. *Edited version broadcast on BBC Radio 3 during tonight's interval*

SUNDAY 18 AUGUST

PROM 48
7.30pm–c.9.30pm • Royal Albert Hall

PRICE BAND Ⓐ *Seats £7.50 to £36*

Ravel
Rapsodie espagnole — *15'*

Matthias Pintscher
Chute d'étoiles — *20'*
London premiere

INTERVAL

Stravinsky
The Firebird — *46'*

Tine Thing Helseth *trumpet*
Marco Blaauw *trumpet*

BBC Scottish Symphony Orchestra
Matthias Pintscher *conductor*

Trumpeters Tine Thing Helseth and Marco Blaauw are the soloists in the London premiere of Matthias Pintscher's *Chute d'étoiles* with the BBC Scottish Symphony Orchestra. The composer makes his Proms conducting debut in his explosive musical homage to the great German artist Anselm Kiefer's 2007 installation in the Grand Palais, Paris, a grand experiment in weight and movement conjuring a shower of falling stars. The Basque melodies of Ravel's *Rapsodie espagnole* and Stravinsky's first Ballet Russes commission *The Firebird* complete a programme of daring orchestral innovations. See 'New Music', pages 62–69.

BROADCAST
RADIO *Live on Radio 3*
ONLINE *Live and 'listen again' options at bbc.co.uk/proms*

PROMS PLUS FAMILY ORCHESTRA & CHORUS
1.00pm • Royal College of Music Create a piece of music together with your family, inspired by the music in this evening's Prom. See pages 80–87 for details of how to sign up.

PROMS PLUS INTRO
5.45pm • Royal College of Music Louise Fryer presents an introduction to tonight's programme with a focus on Stravinsky's *The Firebird*. *Edited version broadcast on BBC Radio 3 during tonight's interval*

17–19 AUGUST

146

BOOK ONLINE AT BBC.CO.UK/PROMS • BY TELEPHONE 0845 401 5040* • IN PERSON AT THE ROYAL ALBERT HALL • BOOKING OPENS 9.00AM ON 11 MAY

MONDAY 19 AUGUST

PROMS CHAMBER MUSIC 6
1.00pm–c2.00pm • Cadogan Hall

Seats £10/£12

Poulenc
Sextet   18'

Imogen Holst
Phantasy Quartet   10'

Warlock
The Curlew   23'

Couperin, arr. T. Adès
Les baricades mistérieuses   3'

Robin Tritschler tenor
London Conchord Ensemble

There will be no interval

More English music at Cadogan Hall as Robin
Tritschler sings Peter Warlock's wistful 1922 setting
of poetry by W. B. Yeats, *The Curlew*, with the
London Conchord Ensemble. Written when she
was still a student, Imogen Holst's nostalgic 1928
Phantasy Quartet could almost be mistaken for a
work by her teacher, Vaughan Williams. Poulenc's
neo-Classical Sextet for wind and piano dates from
the following decade and
was premiered in Paris in
1940. Another modern take
on a much older style of
music comes in Thomas
Adès's richly coloured
arrangement of François
Couperin's *Les baricades
mistérieuses. See 'Small is
Beautiful', pages 96–97.*

ROBIN TRITSCHLER

MONDAY 19 AUGUST

PROM 49
7.00pm–c9.20pm • Royal Albert Hall

PRICE BAND **A** *Seats £7.50 to £36*

Berlioz
Overture 'King Lear'   16'

Mendelssohn
Piano Concerto No. 1 in G minor   21'

INTERVAL

J. S. Bach, orch. G. Benjamin
The Art of Fugue – Canon and Fugue   8'

Beethoven
Symphony No. 3 in E flat major, 'Eroica'   50'

Stephen Hough piano

Scottish Chamber Orchestra
Robin Ticciati conductor

Stephen Hough makes his second festival
appearance this summer playing Mendelssohn's
Piano Concerto No. 1, sight-read by Liszt in the
Érard piano showroom in Paris in 1831 to
Mendelssohn's amazement. Under its
Principal Conductor Robin Ticciati, the
Scottish Chamber Orchestra performs another
work of the same year, Berlioz's *King Lear*
overture, and Beethoven's 'Eroica' Symphony,
described by Berlioz as 'a funeral oration for a great
hero'. George Benjamin
pays tribute to Bach in
orchestrating excerpts
from *The Art of Fugue. See
'Craving the Keyboard',
pages 56–59.*

STEPHEN HOUGH

PROMS PLUS INTRO
5.15pm • Royal College of Music Kenneth Hamilton, concert
pianist and Professor of Music at Cardiff University, looks
at the story of the Romantic piano concerto, and at
Mendelssohn's Piano Concerto in G minor.
Edited version broadcast on BBC Radio 3 during tonight's interval

MONDAY 19 AUGUST

PROM 50
10.15pm–c11.30pm • Royal Albert Hall

PRICE BAND **E** *Seats £12/£16*

John White
Chord-Breaking Machine   10'

Gerald Barry
No other people.   12'
UK premiere

Frederic Rzewski
Piano Concerto   c20'
BBC commission: world premiere

Feldman
Coptic Light   28'

Frederic Rzewski piano

BBC Scottish Symphony Orchestra
Ilan Volkov conductor

There will be no interval

SAME-
DAY SAVER
*Proms 49 & 50
(see page 168)*

Inspired by ancient textiles seen in the Louvre
Museum, Morton Feldman's *Coptic Light*
glows heavily in the air, stopping time. Ilan
Volkov directs the BBC Scottish Symphony
Orchestra in this late masterpiece from the
American modernist and the world premiere of
Frederic Rzewski's Piano Concerto, with the
composer as soloist. English experimentalist John
White's *Chord-Breaking Machine* opens a Late
Night Prom of unusual orchestral textures in which the
Irish composer Gerald Barry's 2008 work *No other
people.* receives its UK premiere.
*See 'Craving the Keyboard',
pages 56–59; 'New Music',
pages 62–69; 'Late Night
Tonic', pages 94–95.*

FREDERIC RZEWSKI

TUESDAY 20 AUGUST

PROM 51
7.30pm–c9.45pm • Royal Albert Hall

PRICE BAND **A** *Seats £7.50 to £36*

Tippett
The Mask of Time – Fanfare No. 5   5'
Concerto for Double String Orchestra   23'

Britten
Les illuminations   25'

INTERVAL

Sibelius
Symphony No. 2 in D major   40'

Ian Bostridge *tenor*

London Symphony Orchestra
Sir Colin Davis *conductor*

Veteran conductor and President of tonight's orchestra, Sir Colin Davis conducts the LSO in repertoire close to his heart. Venetian polychoral motets, Northumbrian bagpipe melodies and the blues can be heard in Tippett's most popular orchestral work, completed, like Britten's flamboyant sequence of Rimbaud settings, in 1939. Fanfare No. 5, from Tippett's vast, humanist oratorio of 1980–82, *The Mask of Time*, opens a concert that ends in the forests of Finland with Sibelius's atmospheric Second Symphony, a signature work for Sir Colin and the LSO. *See 'Revealing Britten', pages 38–43; 'A Composer of Our Time', pages 44–47.*

IAN BOSTRIDGE

BROADCAST
RADIO *Live on Radio 3*
ONLINE *Live and 'listen again' options at bbc.co.uk/proms*
TV *Recorded for broadcast on BBC Four on 25 August*

PROMS PLUS LITERARY
5.45pm • Royal College of Music Benjamin Britten's compositions were inspired by the work of many poets and novelists. Actor Samuel West and writer Alexandra Harris explore the relationship between Britten's words and music. *Edited version broadcast on BBC Radio 3 during tonight's interval*

SPOTLIGHT ON...
Lisa Batiashvili • Prom 52

'There's burning fire inside Sibelius's Violin Concerto,' says Lisa Batiashvili, 'while the outside is a bit glassy. It's a mixture of two extremes. It has an incredible inner strength.' Ever since the Georgian violinist had to prepare the piece at short notice after unexpectedly getting through to the finals of the 1995 Sibelius Violin competition, it's been a work she's loved and played around the world. That first performance was with conductor Sakari Oramo, with whom she'll be appearing again in this Prom. 'Working with him was the best way for me to get to know the piece,' she says. 'I've played it with many other conductors since, but I've always felt that playing it with Sakari is the most natural. There's something straightforward and clear in his understanding of it, and it always sounds fresh. He's a Finnish musician and must love it so much.'

So does Batiashvili see this virtuosic and profound concerto, premiered in 1905 in the version known today, as a Finnish or an international work? 'It is a world-famous concerto but I do hear it as Finnish. I connect it with all my experiences in Finland when I travelled there a lot between the ages of 16 and 20. And I feel Sibelius's music is connected to both Finnish human nature and nature itself.'

WEDNESDAY 21 AUGUST

PROM 52
7.30pm–c9.55pm • Royal Albert Hall

PRICE BAND **A** *Seats £7.50 to £36*

Param Vir
Cave of Luminous Mind   c20'
BBC commission: world premiere

Sibelius
Violin Concerto in D minor   33'

INTERVAL

Bantock
Celtic Symphony   20'

Elgar
'Enigma' Variations   28'

Lisa Batiashvili *violin*

BBC Symphony Orchestra
Sakari Oramo *conductor*

SAKARI ORAMO

Dedicated to the late Jonathan Harvey, Param Vir's *Cave of Luminous Mind* is inspired by the mindfulness of Tibetan Buddhism and the story of Buddhist master Milarepa's penitential progress on the Diamond Path. Chief Conductor and Elgar Medal-winner Sakari Oramo directs the BBC Symphony Orchestra in the world premiere of Vir's work, Elgar's 'Enigma' Variations and Granville Bantock's 1940 *Celtic Symphony* for strings and six harps. Georgian violinist Lisa Batiashvili plays Sibelius's exhilarating Violin Concerto, a work she recorded in 2008 to rave reviews. *See 'Bring out the Bantock', pages 50–51; 'New Music', pages 62–69.*

BROADCAST
RADIO *Live on Radio 3*
ONLINE *Live and 'listen again' options at bbc.co.uk/proms*

PROMS PLUS PORTRAIT
5.45pm • Royal College of Music Param Vir discusses *Cave of Luminous Mind* with Andrew McGregor prior to its world premiere and introduces performances of his chamber works given by musicians from the Royal Academy of Music. *Edited version broadcast on BBC Radio 3 after tonight's Prom*

148

20–22 AUGUST

BOOK ONLINE AT BBC.CO.UK/PROMS • BY TELEPHONE 0845 401 5040* • IN PERSON AT THE ROYAL ALBERT HALL • BOOKING OPENS 9.00AM ON 11 MAY

THURSDAY 22 AUGUST

PROM 53
7.00pm–c9.05pm • Royal Albert Hall

PRICE BAND **B** *Seats £9.50 to £46*

Tchaikovsky
Fantasy-Overture 'Romeo and Juliet'   *21'*

Wagner
Wesendonck-Lieder   *21'*

INTERVAL

Prokofiev
Symphony No. 5 in B flat major   *40'*

Anna Caterina Antonacci *soprano*

Rotterdam Philharmonic Orchestra
Yannick Nézet-Séguin *conductor*

Charismatic Italian soprano Anna Caterina
Antonacci joins the young Canadian Yannick
Nézet-Séguin, Music Director of the
Rotterdam Philharmonic Orchestra, for
Wagner's *Wesendonck-Lieder*, a song-cycle thick
with musical references to what would become
Tristan and Isolde and written when the composer
was infatuated with Mathilde Wesendonck, author
of the poems and wife of Wagner's patron.
Tchaikovsky's *Romeo and Juliet* relates another
doomed love, while
Prokofiev's Fifth Symphony
has a brightness and energy
beyond the requirements
of Soviet war-time
propaganda. See 'Tchaikovsky
and the Russian Symphony',
pages 22–27.

BROADCAST
RADIO *Live on Radio 3*
ONLINE *Live and 'listen again'*
options at bbc.co.uk/proms
TV *Broadcast on BBC Four at 7.30pm*

ANNA CATERINA
ANTONACCI

PROMS PLUS INTRO
5.15pm • Royal College of Music James Jolly talks to
Fiona McKnight, Archivist of the Serge Prokofiev Archive
at Goldsmiths, University of London, about Prokofiev and
his Fifth Symphony.
Edited version broadcast on BBC Radio 3 during tonight's interval

---

THURSDAY 22 AUGUST

PROM 54
10.00pm–c11.15pm • Royal Albert Hall

PRICE BAND **E** *Seats £12/£16*

WORLD ROUTES PROM

Fidan Hajiyeva *vocalist*
Gochaq Askarov *vocalist*
Bassekou Kouyaté & Ngoni Ba
Tinariwen

There will be no interval

Following last year's riotous celebration of
Colombian music, this year BBC Radio 3's World
Routes Academy turns east to the former Soviet
state of Azerbaijan. Eighteen-year-old Baku-born
London resident Fidan Hajiyeva performs alongside
her mentor, the Azerbaijani singer Gochaq
Askarov. One of the most distinguished and
eloquent exponents of the ancient mugham
form, Askarov has worked closely with
Fidan during a recent three-week period of
teaching and performance in Azerbaijan. Also
featuring on the bill are the guitar-driven 'desert
blues' of Tinariwen, from the Sahara Desert region
of northern Mali, and the central Malian singer/ngoni
(lute) player Bassekou Kouyaté with his band Ngoni
Ba – two celebrated groups fusing traditional and
popular styles, who have taken the world music
scene by storm.

BROADCAST
RADIO *Live on Radio 3*
ONLINE *Live and 'listen again' options at bbc.co.uk/proms*

SAME-
DAY SAVER
Proms 53 & 54
(see page 168)

FIDAN HAJIYEVA AND GOCHAQ ASKAROV

SPOTLIGHT ON...
World Routes • Prom 54

'Her voice has a rich timbre, and she's not afraid
of the stage. I think Fidan is a fighter by nature.
If she decides to be a singer, she will succeed.'
So says Gochaq Askarov, the Azerbaijani singer
known as the 'prince of mugham' who is
mentoring the young Fidan Hajiyeva for this
year's World Routes Prom. Fidan was born in
Azerbaijan but moved to Hackney as a young
child. She started singing Azeri music at 13,
inspired by the music her father listened to.
'It's very dramatic – there's a story behind every
song which expresses something very powerful,'
she explains. 'Even if you don't understand the
language, it can make you cry.' She's now
considering a musical career: 'I've realised I have
a voice. I've had lessons with Gochaq in video
calls online and he's made me feel comfortable,
although he's very famous in Azerbaijan. I'm
looking forward to going there for lessons.'
Askarov himself fought hard to become a
musician, running away from home to attend
a music school and making his own way to the
music college in Baku. He will train the young
teenager in the 'mugham' style, a complex form
of Azerbaijani song with instrumental
accompaniment. 'I'm planning to teach her
Mugham Qatar, which will fit her high-pitched
voice. It's a sophisticated music in every sense,
requiring a voice inclined to coloratura, special
vocal technique and a sublime artistic nature.'

FRIDAY 23 AUGUST

PROM 55
7.30pm–c10.05pm • Royal Albert Hall

PRICE BAND Ⓐ *Seats £7.50 to £36*

Lutosławski
Concerto for Orchestra   30'

Shostakovich
Piano Concerto No. 2 in F major   19'

INTERVAL

Panufnik
Tragic Overture   9'

Lullaby   8'

Shostakovich
Symphony No. 6 in B minor   35'

Alexander Melnikov *piano*

Warsaw Philharmonic Orchestra
Antoni Wit *conductor*

Antoni Wit and the Warsaw Philharmonic Orchestra
make their Proms debuts as the festival continues its
focus on Polish music during Lutosławski's centenary
year. Written for the Warsaw Philharmonic in 1954,
Lutosławski's virtuosic folk-inflected *Concerto for
Orchestra* creates a unique sound-world. Lauded
for his recording of Shostakovich's Preludes and
Fugues, pianist Alexander Melnikov is the soloist
in the composer's buoyant Piano Concerto No. 2.
Andrzej Panufnik's *Tragic Overture* and *Lullaby* and
Shostakovich's Sixth Symphony paint a vivid picture
of two nations in parallel periods of anxiety. *See
'A Polish Awakening', pages 30–35.*

BROADCAST
RADIO *Live on Radio 3*
ONLINE *Live and 'listen again' options at bbc.co.uk/proms*

PROMS PLUS INTRO
5.45pm • Royal College of Music Andrew McGregor talks to
Nick Reyland about Lutosławski, Panufnik and their place in
the history of Polish culture.
Edited version broadcast on BBC Radio 3 during tonight's interval

PROMS PLUS LATE
Elgar Room, Royal Albert Hall Informal post-Prom music
and poetry. For details see bbc.co.uk/proms

SATURDAY 24 AUGUST

PROMS SATURDAY MATINEE 4
3.00pm–c4.30pm • Cadogan Hall

Seats £10 / £12

Purcell, arr. Britten
Chacony   7'

Lutosławski
Paroles tissées   15'

**L. Berkeley, Britten, Oldham,
Searle, Tippett, Walton**
Variations on an Elizabethan Theme
(Sellinger's Round)
with new variations by **Tansy Davies**
and **John Woolrich**   c24'
BBC commission: world premiere

Britten
Serenade for tenor, horn and strings   25'

Ben Johnson *tenor*
Richard Watkins *horn*

English Chamber Orchestra
Paul Watkins *conductor*

There will be no interval

To mark the coronation in
1953, Lennox Berkeley, Britten,
Arthur Oldham, Humphrey
Searle, Tippett and Walton
composed a series of variations
on 'Sellinger's Round', a
melody harmonised four
centuries earlier by William
Byrd and orchestrated in 1953
by Imogen Holst. Today the
English Chamber Orchestra adds two new
variations to the set, by John Woolrich and Tansy
Davies, in a matinee that also features two vivid
works written for tenor Peter Pears: Britten's
Serenade for tenor, horn and strings and Lutosławski's
*Paroles tissées. See 'A Polish Awakening', pages 30–35;
'Revealing Britten', pages 38–43; 'Orb and Sceptre',
pages 52–53; 'New Music', pages 62–69; 'Small is
Beautiful', pages 96–97.*

PAUL WATKINS

BROADCAST
RADIO *Live on Radio 3*
ONLINE *Live and 'listen again' options at bbc.co.uk/proms*

SPOTLIGHT ON...

Ben Johnson • PSM 4

Young British tenor Ben Johnson sings two
works written for Peter Pears in his Saturday
Matinee concert: Britten's *Serenade for tenor,
horn and strings* and Lutosławski's *Paroles
tissées.* He notes that they are both not only
brilliant settings but very wordy ones: 'Pears
was so skilful in the way he delivered text.
I studied with Neil Mackie at the Royal College
of Music, who was a student of Pears, and he
always encouraged me to sing a lot of the
works, so I feel close to Britten's music.'

His favourite moment of the *Serenade*, he
says, is 'my very first note in the "Pastoral", that
high *pianissimo* A flat that magically flows in
on a warm cushion of strings. Then there's the
remarkable setting of Keats's sonnet "To Sleep"
just before the end. It's perfectly placed: when
you finish there's nothing left to say and the
offstage horn allows the intensity to sink in.'

He observes that Pears found great lyricism
in Lutosławski's *Paroles tissées.* 'It can be
recreated in a unique way each time: there
are elements of freedom. The tenor is part of
a chamber music texture and you need to find
a wide palette of colours; sometimes you're
singing, sometimes it's more like oratory.'

It's a big year for Johnson, who will be
competing at the Cardiff Singer of the World
in June – and getting married in September.
'There's a lot to think about!'

SATURDAY 24 AUGUST

PROM 56
7.30pm–c9.40pm • Royal Albert Hall

PRICE BAND **B** *Seats £9.50 to £46*

Wagner
Rienzi – overture   *12'*

Ravel
Piano Concerto in G major   *22'*

INTERVAL

Shostakovich
Symphony No. 5 in D minor   *49'*

Jean-Yves Thibaudet *piano*

Gustav Mahler Jugendorchester
Philippe Jordan *conductor*

Founded by Claudio Abbado in 1986, the
pan-European Gustav Mahler Jugendorchester
remains one of the most musically exciting and
technically polished youth orchestras in the world.
Tonight, Philippe Jordan directs the GMJO in the
overture to Wagner's *Rienzi* and Shostakovich's
Fifth Symphony, written in an atmosphere of intense
scrutiny and artistic repression, after the public
denouncement of his opera *The Lady Macbeth
of the Mtsensk District*. Ravel's jazz-inflected Piano
Concerto in G major completes the programme,
with the flamboyant French pianist Jean-Yves
Thibaudet as the soloist. See 'Craving the Keyboard',
pages 56–59.

BROADCAST
RADIO *Live on Radio 3*
ONLINE *Live and
'listen again' options at
bbc.co.uk/proms*
TV *Recorded for
broadcast on BBC Four
on 29 August*

PHILIPPE JORDAN

PROMS PLUS FAMILY
5.30pm • Royal College of Music Join Rachel Leach and
professional musicians to discover the hidden stories within
the music of tonight's Prom. Bring your instrument and join in!

SPOTLIGHT ON...

Jean-Yves Thibaudet • Prom 56

Jean-Yves Thibaudet first came to the
Proms in 1992, playing Rachmaninov's
Piano Concerto No. 3, and has been back
on a dozen occasions since, playing concertos
by composers ranging from Mendelssohn
and Grieg to Gershwin and Messiaen. 'I've
always enjoyed it; the atmosphere is electric.
I was lucky enough to play on the Last Night
once – that was a Prom on steroids! I can't
think of any event in the world like it.'

The Lyons-born pianist has naturally been
been drawn to the French repertoire and he
returns to the Proms this year to perform
Ravel's Piano Concerto in G major, a work
which has been with him since childhood:
'I was 11 the first time I played it and every
single time I play it again, I find it as fresh as
the first time. To me, it's somehow perfection:
I wouldn't add a note or take out a note! Ravel
wrote in this concerto "to have fun", so that
should be the main feeling. The challenge,
I think, rests in its simplicity. The second
movement may look simple, but you can
move people to tears with its profundity.'

Thibaudet's connection with Ravel's
music goes beyond the piano works, though.
'If I had to take one work of Ravel, it would
be the complete ballet of *Daphnis and Chloe*.
It's an entire cycle of life; it moves me every
time I hear it.'

SUNDAY 25 AUGUST

PROM 57
4.30pm–c10.10pm • Royal Albert Hall

PRICE BAND **B** *Seats £9.50 to £46*

Wagner Parsifal   *235'*
(concert performance; sung in German)

Lars Cleveman *Parsifal*
Katarina Dalayman *Kundry*
Robert Holl *Gurnemanz*
Iain Paterson *Amfortas*
Tom Fox *Klingsor*
Reinhard Hagen *Titurel*
Robert Murray *Knight 1*
Andrew Greenan *Knight 2*
Sarah Castle *Squire 1/Flower Maiden 3*
Madeleine Shaw *Squire 2/Flower Maiden 6/
Voice from Above*
Andrew Rees *Squire 3*
Joshua Ellicott *Squire 4*
Elizabeth Cragg *Flower Maiden 1*
Anita Watson *Flower Maiden 2*
Sarah-Jane Brandon *Flower Maiden 5*

Choirs to include:
Trinity Boys Choir
Hallé Youth Choir

Hallé
Sir Mark Elder *conductor*

There will be two intervals, of 50 and 35 minutes

Sir Mark Elder conducts the Hallé in *Parsifal*,
Wagner's final epic drama of renunciation and
redemption, with Robert Holl as Gurnemanz,
the veteran Knight of the Grail. Lars Cleveman is
the Holy Fool Parsifal and Katarina Dalayman the
penitential Magdalen figure, Kundry. See 'All Around
the Ring', pages 14–19.

BROADCAST
RADIO *Live on Radio 3*
ONLINE *Live and 'listen again' options at bbc.co.uk/proms*

PROMS PLUS INTRO
2.45pm • Royal College of Music Martin Handley presents
an introduction to Wagner's epic and final opera, *Parsifal*,
with Stephen Johnson.
Edited version broadcast on BBC Radio 3 during tonight's first interval

PROMS CHAMBER MUSIC 7
1.00pm–c2.00pm • Cadogan Hall

Seats £10 / £12

Maconchy
String Quartet No. 3   11'

Brahms
Piano Quintet in F minor   40'

Signum Quartet
Christian Ihle Hadland piano

There will be no interval

Nearly 21 years after her death, Elizabeth Maconchy
remains one of 20th-century Britain's most alluring
forgotten voices. International in outlook, she wrote
music of great lyricism and subtlety, closer to the
sound-world of Central Europe than to that of the
English musical establishment. Today the Signum
Quartet, one of BBC Radio 3's New Generation
Artists, pairs Maconchy's Bartók-influenced String
Quartet No. 3 with another work of meticulously
compressed emotionalism, Brahms's F minor Piano
Quintet. Norwegian pianist and fellow NGA
Christian Ihle Hadland joins them. See 'Small is
Beautiful', pages 96–97.

BROADCAST
RADIO Live on Radio 3
ONLINE Live and 'listen again' options at bbc.co.uk/proms

CHRISTIAN IHLE HADLAND

SPOTLIGHT ON...
Richard Hills • Prom 58

'I love a good tune,' says British organist
Richard Hills, whose work straddles both the
church and theatre organ worlds. 'This Prom
is all about the musical age where melody was
king.' It's a handy introduction to this light
music concert, which showcases just how
versatile the organ can be. Hills has put
together a programme delving into repertoire
popular in the 1930s, 1940s and 1950s.
'I tried to choose music that could be
successfully realised on the Royal Albert Hall
instrument. It's a very orchestral organ,' he
says of the Henry Willis instrument, originally
completed in 1871, but substantially rebuilt in
the early 2000s. 'The stops include things like
French horns and strings, even tubular chimes
and bass drums. It will be great fun to explore
using the organ in this way.'
    After its heyday in the era of the silent
cinema and daily broadcasts on the BBC, the
theatre organ fell out of fashion. So why does
it appeal to Hills? 'It's hugely satisfying and
great fun. The sound grabs holds of you.
I remember hearing my first Wurlitzer at the
age of 7, and I was speechless at the big, warm
and vibrant effect. It's possible to capture
every nuance on the theatre organ: you can
have pathos, tragedy, ecstatic joy. All these
emotions can be portrayed: indeed, this was
its job in accompanying silent films.'

PROM 58
4.30pm–c5.30pm • Royal Albert Hall

PRICE BAND E Seats £12/£16

LIGHT ORGAN PROM

Programme to include:

Coates
March 'Sound and Vision'   4'

Sullivan, arr. R. Hills
Mikado Memories   7'

Ireland
Miniature Suite – Villanella   4'

Mayerl
Four Aces Suite – Ace of Hearts   3'

German
Three Dances from Nell Gwyn   12'

Waller
A Handful of Keys   3'

Richard Hills organ

There will be no interval

A chance to revel in the breathtaking versatility of
the 'king of instruments'! The art of performing
classical favourites on the organ has a long and
distinguished history and in this Bank Holiday
matinee Prom, Richard Hills brings together the
traditions of the great theatre organist-entertainers
and the Town Hall recitalists – with the accent on
melody and virtuosity.

BROADCAST
RADIO Live on Radio 3
ONLINE Live and 'listen again' options
at bbc.co.uk/proms

SAME-
DAY SAVER
Proms 58 & 59
(see page 168)

PROMS PLUS SING
2.30pm • Royal College of Music Join Mary King for a sing
through some great tunes from musicals and movies to
get you in the toe-tapping mood for this afternoon's
Light Organ Prom! Suitable for all. See pages 80–87
for details of how to sign up.

26–27 AUGUST

152

BOOK ONLINE AT BBC.CO.UK/PROMS • BY TELEPHONE 0845 401 5040* • IN PERSON AT THE ROYAL ALBERT HALL • BOOKING OPENS 9.00AM ON 11 MAY

MONDAY 26 AUGUST

PROM 59
7.30pm–c9.45pm • Royal Albert Hall

PRICE BAND **C** *Seats £14 to £57*

HOLLYWOOD RHAPSODY PROM

John Wilson Orchestra
John Wilson *conductor*

There will be one interval

John Wilson and his orchestra return to the Proms in a celebration of the Hollywood film scores that Wilson describes as 'literally unsung' and a medley of theme songs (featuring distinguished vocalists) from otherwise non-musical movies. Connecticut-born child prodigy Alfred Newman's 'Street Scene', from *How to Marry a Millionaire*, contrasts with the music of Jewish émigrés Erich Korngold, Max Steiner and Franz Waxman, with suites from Korngold's swashbuckling score for *Robin Hood*, Steiner's nostalgic music for *Casablanca* and Waxman's brooding score for *A Place in the Sun* – all of them Academy Award-winners – making for a red-carpet event at the Royal Albert Hall.

BROADCAST
RADIO *Live on Radio 3*
ONLINE *Live and 'listen again' options at bbc.co.uk/proms*
TV *Recorded for broadcast on BBC Four on 30 August*

SAME-DAY SAVER
Proms 58 & 59
(see page 168)

PROMS PLUS LITERARY
5.45pm • Royal College of Music Film composer Debbie Wiseman and writer David Benedict talk to Matthew Sweet about the ways in which film-makers have created mood with music from the very first days of silent film to the contemporary CGI blockbuster.
Edited version broadcast on BBC Radio 3 during tonight's interval

---

SPOTLIGHT ON...
John Wilson • Prom 59

It was back in 2009 that John Wilson and his orchestra first caught the public imagination with their MGM Musicals Prom. In 2010 their Rodgers and Hammerstein Prom was just as big a hit. Now a Proms regular, this year Wilson is turning his attention to the composers who wrote for films away from the musicals: 'I want to put the spotlight back on to the orchestral players. There are things we can do that we've not really done at the Proms yet, such as the really lavishly wrought scores of Korngold.'

Wilson's Prom explores the film score's development from the first film composers, including Max Steiner and Alfred Newman, to the end of the golden age, focusing on the 'significant amount of music that really does stand up in concert'. And it's a programme that demands versatility and virtuosity from his orchestra: 'It's a symphony orchestra with an old-fashioned dance band in the middle – just about the most adaptable combination of players. We'll need it here, to go from those rich idioms of Richard Strauss and French Impressionism to American hot jazz.'

And how will it feel to be back in the Royal Albert Hall? 'Playing at the Proms is the musical equivalent of entering the kingdom of heaven. As long as there's a slot for us, we'll do our damnedest to be worthy of the institution.'

TUESDAY 27 AUGUST

PROM 60
7.00pm–c10.15pm • Royal Albert Hall

PRICE BAND **C** *Seats £14 to £57*

Britten
Billy Budd   160'
(semi-staged)

Jacques Imbrailo *Billy Budd*
Mark Padmore *Captain Vere*
Brindley Sherratt *John Claggart*
Stephen Gadd *Mr Redburn*
David Soar *Mr Flint*
Darren Jeffery *Lieutenant Radcliffe*
Alasdair Elliott *Red Whiskers*
John Moore *Donald*
Jeremy White *Dansker*
Peter Gijsbertsen *The Novice*
Colin Judson *Squeak*
Richard Mosley-Evans *Bosun*

Glyndebourne Festival Opera
London Philharmonic Orchestra
Sir Andrew Davis *conductor*

There will be one interval

Sir Andrew Davis conducts the London Philharmonic Orchestra and the cast and chorus of Glyndebourne Festival's production of Britten's *Billy Budd*. Adapted by E. M. Forster and Eric Crozier from Herman Melville's unfinished novella, Britten's 1951 opera on the persecution and destruction of pure-hearted sailor Billy by a predatory master-at-arms is a tragedy of 'sexual discharge gone evil' in the Napoleonic Wars. Jacques Imbrailo sings the title-role, with Brindley Sherratt as the sinister Claggart and Mark Padmore as the rule-bound Pontius Pilate figure, Captain 'Starry' Vere. See 'Revealing Britten', pages 38–43.

BROADCAST
RADIO *Live on Radio 3*
ONLINE *Live and 'listen again' options at bbc.co.uk/proms*

PROMS PLUS LITERARY
5.15pm • Royal College of Music Writers Philip Hoare and Kate Mosse talk to Rana Mitter about the themes of good and evil, justice and the law in Melville's novella *Billy Budd*.
Edited version broadcast on BBC Radio 3 during tonight's interval

WEDNESDAY 28 AUGUST

PROM 61
7.00pm–c9.25pm • Royal Albert Hall

PRICE BAND Ⓐ *Seats £7.50 to £36*

Stravinsky
Scherzo à la russe   4'
Ave Maria   2'
Pater noster   2'

Brahms
Violin Concerto in D major   40'

INTERVAL

Charlotte Seither
Language of Leaving   c18'
BBC commission: world premiere

Stravinsky
Petrushka (1947 version)   30'

Frank Peter Zimmermann *violin*

BBC Singers
BBC Symphony Orchestra
Josep Pons *conductor*

German composer Charlotte Seither
adapts the words of the 17th-century poet
Francesco de Lemene in a new work for the
BBC Singers and the BBC Symphony Orchestra,
using voices and syllables as spots of 'human colour'.
Josep Pons conducts this world premiere alongside
the 1947 version of Stravinsky's *Petrushka*, the *a
cappella* motets *Ave Maria* and *Pater noster*, and the
four-minute novelty *Scherzo à la russe*, written
in Hollywood for the bandleader Paul Whiteman.
Frank Peter Zimmermann is the soloist in Brahms's
much-loved Violin Concerto. See 'New Music',
pages 62–69.

BROADCAST
RADIO *Live on Radio 3*
ONLINE *Live and 'listen again' options at bbc.co.uk/proms*

PROMS PLUS PORTRAIT
5.15pm • Royal College of Music Charlotte Seither discusses
her commisssion with Andrew McGregor and introduces
performances of her chamber works given by musicians
from the Royal Conservatoire of Scotland.
Edited version broadcast on BBC Radio 3 after tonight's Prom

WEDNESDAY 28 AUGUST

PROM 62
10.15pm–c11.30pm • Royal Albert Hall

PRICE BAND Ⓔ *Seats £12/£16*

A CELEBRATION OF CHARLIE PARKER

Programme to include:

Django Bates
The Study of Touch   10'
UK premiere

Belovèd
Django Bates *piano*
Petter Eldh *double bass*
Peter Bruun *drums*

Norrbotten Big Band
with guest vocalist **Ashley Slater**

There will be no interval

Twenty-six years after his first Proms appearance,
with his big band Loose Tubes, jazz pianist and
composer Django Bates returns with his own trio
in a new partnership with the Grammy-nominated
Norrbotten Big Band from northern Sweden.
Together they present a celebration of
Charlie 'Bird' Parker – bebop pioneer and
beloved hero of Bates – adding their own
spin on Parker classics such as 'Confirmation',
'Scrapple from the Apple' and 'Donna Lee',
interleaved with Bates's own compositions, fast
becoming part of the jazz canon. See 'New Music',
pages 62–69; 'Late Night Tonic', pages 94–95.

BROADCAST
RADIO *Live on Radio 3*
ONLINE *Live and 'listen again' options at bbc.co.uk/proms*

SAME-
DAY SAVER
Proms 61 & 62
(see page 168)

NORRBOTTEN BIG BAND

Inimitable jazz leader-composer Django Bates
has spent the last few years exploring the legacy
of Charlie Parker, resulting in two albums,
Belovèd Bird and *Confirmation*. But the love
affair dates back much further: 'Charlie Parker
was my childhood hero. Just as birdsong makes
humans happy, Parker's compositions and
improvisations were like birdsong to me; they
flow freely in and out of the pulse, they burble
very fast but with immense clarity, they
understand but are not bound by harmonic
structure, they communicate joy.'

Bates's trio Belovèd was formed at
Copenhagen's Rhythmic Music Conservatory,
where he was a professor. 'I decided long ago
I'd never have a piano trio, until I walked past
a room where Petter Eldh and Peter Bruun were
the rhythm section for a small concert. At that
moment I changed my mind. I chose Petter and
Peter not just for their great instrumental skills
but for their personalities, wide-ranging
musical interests and for the intensity they
bring to every note and brush stroke.' For this
Prom, Belovèd joins forces with the Norrbotten
Big Band. 'We'll be performing versions of
Belovèd's recent material on a grander scale:
14 horns creating new colours and textures
alongside the trio, with bigger venues to
provide a new context – and they don't get
much bigger than the Royal Albert Hall!'

154

28–30 AUGUST

BOOK ONLINE AT BBC.CO.UK/PROMS • BY TELEPHONE 0845 401 5040* • IN PERSON AT THE ROYAL ALBERT HALL • BOOKING OPENS 9.00AM ON 11 MAY

THURSDAY 29 AUGUST

PROM 63
7.30pm–c9.50pm • Royal Albert Hall

PRICE BAND **A** *Seats £7.50 to £36*

Mozart
Der Schauspieldirektor – overture   4'

Peter Eötvös
DoReMi   21'
*BBC co-commission with the Los Angeles
Philharmonic and the Leipzig Gewandhaus:
UK premiere*

INTERVAL

Bruckner
Symphony No. 7 in E major   70'

Midori *violin*

Philharmonia Orchestra
Esa-Pekka Salonen *conductor*

Described by the violinist
Midori as 'so rhapsodic
and so individual', *DoReMi* is
Hungarian composer Peter
Eötvös's second violin
concerto. Esa-Pekka
Salonen conducts the
Philharmonia Orchestra in
the UK premiere of a work
first heard in Los Angeles

MIDORI

this January. Eötvös's 'world of simple things' and
the sparkling overture to Mozart's 1786 backstage
comedy of artistic tantrums and overblown egos,
Der Schauspieldirektor, contrast with the misty
melancholy of Bruckner's great tribute to Wagner,
the Seventh Symphony, its orchestration permeated
by the sound of four Wagner tubas. *See 'New Music',
pages 62–69.*

BROADCAST
RADIO *Live on Radio 3*
ONLINE *Live and 'listen again' options at bbc.co.uk/proms*

PROMS PLUS INTRO
5.45pm • Royal College of Music Stephen Johnson talks
about Peter Eötvös's *DoReMi* and introduces Bruckner's
Symphony No. 7
Edited version broadcast on BBC Radio 3 during tonight's interval

---

FRIDAY 30 AUGUST

PROM 64
7.30pm–c9.45pm • Royal Albert Hall

PRICE BAND **A** *Seats £7.50 to £36*

Bantock
The Witch of Atlas   15'

Prokofiev
Piano Concerto No. 3 in C major   28'

INTERVAL

Sibelius
Pohjola's Daughter   14'

R. Strauss
Also sprach Zarathustra   32'

Anika Vavic *piano*

London Philharmonic Orchestra
Vladimir Jurowski *conductor*

Vladimir Jurowski and the London Philharmonic
Orchestra trace the development of the tone-poem
in works inspired by Nietzsche, Shelley and the
Finnish epic, the *Kalevala*. Natural and supernatural
imagery collide in the great sunrise of Richard
Strauss's *Also sprach Zarathustra*, the fire and snow
of Granville Bantock's 1902 tone-poem *The Witch
of Atlas* and the rainbows of Sibelius's fantasy
Pohjola's Daughter. Serbian-born Anika Vavic makes
her Proms debut in Prokofiev's crisp and virtuosic
Piano Concerto No. 3,
premiered in Chicago in
1921 with the composer at
the keyboard. *See 'Bring out
the Bantock', pages 50–51;
'Craving the Keyboard',
pages 56–59.*

VLADIMIR JUROWSKI

BROADCAST
RADIO *Live on Radio 3*
ONLINE *Live and 'listen again'
options at bbc.co.uk/proms*

PROMS PLUS FAMILY
5.30pm • Royal College of Music Find out the real meaning
of Strauss's epic *Also sprach Zarathustra*, along with the
stories behind *The Witch of Atlas* and *Pohjola's Daughter*
in this introductory talk for families with Rachel Leach.

SPOTLIGHT ON...
Anika Vavic • Prom 64

'Prokofiev's five piano concertos have such
variety, each is a different world. The first is
youthful and Romantic, the second angry
and sad, the third full of vitality – it's bright,
compact and brilliant,' says Serbian-born
pianist Anika Vavic, who'll perform it under
Vladimir Jurowski's baton. 'Prokofiev wrote
it during a summer in Brittany and you can
almost sense a succession of beautiful days
playing chess, visiting the beach. I love how
the pianist's syncopations drive against the
orchestra. When you finish you feel energised.'

Her relationship with the music of Prokofiev
is entwined with her friendship with Mstislav
Rostropovich, which began in her Viennese
student days: 'A cellist rushed up to me and said
that the maestro was giving him a lesson and
I must accompany him. I ran to the Musikverein
and "Slava" ended up playing Shostakovich's
Cello Sonata with me. Afterwards he said:
"Learn Prokofiev's Eighth Piano Sonata, meet
me in Moscow in three weeks and I'll tell you
a secret!" From there I began working with
him on many scores, learning first-hand about
Prokofiev and Shostakovich. He gave me the
idea that one has to see strong pictures and
be true to every detail in the score. Through
him I felt I had somehow made friends with
Prokofiev, and when you are friends with
someone, you must do them justice!'

SATURDAY 31 AUGUST

PROMS SATURDAY MATINEE 5
3.00pm–c4.30pm • Cadogan Hall

Seats £10 / £12

Britten
Simple Symphony   17'

Tippett
Little Music for strings   11'

Britten
Elegy for strings   c8'
world premiere

Lachrymae   15'

Walton
Sonata for strings   27'

Catherine Bullock viola

Camerata Nordica
Terje Tønnesen violin/director

There will be no interval

The focus on Benjamin Britten and his
contemporaries continues with the world premiere
of his Elegy for strings. Written six years before the
Simple Symphony, this eloquent early miniature is
contrasted with works by
Tippett and Walton in the
Proms debut of Camerata
Nordica. Violinist Terje
Tønnesen directs the
Swedish ensemble as well
as viola player Catherine
Bullock in *Lachrymae*,
arranged for string
orchestra by Britten in the
last year of his life. Tippett's

TERJE TØNNESEN

Little Music for strings and
Walton's Sonata for strings, another 1970s
arrangement of a 1940s work, complete an
all-British string ensemble matinee. See 'Revealing
Britten', pages 38–43; 'A Composer of Our Time',
pages 44–47; 'New Music', pages 62–69; 'Small
is Beautiful', pages 96–97 .

BROADCAST
RADIO Live on Radio 3
ONLINE Live and 'listen again' options at bbc.co.uk/proms

SATURDAY 31 AUGUST

PROM 65
7.30pm–c9.45pm • Royal Albert Hall

PRICE BAND **B** Seats £9.50 to £46

FILM MUSIC PROM

Programme to include:

Addinsell
Warsaw Concerto (from 'Dangerous
Moonlight')   10'

Alwyn
The True Glory – March   3'

Bennett
Lady Caroline Lamb – suite   17'

Lucas
Ice Cold in Alex – March   3'

Walton
Battle of Britain – excerpts   11'

*and music from space and science-fiction titles,
including '2001: A Space Odyssey', 'Alien',
'Independence Day', 'Star Wars' and 'Superman'*

Valentina Lisitsa piano
Lawrence Power viola

BBC Concert Orchestra
Keith Lockhart conductor

A parade of excerpts from great British film scores
conjures up a world of stiff upper lips and suicide
missions, while the late Richard Rodney Bennett's
lyrical *Lady Caroline Lamb* suite portrays the
literary adventuress who captured Byron's heart.
Superheroes and space travellers dominate the
second half, with music by Richard Strauss, Johann
Strauss, John Williams and Jerry Goldsmith.

BROADCAST
RADIO Live on Radio 3
ONLINE Live and 'listen again' options at bbc.co.uk/proms
TV Recorded for broadcast on BBC Four

PROMS PLUS LITERARY
5.45pm • Royal College of Music Matthew Sweet considers
the ways in which film composers have risen to the challenge
of capturing the sound of dark matter and distant planets.
Edited version broadcast on BBC Radio 3 during tonight's interval

SUNDAY 1 SEPTEMBER

PROM 66
4.00pm–c5.50pm • Royal Albert Hall

PRICE BAND **H** Seats £6/£12

FAMILY MATINEE:
THE BIG PROMS BEAR HUNT

*Programme to include music by Mussorgsky,
Grieg and Stravinsky*

Michael Rosen storyteller
Tony Ross illustrator

In Harmony Liverpool
**Liverpool Philharmonic
Children's Choirs**
**Royal Liverpool Philharmonic
Orchestra**
Matthew Coorey conductor

We're going on a bear hunt! There's fun for all the
family as Michael Rosen takes his much-loved book
as the starting point for a whole new set of
adventures. Along the way, illustrator Tony Ross
conjures up pictures live on big screens and
the RLPO and children from In
Harmony plunder the music of
composers including Mussorgsky,
Grieg and Stravinsky to find the most
exciting, most dreamy and most scary
tunes. And there will be lots of opportunities for
the audience to join in.
See 'New Adventures',
pages 80–87.

SAME-
DAY SAVER
Proms 66 & 67
(see page 168)

Signed Prom (Dr Paul
Whittaker, Artistic
Director of Music for
the Deaf)

MICHAEL ROSEN

BROADCAST
RADIO Live on Radio 3
ONLINE Live and
'listen again' options at
bbc.co.uk/proms

PROMS PLUS FAMILY ORCHESTRA & CHORUS
1.00pm • Royal College of Music Create, explore and
play music inspired by today's Family Prom with a team
of professional musicians. Suitable for all the family.
See pages 80–87 for details of how to sign up.

SUNDAY 1 SEPTEMBER

PROM 67

7.30pm–c9.50pm • Royal Albert Hall

PRICE BAND **C** *Seats £14 to £57*

Arvo Pärt
Cantus in memoriam Benjamin Britten 6'

Britten
Violin Concerto 36'

INTERVAL

Berlioz
Overture 'Le corsaire' 10'

Saint-Saëns
Symphony No. 3 in C minor, 'Organ' 36'

Janine Jansen *violin*
Thierry Escaich *organ*

Orchestre de Paris
Paavo Järvi *conductor*

SAME-DAY SAVER
Proms 66 & 67
(see page 168)

Paavo Järvi directs his Orchestre de Paris in Arvo Pärt's meditative *Cantus in memoriam Benjamin Britten.* Janine Jansen is the soloist in Britten's Violin Concerto, written during the composer's war-time years in New York. 'I feel so deeply about this piece … one experiences the incredible strength of it,' Jansen says. The Mediterranean verve of Berlioz's overture *Le corsaire* and the shimmering weight of full orchestra and organ in Saint-Saëns's Third Symphony complete a programme of introspective reflection and extrovert display. *See 'Revealing Britten', pages 38–43.*

BROADCAST
RADIO *Live on Radio 3*
ONLINE *Live and 'listen again' options at bbc.co.uk/proms*
TV *Recorded for broadcast on BBC Four*

JANINE JANSEN

PROMS PLUS INTRO
5.45pm • Royal College of Music Martin Handley talks to Paul Kildea about Britten and his place in 20th-century music. *Edited version broadcast on BBC Radio 3 during tonight's interval*

MONDAY 2 SEPTEMBER

PROMS CHAMBER MUSIC 8

1.00pm–c2.00pm • Cadogan Hall

Seats £10/£12

Dowland
The King of Denmark's Galliard 2'

Can she excuse my wrongs (The Earl of Essex's Galliard) 4'

Flow, my tears (Lachrimae antiquae) 4'

My thoughts are winged with hopes (Sir John Souch's Galliard) 4'

Farewell Fancy (Chromatic fantasia) 5'

Sorrow, stay, lend true repentant tears 4'

Come again, sweet love doth now invite 3'

Mr John Langton's Pavan 5'

I saw my lady weep 6'

Lachrimae amantis 3'

If my complaints could passions move (Captain Digorie Piper's Galliard) 4'

Lachrimae tristes 5'

In darkness let me dwell 3'

Shall I strive with words to move (Sir Henry Noel's Galliard) 3'

Fretwork
Ian Bostridge *tenor*
Elizabeth Kenny *lute*

There will be no interval

The laureate of the lute song, John Dowland is chiefly remembered for the burnished melancholy of 'Flow, my tears'. In the last Cadogan Hall concert of the 2013 Proms, tenor Ian Bostridge, lutenist Elizabeth Kenny and the viol consort Fretwork mark the 450th anniversary of Dowland's birth in a programme that explores his work at its saddest, most seductive, and most light-hearted. An hour of lachrimaes, love songs and dances amid the painters (Sir John Souch), courtiers (Henry Noel) and soldiers (Captain Digorie Piper) of Elizabethan England. *See 'Small is Beautiful', pages 96–97.*

BROADCAST
RADIO *Live on Radio 3*
ONLINE *Live and 'listen again' options at bbc.co.uk/proms*

MONDAY 2 SEPTEMBER

PROM 68

7.30pm–c10.00pm • Royal Albert Hall

PRICE BAND **C** *Seats £14 to £57*

Tchaikovsky
Symphony No. 1 in G minor, 'Winter Daydreams' 44'

INTERVAL

Szymanowski
Violin Concerto No. 1 24'

Rachmaninov
Symphonic Dances 36'

Baiba Skride *violin*

Oslo Philharmonic Orchestra
Vasily Petrenko *conductor*

Proms debut violinist Baiba Skride joins the Oslo Philharmonic and its new Chief Conductor, Vasily Petrenko, to continue the Proms focus on Polish music in their performance of Szymanowski's Violin Concerto No. 1, an opulent nocturnal fantasy from a composer enchanted by the sound-worlds and peoples of North Africa and the southern Mediterranean, and inspired by the 'amorous conflagration' of Tadeusz Miciński's poem 'May Night'. Tchaikovsky's youthful Symphony No. 1, 'Winter Daydreams', and Rachmaninov's nostalgic final work, the *Symphonic Dances* of 1940, frame the concerto in a programme rich with dreams. *See 'Tchaikovsky and the Russian Symphony', pages 22–27; 'A Polish Awakening', pages 30–35.*

BAIBA SKRIDE

BROADCAST
RADIO *Live on Radio 3*
ONLINE *Live and 'listen again' options at bbc.co.uk/proms*

PROMS PLUS LITERARY
5.45pm • **Royal College of Music** Andrew Motion, former Poet Laureate, and poet Paul Farley discuss one of the most influential of the Thirties Poets, Louis MacNeice, who worked with Benjamin Britten during his time as a BBC producer. *Edited version broadcast on BBC Radio 3 during tonight's interval*

PROM 69
7.00pm–c9.20pm • Royal Albert Hall

PRICE BAND Ⓒ *Seats £14 to £57*

Beethoven
Piano Concerto No. 2 in B flat major   29'

INTERVAL

Bruckner
Symphony No. 4 in E flat major,
'Romantic'   70'

Christian Ihle Hadland *piano*

Oslo Philharmonic Orchestra
Vasily Petrenko *conductor*

In their second Proms appearance this summer
Vasily Petrenko and the Oslo Philharmonic explore
the Romantic landscape and Schubertian echoes
of Bruckner's Fourth Symphony. Repeatedly
revised by the composer during his lifetime,
the symphony opens with a radiant sunrise.
Last heard playing Brahms with the Signum
Quartet (PCM 7), Christian Ihle Hadland joins
Petrenko and the orchestra for Beethoven's
Second Piano Concerto, built on the Mozartian
model but already pointing to the bold gestures
of the composer's maturity. See 'Craving the
Keyboard', pages 56–59.

BROADCAST
RADIO *Live on Radio 3*
ONLINE *Live and*
'listen again' options at
bbc.co.uk/proms

VASILY PETRENKO

PROMS PLUS INTRO
5.45pm • Royal College of Music An introduction to
Bruckner the man, and his influences and inspirations
at the time of writing the 'Romantic' Symphony.
Edited version broadcast on BBC Radio 3 during tonight's interval

---

PROM 70
10.00pm–c11.30pm • Royal Albert Hall

PRICE BAND Ⓔ *Seats £12/£16*

Britten
A Boy was Born   30'

Lloyd
Requiem   52'
London premiere

Iestyn Davies *counter-tenor*
Greg Morris *organ*

Choristers of the Temple Church
BBC Singers
David Hill *conductor*

There will be no interval

SAME-DAY SAVER
Proms 69 & 70
(see page 168)

David Hill conducts an early and a late work
respectively by two centenary composers.
Britten's *A Boy was Born* was written when
the composer was just 19 years old and
first broadcast on the day of Edward Elgar's
death. It is shot through with what John Bridcut
described in his book, *Britten's Children*, as 'an
apparently childlike simplicity'. George Lloyd's
Requiem – his final work, written in memory of
Diana, Princess of Wales – receives its London
premiere. See 'Revealing Britten', pages 38–43; 'New
Music', pages 62–69; 'Late Night Tonic', pages 94–95.

BROADCAST
RADIO *Live on Radio 3*
ONLINE *Live and 'listen again' options at bbc.co.uk/proms*

BBC SINGERS

PROM 71
7.30pm–c10.05pm • Royal Albert Hall

PRICE BAND Ⓐ *Seats £7.50 to £36*

Górecki
Symphony No. 3,
'Symphony of Sorrowful Songs'   60'

INTERVAL

Vaughan Williams, orch. A. Payne
Four Last Songs   c12'
BBC commission: world premiere

Tchaikovsky
Symphony No. 6 in B minor, 'Pathétique' 48'

Ruby Hughes *soprano*
Jennifer Johnston *mezzo-soprano*

BBC Symphony Orchestra
Osmo Vänskä *conductor*

A series of farewells as Osmo Vänskä concludes
the season's focus on Polish music and conducts
the premiere of Anthony Payne's orchestration of
Vaughan Williams's *Four Last Songs*. BBC Radio 3
New Generation Artists Ruby Hughes and Jennifer
Johnston are the soloists, Hughes singing the three
Polish texts of Henryk Górecki's 'Symphony of
Sorrowful Songs', Johnston singing 'Procris',
'Menelaus', 'Tired' and 'Hands, Eyes and Heart'
that make up the Vaughan Williams. Tchaikovsky's
heartfelt 'Pathétique' is the penultimate instalment
of this summer's cycle of his symphonies.
See 'Tchaikovsky and the
Russian Symphony', pages
22–27; 'A Polish Awakening',
pages 30–35; 'New Music',
pages 62–69.

BROADCAST
RADIO *Live on Radio 3*
ONLINE *Live and 'listen again'*
options at bbc.co.uk/proms

RUBY HUGHES

PROMS PLUS INTRO
5.45pm • Royal College of Music Join Proms Director
Roger Wright and Chris Cotton, Chief Executive of the
Royal Albert Hall, as they look back over the 2013 season
with Petroc Trelawny.

Joseph Calleja • Prom 72

Maltese tenor Joseph Calleja has become something of a Proms favourite in recent years: who will forget his entrance at last year's Last Night in an Olympic shell suit, throwing Maltese Cross caps at the audience and bringing the house down in 'Nessun dorma'? As one critic remarked, 'big of frame and generous of voice, he … seemed absolutely in his element in these show-stopping numbers'. He sang in Verdi's *Simon Boccanegra* at the Proms in 2010 and in the *Requiem* in 2011. This year he'll present a feast of Verdi arias – mostly from roles he has vividly enacted on stage, particularly his searing Adorno in *Simon Boccanegra* and the Duke in *Rigoletto* – as well as highlights from *I vespri siciliani* and *Luisa Miller*.

Calleja spent his youth listening to old recordings of Italian singers such as Alessandro Bonci and Tito Schipa, absorbing the style of that particular 'golden age'. 'The vocal line they had was absolutely unrivalled,' he feels. 'The Italians call it the *linea di canto* – the "singing line". If you listen to people like Schipa, it's like being in a dream, the way they approach a phrase and the way they spin it.' Many have commented on the closeness of Calleja's sound to these singers, which sets him apart among elite operatic tenors today.

THURSDAY 5 SEPTEMBER

PROM 72
7.00pm–c9.30pm • Royal Albert Hall

PRICE BAND **C** *Seats £14 to £57*

Verdi

La forza del destino – overture	8'
Attila – 'O dolore! ed io vivea'	3'
I vespri siciliani – 'À toi que j'ai chérie'	4'
La traviata – Prelude (Act 1)	4'
Simon Boccanegra – 'O inferno! … Sento avvampar nell'anima'	5'
Aida – Triumphal March (Act 2)	6'
Luisa Miller – 'O! fede negar potessi … Quando le sere al placido'	6'
Rigoletto – 'La donna è mobile'	3'

INTERVAL

Tchaikovsky

Manfred	55'

Joseph Calleja *tenor*

Orchestra Sinfonica di Milano Giuseppe Verdi
Xian Zhang *conductor*

Tchaikovsky's *Manfred* depicts the death of a tormented Faustian hero with supernatural gifts and a guilty secret. Chinese-American conductor Xian Zhang directs the Orchestra Sinfonica di Milano Giuseppe Verdi in the Byronic epic that closes the season's Tchaikovsky symphony cycle, and also in a selection of Verdi's operatic overtures and arias featuring last year's star of the Last Night of the Proms, the Maltese tenor Joseph Calleja. See *'Tchaikovsky and the Russian Symphony'*, pages 22–27.

BROADCAST
RADIO *Live on Radio 3*
ONLINE *Live and 'listen again' options at bbc.co.uk/proms*
TV *Broadcast on BBC Four at 7.30pm*

PROMS PLUS INTRO
5.45pm • Royal College of Music Ian Skelly presents a discussion on Verdi and the orchestra, plus an introduction to Tchaikovsky's *Manfred*.
Edited version broadcast on BBC Radio 3 during tonight's interval

THURSDAY 5 SEPTEMBER

PROM 73
10.15pm–c11.30pm • Royal Albert Hall

PRICE BAND **F** *Seats £18/£24*

Schubert

Piano Sonata in C minor, D958	33'
Piano Sonata in C major, D812, 'Grand Duo'	39'

Imogen Cooper *piano*
Paul Lewis *piano*

There will be no interval

Pianists Imogen Cooper and Paul Lewis return for the final Late Night Prom of the festival. Cooper plays Schubert's late, great Piano Sonata in C minor, its scherzo still informed by the Rossinian *joie de vivre* of the early symphonies, the surrounding movements infused with the sorrow and resignation of the song-cycles *Winterreise* and *Schwanengesang*. Published posthumously, the symphonically conceived 'Grand Duo' dates from the summer of 1824, when the composer was engaged as music master to Marie and Caroline Esterházy on the family's Slovakian estate. See 'Late Night Tonic', pages 94–95.

SAME-DAY SAVER
Proms 72 & 73
(see page 168)

BROADCAST
RADIO *Live on Radio 3*
ONLINE *Live and 'listen again' options at bbc.co.uk/proms*

IMOGEN COOPER   PAUL LEWIS

FRIDAY 6 SEPTEMBER

PROM 74
7.30pm–c9.35pm • Royal Albert Hall

PRICE BAND **D** *Seats £18 to £68*

J. S. Bach, arr. A. Guilmant
Cantata 'Wir danken dir, Gott,
wir danken dir', BWV 29 – Sinfonia   5'

J. S. Bach
Chorale Prelude 'Allein Gott in der
Höh' sei Ehr', BWV 662   8'

Chorale Prelude 'Komm, Gott Schöpfer,
heiliger Geist', BWV 667   3'

Chorale Prelude 'Vor deinem Thron tret'
ich hiermit', BWV 668   5'

Prelude and Fugue in A minor, BWV 543 10'

INTERVAL

Bruckner
Symphony No. 8 in C minor (1890 version,
ed. Nowak)   85'

Klaus Sonnleitner *organ*

Vienna Philharmonic Orchestra
Lorin Maazel *conductor*

Who better to open tonight's Prom than Klaus
Sonnleitner, present-day organist at St Florian's Abbey,
Linz, where Bruckner himself became organist almost
160 years ago. Lorin Maazel conducts the Vienna
Philharmonic in Bruckner's Eighth Symphony, a vivid
realisation of the self-doubting composer's lifelong
ambition to build upon the legacies of Beethoven,
Schubert and Wagner.

BROADCAST
RADIO *Live on Radio 3*
ONLINE *Live and 'listen again' options at bbc.co.uk/proms*

PROMS PLUS LITERARY
5.45pm • Royal College of Music Poet Don Paterson and
poet and Radio 3 presenter Ian McMillan introduce the
winning entries in this year's Proms Poetry competition.
Edited version broadcast on BBC Radio 3 during tonight's interval

PROMS PLUS LATE
Elgar Room, Royal Albert Hall Informal post-Prom music
and poetry. For details see bbc.co.uk/proms

SATURDAY 7 SEPTEMBER

PROM 75
7.30pm–c10.40pm • Royal Albert Hall

PRICE BAND **G** *Seats £27 to £95*

THE LAST NIGHT OF THE PROMS 2013

Anna Clyne
Masquerade   c5'
BBC commission: world premiere

Wagner
The Mastersingers of Nuremberg
– overture   10'

Bernstein
Chichester Psalms   19'

Vaughan Williams
The Lark Ascending   12'

Britten
The Building of the House   5'

Bernstein
Candide – 'Make our Garden Grow'   5'

Massenet
Chérubin – 'Je suis gris! je suis ivre!'   2'

Handel
Xerxes – 'Frondi tenere e belle …
Ombra mai fù'   4'

Rossini
La donna del lago – 'Tanti affetti in
tal momento!'   4'

INTERVAL

Bernstein
Candide – overture   5'

Verdi
Nabucco – 'Va, pensiero'
(Chorus of the Hebrew Slaves)   4'

Arlen
Over the Rainbow   5'

Monti
Csárdás   6'

Trad.
Londonderry Air (Danny Boy)   4'

Rodgers
Carousel – 'You'll never walk alone'   6'

Bantock
Sea Reivers   4'

Lloyd
HMS Trinidad March   4'
UK premiere of this version

Arne
Rule, Britannia!   7'

Elgar
Pomp and Circumstance March No. 1 in
D major ('Land of Hope and Glory')   6'

Parry, orch. Elgar
Jerusalem   4'

The National Anthem (arr. Britten)

Joyce DiDonato *mezzo-soprano*
Nigel Kennedy *violin*

BBC Symphony Chorus
BBC Symphony Orchestra
Marin Alsop *conductor*

The Last Night begins with a celebratory new work
by Anna Clyne and includes a rare performance of
Britten's 1967 overture for chorus and orchestra
The Building of the House, a touch of Broadway magic
and the sound of a glass ceiling being broken as
Marin Alsop takes charge of her first Last Night.
Nigel Kennedy and Joyce DiDonato are the star
soloists in a programme that picks up sea-faring
themes from Bantock and George Lloyd and
includes a transatlantic flavour. *See 'All Around the
Ring', pages 14–19; 'Revealing Britten', pages 38–43;
'Bring out the Bantock', pages 50–51; 'New Music',
pages 62–69; 'Last But Not Least', pages 74–77;
'Passing the Baton', pages 102–103.*

BROADCAST
RADIO *Live on Radio 3*
ONLINE *Live and 'listen again' options at bbc.co.uk/proms*
TV *First half live on BBC Two, second half live on BBC One*

PROMS PLUS SING
5.00pm • Royal College of Music A fun workshop with
Mary King to get you ready for vocal action at the
Last Night singalong.

BBC Proms

IN THE PARK

JOSEPH CALLEJA

NIGEL KENNEDY

RED HOT CHILLI PIPERS

SIR TERRY WOGAN

TICKETS £35 (under-3s free)

SATURDAY 7 SEPTEMBER
HYDE PARK, LONDON

JOSEPH CALLEJA *tenor*
NIGEL KENNEDY *violin*
ROYAL CHORAL SOCIETY
BBC CONCERT ORCHESTRA
RICHARD BALCOMBE *conductor*
SIR TERRY WOGAN *presenter*

Join in the Last Night of the Proms celebrations in Hyde Park, hosted by Proms in the Park favourite Sir Terry Wogan. The open-air concert features a host of musical stars, including world-famous tenor **Joseph Calleja**, the **BBC Concert Orchestra** and violin virtuoso **Nigel Kennedy**, who makes a special appearance on the Hyde Park stage before performing at the Last Night in the Royal Albert Hall! Further artists to be announced. Presenter **Tony Blackburn** joins us again to get this year's party under way, introducing a range of artists, including **Red Hot Chilli Pipers** and **Craig Charles and the Fantasy Funk Band**.

Gates open 3.30pm;
entertainment from 5.15pm

For details of how to order a picnic hamper for collection on the day, or to find out about VIP packages and corporate hospitality, visit bbc.co.uk/promsinthepark.

Tickets £35 (under-3s free) – *now available*

ONLINE via bbc.co.uk/promsinthepark

BY PHONE from **SEE Tickets** on **0844 209 7353** * *(a transaction fee of £2.00, plus a booking fee of £1.35 per ticket applies);* from the **Royal Albert Hall** on **0845 401 5040** * *(a booking fee of 2% of the total value plus £1.00 per ticket up to a maximum of £10 applies for telephone bookings)*

IN PERSON at the Royal Albert Hall Box Office *(a booking fee of 2% of the total value applies to in-person bookings for more than two tickets, if paying by credit/debit card)*

BY POST see page 166

PLEASE NOTE: in the interest of safety, please do not bring glass items (including bottles), barbeques or flaming torches to the event

* Calls cost up to 5p/min from most landlines (an additional connection fee may also apply). Calls from mobiles may be considerably more. (All calls to the Royal Albert Hall Box Office will be recorded and may be monitored for quality-control purposes.)

with thanks to

THE ROYAL PARKS

EXPERIENCE THE LAST NIGHT MAGIC, LIVE IN THE OPEN AIR!

The BBC Proms in the Park event offers a live, open-air concert featuring high-profile artists and well-loved presenters, culminating in a fireworks finale and a BBC Big Screen link-up to the Royal Albert Hall. So gather your friends and your Last Night spirit for an unforgettable evening.

Further Last Night celebrations around the UK will be announced on **bbc.co.uk/promsinthepark** so keep checking for details.

Highlights of the Hyde Park concert will be included as part of the live coverage of the Last Night on BBC One and BBC Two. Digital viewers can also access Proms in the Park content via the red button.

BROADCAST
RADIO Live on BBC Radio 2
ONLINE Live and 'listen again' options at bbc.co.uk/proms
TV Live via the red button on BBC Television

BBC Radio 2 LIVE in Hyde Park

A Festival in a Day
Sunday 8 September 2013

Tickets on sale Friday 24 May
£35 plus booking fee

bbc.co.uk/radio2

BBC RADIO

HOW TO PROM

WHAT IS PROMMING?

The popular tradition of Promming (standing in the Arena or Gallery areas of the Royal Albert Hall) is central to the unique and informal atmosphere of the BBC Proms.

Up to 1,400 standing places are available for each Proms concert at the Royal Albert Hall. The traditionally low prices allow you to enjoy world-class performances for just £5.00 each (or even less with a Season Ticket or Weekly Promming Pass). There are two standing areas: the Arena, located directly in front of the stage, and the Gallery, running round the top of the Hall. All spaces are unreserved.

DAY PROMMERS

Over 500 Arena and Gallery tickets (priced £5.00) are available for every Prom. These tickets are available on the day and cannot be booked in advance, so even if all seats have been sold, you always have a good chance of getting in (although early queuing is advisable for the more popular concerts). You must buy your ticket in person and must pay by cash.

A limited number of Arena tickets will usually be sold to the Day Queue from two and a half hours before each performance. The remaining Day Promming tickets will then be sold from Door 11 (Arena) and Door 10 (Gallery) from 45 minutes before the performance to those queuing. Tickets for Late Night Proms are available only on the doors, from 30 minutes before the performance. Arena and Gallery tickets are available only at Door 11 and Door 10, not at the Box Office.

Wheelchair-users who wish to Prom (Gallery only) should queue in the same way but will be redirected to Door 8 once their ticket is purchased. For further information for disabled concert-goers, see page 169.

If you are in doubt about where to go, Royal Albert Hall stewards will point you in the right direction.

PROMMING SEASON TICKETS, OPENING WEEKEND AND WEEKLY PROMMING PASSES

Frequent Prommers can save money by purchasing a Season Ticket covering the whole Proms season (including the Last Night), or an Opening Weekend or Weekly Promming Pass. These allow access to either the Arena or Gallery.

Season Ticket- and Promming Pass-holders benefit from:

- guaranteed entrance (until 20 minutes before each concert)
- great savings – prices can work out at less than £2.60 per concert

Season Ticket-holders also benefit from guaranteed entrance to the Last Night (until 20 minutes before the concert).

Important information: Season Ticket- and Promming Pass-holders arriving at the Hall less than 20 minutes before a concert are not guaranteed entry and should join the back of the Day Queue.

Season Tickets and Promming Passes are not valid for concerts at Cadogan Hall.

For further details and prices of whole Season Tickets, Opening Weekend and Weekly Promming Passes, see page 168.

PROMS AT CADOGAN HALL

For Cadogan Hall Day Seats (priced £5.00) and Proms Chamber Music Series Passes, see pages 164 and 168 respectively.

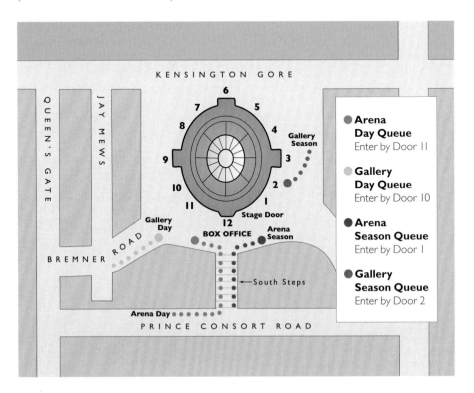

BOOKING INFORMATION

THE LAST NIGHT OF THE PROMS

The majority of tickets for the Last Night of the Proms will be allocated by ballot to customers who have bought tickets to at least five other Proms concerts at the Royal Albert Hall. A further 200 tickets will be allocated by the Open Ballot (see far right).

The Five-Concert Ballot To be eligible to enter the Five-Concert Ballot, you must book tickets for at least five other concerts. (The Free Prom, Beethoven's Ninth Symphony [Prom 38], concerts at Cadogan Hall and Proms in the Park do not count towards the Five-Concert Ballot.) You can apply to buy a maximum of two tickets for the Last Night. If you are successful in the Ballot, you will not be obliged to buy Last Night tickets should your preferred seating area not be available.

Please note: you must tick the Ballot opt-in box when booking online, or inform the Box Office that you wish to enter this Ballot when booking by telephone, in person or by post.

If you require a wheelchair space for the Last Night of the Proms, you will still need to book for five other concerts but you must phone the Access Information Line (020 7070 4410) by Thursday 23 May and ask to be entered into the separate Ballot for wheelchair spaces. This Ballot cannot be entered online.

The Five-Concert Ballot closes on Thursday 23 May and you will be informed by Friday 31 May whether or not you have been successful. If you are successful, **please note that your Last Night Tickets will not be issued until Friday 30 August.** We regret that, if you are unsuccessful in the Five-Concert Ballot, no refunds for other tickets purchased will be payable.

GENERAL AVAILABILITY FOR THE LAST NIGHT

Any tickets not allocated by the Five-Concert Ballot or the Open Ballot will go on sale on Friday 5 July. There is exceptionally high demand for Last Night tickets, but returns occasionally become available, so it is always worth checking with the Box Office.

Please note: for all Last Night bookings, only one application (for a maximum of two tickets) can be made per household.

PROMMING AT THE LAST NIGHT

Day Prommers, Opening Weekend and Weekly Promming Pass-holders who have attended five or more concerts (in either the Arena or the Gallery) are eligible to purchase one ticket each for the Last Night (priced £5.00) on presentation of their used tickets (which will be retained) at the Box Office. A number of tickets will go on sale on Wednesday 17 July; a further allocation will be released on Wednesday 14 August; and a final, smaller allocation on Friday 30 August.

Season Ticket-Holders Whole Season Tickets include admission to the Last Night.

Queuing All Prommers (Day or Season) with Last Night tickets should queue on the South Steps, west side (Arena), or the top of Bremner Road, south side (Gallery). Whole Season Ticket- and Promming Pass-holders are guaranteed entrance until 20 minutes before the concert. Whole Season Ticket- and Promming Pass-holders who arrive less than 20 minutes before the concert should join the back of the Day Queue on the South Steps, east side (Arena), or the top of Bremner Road, north side (Gallery).

Sleeping Out Please note it is not necessary for Prommers with Last Night tickets to camp out overnight to secure their preferred standing place inside the Hall. Ticket-holders may add their name to a list which will be held at the Stage Door at the Royal Albert Hall from 4.00pm on Friday 6 September. They then need to return to the queue in list order by 10.00am on Saturday 7 September.

On the Night A limited number of standing tickets are available on the Last Night itself (priced £5.00, one per person). No previous ticket purchases are necessary. Just join the queue on the South Steps, east side (Arena), or the top of Bremner Road, north side (Gallery), and you may well be lucky.

2013 Open Ballot Form

One hundred Centre Stalls seats (priced £87.50 each) and 100 Front Circle seats (priced £57.00 each) for the Last Night of the Proms at the Royal Albert Hall will be allocated by Open Ballot. The Five-Concert Ballot rule does not apply: no other ticket purchases are necessary. Only one application (for a maximum of two tickets) may be made per household.

If you would like to apply for tickets by Open Ballot, please complete the official Open Ballot Form on the back of this slip and send it by post only – to arrive no later than Thursday 27 June – to:

BBC Proms Open Ballot
Box Office
Royal Albert Hall
London SW7 2AP

Note that the Open Ballot application is completely separate from other Proms booking procedures. Envelopes should be clearly addressed to 'BBC Proms Open Ballot' and should contain only this official Open Ballot Form. The Open Ballot takes place on Friday 28 June and successful applicants will be contacted by Thursday 4 July.

This form is also available to download from bbc.co.uk/proms; or call 020 7765 2044 to receive a copy by post.

Please note: if you are successful in the Five-Concert Ballot, you will not be eligible for Last Night tickets via the Open Ballot.

2013 Open Ballot Form

Title _____ Initial(s) _____

Surname _____

Address _____

_____

_____

_____

Postcode _____

Country _____

Daytime tel. _____

Evening tel. _____

Mobile tel. _____

Email _____

_____

_____

**Please indicate your preferred
seating option** ‡

☐ I wish to apply for one Centre Stalls ticket (£87.50)

☐ I wish to apply for two Centre Stalls tickets (£175.00)

☐ I wish to apply for one Front Circle ticket (£57.00)

☐ I wish to apply for two Front Circle tickets (£114.00)

‡ *We cannot guarantee that you will be offered
tickets in your preferred seating section. You will not
be obliged to buy tickets outside your preference,
but we regret we cannot offer alternatives.*

The personal information given on this form will not be used for any
purpose by the BBC or the Royal Albert Hall other than this Ballot.

TICKET PRICES

ROYAL ALBERT HALL

Concerts fall into one of eight price bands, indicated below each concert listing on pages 122–160.

	A	B	C	D	E	F	G	H
Grand Tier Boxes 12 seats, price per seat	£36.00	£46.00	£57.00	£68.00	£16.00	£24.00	£95.00	
	(As most grand tier boxes are privately owned, availability is limited)							
Centre Stalls	£28.00	£38.00	£48.00	£58.00	£16.00	£24.00	£87.50	
Side Stalls	£24.00	£34.00	£44.00	£54.00	£16.00	£24.00	£85.00	
Loggia Boxes 8 seats, price per seat	£32.00	£42.00	£52.00	£62.00	£16.00	£24.00	£90.00	ALL SEATS £12.00 (UNDER-18s £6.00)
2nd Tier Boxes 5 seats, price per seat	£25.00	£35.00	£45.00	£55.00	£16.00	£24.00	£86.00	
Mid Choir	£18.00	£22.00	£32.00	£42.00	£16.00	£18.00	£65.00	
Upper Choir	£16.00	£20.00	£27.00	£35.00	£12.00	£18.00	£62.00	
Front Circle	£15.00	£19.00	£23.00	£27.00	£12.00	£18.00	£57.00	
Rear Circle	£12.00	£15.00	£19.00	£24.00	£12.00	£18.00	£47.00	
Restricted View Circle	£7.50	£9.50	£14.00	£18.00	N/A	N/A	£27.00	

PROMMING **Standing places are available in the Arena and Gallery on the day for £5.00
(see page 162).** Save by buying an Opening Weekend or Weekly Promming Pass, or a Full Season Ticket *(see page 168 for details). Please note: a booking fee of 2% of the total value (plus £1.00 per ticket up to a maximum of £10.00) applies to all bookings, other than those made in person at the Royal Albert Hall. (For Proms in the Park booking fee information, see below.)*

CADOGAN HALL (PROMS CHAMBER MUSIC AND PROMS SATURDAY MATINEES)
Stalls: £12.00, Centre Gallery: £10.00, Day Seats: £5.00

Cadogan Hall tickets are available to book from 9.00 am on Saturday 11 May and may be included in the Proms Planner (see page 166). From Saturday 18 May Cadogan Hall tickets can be bought from Cadogan Hall (020 7730 4500) as well as from the Royal Albert Hall Box Office. On the day of the concert, tickets can be bought at Cadogan Hall only – from 10.00am. At least 150 Day Seats (Side Gallery bench seats) are available from 10.00am on the day of the concert. They must be purchased in person, with cash only, and are limited to two tickets per transaction.

Save by buying a Proms Chamber Music Series Pass (see page 168 for details).
Unwanted tickets for all Royal Albert Hall and Cadogan Hall Proms may be exchanged for tickets to other Proms concerts (subject to availability). A fee of £1.00 per ticket will be charged for this service. Call the Royal Albert Hall Box Office (0845 401 5040) for further details.*

BBC PROMS IN THE PARK, HYDE PARK, LONDON, SATURDAY 7 SEPTEMBER
All tickets £35.00 (under-3s free) *A booking fee of 2% of the total value (plus £1.00 per ticket up to a maximum of £10.00) applies, unless booking in person at the Royal Albert Hall and paying by cash or cheque. A booking fee of 2% of the total value applies to in-person bookings for more than two tickets, if paying by credit/debit card. (The maximum charge of £10.00 can apply to Proms and Proms in the Park bookings combined.) See page 161 for details on how to book and booking fee information for SEE Tickets.*

CHOOSE YOUR SEAT

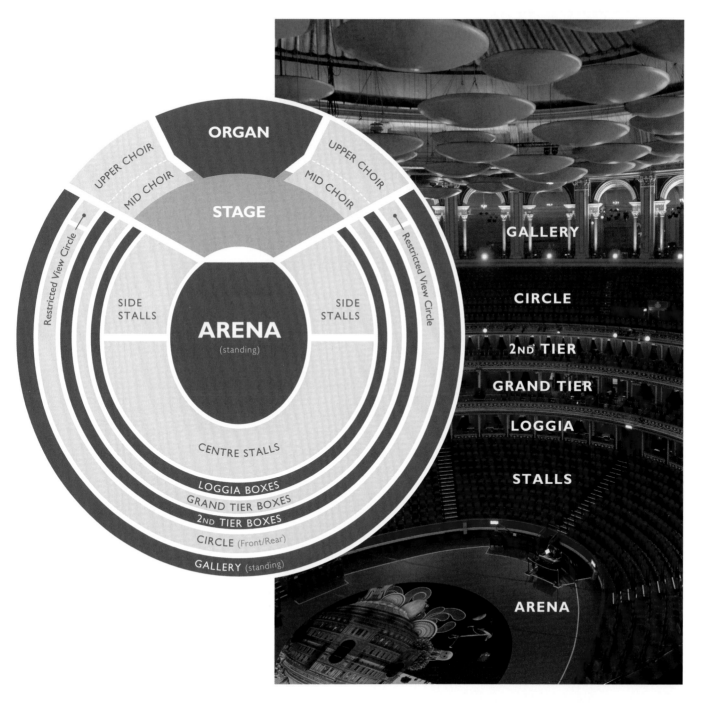

ORGAN

UPPER CHOIR

MID CHOIR

UPPER CHOIR

MID CHOIR

STAGE

Restricted View Circle

Restricted View Circle

SIDE STALLS

SIDE STALLS

ARENA
(standing)

CENTRE STALLS

LOGGIA BOXES

GRAND TIER BOXES

2ND TIER BOXES

CIRCLE (Front/Rear)

GALLERY (standing)

GALLERY

CIRCLE

2ND TIER

GRAND TIER

LOGGIA

STALLS

ARENA

HOW TO BOOK

Booking opens on Saturday 11 May at 9.00am – online, by telephone and in person. Tickets may also be requested by post.

For Promming (standing) tickets in the Arena and Gallery, priced £5.00, see page 162.

Owing to high demand, special booking arrangements apply to Last Night of the Proms tickets: see page 163.

For Proms in the Park tickets, see page 161.

Tickets for the Free Prom (Prom 38) are available from Friday 28 June.

ONLINE

Thursday 18 April (2.00pm) to Friday 10 May (midnight)

Use the **Proms Planner**, accessible via bbc.co.uk/proms (see instructions below), to create your personal Proms Plan. Once completed, this is ready for you to submit as soon as booking opens at 9.00am on Saturday 11 May. The Proms Planner allows you to create and amend your personal Proms Plan at your leisure before tickets go on sale, at any time from 2.00pm on Thursday 18 April until midnight on Friday 10 May. Submitting your Proms Plan as soon as booking opens speeds up the booking process and means that you may be more successful in securing your preferred tickets for concerts in high demand.

However, should you not wish to use the Proms Planner, you can visit www.royalalberthall.com from 9.00am on Saturday 11 May to book your tickets online. Please note that the website is likely to experience very high demand for tickets that day, so you may be placed in a queue.

How to use the Proms Planner

- From 2.00pm on Thursday 18 April select 'Plan Your Proms Tickets' at bbc.co.uk/proms. (You will be redirected to www.royalalberthall.com.)
- Select 'Create My Proms Plan'. Then create an account (or log in if you are an existing

user) and start choosing the concerts you would like to attend, along with the number of tickets and preferred seating area. You can amend your Proms Plan at any time until midnight on Friday 10 May.

Please note: this is a request system and there is no guarantee that the tickets you select in your Proms Plan will be available once booking has opened.

- From 9.00am on Saturday 11 May visit www.royalalberthall.com and log in to your Proms Plan in order to submit it. In the case of exceptionally high demand you may be held in an online waiting room before you are able to log in: you will be informed how many people precede you in the queue (you do not need to refresh the page). **You must submit your Proms Plan in order to make a booking.**
- Your Proms Plan will now have been updated to reflect live ticket availability and you will be given the chance to cancel tickets or choose alternatives should your selected tickets or seating areas have become unavailable.
- Confirm your online booking by submitting your Proms Plan and entering your payment details.
- Your booking will be confirmed by email.

Please note: it is not possible to book entire boxes online. If you would like to book a full box, call the Box Office on 0845 401 5040 from 9.00am on Saturday 11 May.*

The 'Select Your Own Seat' option is not available via the Proms Planner or during the first few days that Proms tickets are on sale. You will be allocated the best available places within your chosen seating area. This is to allow as many customers as possible to book as efficiently as possible and to speed up the queue during the period of high demand.

If you have any queries about how to use the Proms Planner, call the Royal Albert Hall Box Office on **0845 401 5040***.

From 9.00am on Saturday 11 May

From 9.00am on Saturday 11 May you can book online at **www.royalalberthall.com**. If you already have a Proms Plan, you can redeem

your plan and process your booking. If you do not have a Proms Plan, you can just book online. You will not be able to create a Proms Plan at this time.

A booking fee of 2% of the total value (plus £1.00 per ticket up to a maximum of £10.00 per booking) applies. (For Proms in the Park booking fee information, see page 161.)

BY TELEPHONE

From 9.00am on Saturday 11 May, call the Royal Albert Hall Box Office on **0845 401 5040*** (open 9.00am–9.00pm daily). From outside the UK, please call +44 20 7589 8912.

A booking fee of 2% of the total value (plus £1.00 per ticket up to a maximum of £10.00 per booking) applies. (For Proms in the Park booking fee information, see page 161)

IN PERSON

From 9.00am on Saturday 11 May, visit the Royal Albert Hall Box Office. Please note that the Box Office will be located at Door 4 until the end of May; thereafter it will return to Door 12. (The Box Office is open 9.00am–9.00pm daily.)

No booking fee applies to tickets bought in person. (For Proms in the Park booking fee information, see page 161.)

BY POST

Please write to BBC Proms, Box Office, Royal Albert Hall, London SW7 2AP with the following details:

- your name, address, telephone number(s) and email address (if applicable)
- the concerts you wish to attend
- number of tickets required
- preferred seating section, preferably with alternatives (see ticket prices on page 164 and seating plan on page 165)
- applicable discounts (see pages 168 & 169)
- a cheque, payable to 'Royal Albert Hall' and made out for the maximum amount (including booking fees); or your credit card details, including type of card, name on the

HOW TO BOOK

card, card number, issue number (Maestro only), start date, expiry date and security code (last three digits on back of Visa/Mastercard or last four digits on front of American Express).

Your details will be held securely. Postal bookings will start to be processed from 9.00am on Saturday 11 May, when booking opens.

A booking fee of 2% of the total value (plus £1.00 per ticket up to a maximum of £10.00 per booking) applies. (For Proms in the Park booking fee information, see page 161.)

* Calls cost up to 5p/min from most landlines (an additional connection fee may also apply). Calls from mobiles may cost considerably more. All calls will be recorded and may be monitored for training and quality-control purposes.

TICKETS SOLD OUT? DON'T GIVE UP!

If you are unable to get tickets for a popular Prom, **keep trying** at bbc.co.uk/proms or the Royal Albert Hall Box Office, as returns often become available. In addition, many boxes and some seats at the Royal Albert Hall are privately owned, and these seats may be returned for general sale in the period leading up to the concert. The Royal Albert Hall does not operate a waiting list.

If you can't sit, stand
Up to 1,400 Promming (standing) places are available in the Arena and Gallery on the day for every Prom at the Royal Albert Hall. If you arrive early enough on the day of the concert, you have a very good chance of getting in. For more details, see page 162.

SPECIAL OFFERS

SAME-DAY SAVERS

Book seats for more than one concert on the same day, and save up to £4.00 per ticket for the later concert. This discount is available through all booking methods, including online and via the Proms Planner. When booking online, it will be applied automatically at the checkout stage.

This offer applies to performances at the Royal Albert Hall only, excluding the Arena and Gallery standing areas and the Restricted View Circle seating area. Please note that Prom 38 (the Free Prom) is excluded from this offer. *See page 164 for ticket prices.*

UNDER-18s GO HALF-PRICE

The Proms are a great way to discover live music and we encourage anyone over 5 years old to attend. Tickets for under-18s can be purchased at half price in any seating area for all Proms except the Last Night (Prom 75). This discount is available through all booking methods, including online and via the Proms Planner.

GREAT SAVINGS FOR GROUPS

Groups of 10 or more can claim a 10% discount (5% for C-band and D-band concerts) on the price of Centre/Side Stalls or Front/Rear Circle tickets (excluding the Last Night). *See page 164 for ticket prices.*

Please note: group bookings can only be made by phone or in person at the Royal Albert Hall.
To make a group booking, or for more information, call the Group Booking Information Line on 020 7070 4408 (from 9.00am on Saturday 11 May).

PROMMING SEASON TICKETS, OPENING WEEKEND AND WEEKLY PROMMING PASSES

With the Promming Season Tickets, Opening Weekend and Weekly Promming Passes you can save money and get guaranteed entrance up to 20 minutes before the start-time to the Arena or Gallery standing areas.

Whole Season Tickets are non-transferable and two passport-sized photographs must be provided before tickets can be issued.

Opening Weekend and Weekly Promming Passes can be purchased online, by phone or in person at the Royal Albert Hall Box Office from 9.00am on Saturday 11 May, and planned online via the Proms Planner from 2.00pm on Thursday 18 April. Passes must be purchased a minimum of two hours before the start of the first concert covered. Prices vary for each week depending on the number of concerts covered – see box right.

Please note: you may purchase a maximum of four passes per week.

There is no Weekly Promming Pass covering Prom 75. Weekly Promming Passes are not valid for concerts at Cadogan Hall.

The Opening Weekend and Weekly Promming Passes replace Half Season Tickets and Weekend Promming Passes.

Passes are non-transferable and ID may be requested upon entry. Purchase of an Opening Weekend or Weekly Promming Pass does not guarantee entry to the Last Night, but tickets may be counted towards the Five-Concert Ballot *(see page 163)* in conjunction with further Passes or Day Ticket stubs.

Please note: holders of Promming Season Tickets, Opening Weekend and Weekly Promming Passes arriving at the Hall less than 20 minutes before a concert are not guaranteed entry and should join the back of the Day Queue.

All Promming Season Tickets, Opening Weekend and Weekly Promming Passes are subject to availability.

Promming Season Tickets, Opening Weekend and Weekly Promming Pass prices		
Whole Season	Proms 1–75	£190.00
Opening Weekend	Proms 1, 2 & 4	£12.50
Week 1	Proms 5–13	£42.50
Week 2	Proms 14–20 *(includes the Proms 'Ring' cycle)*	£32.50
Week 3	Proms 21–29	£42.50
Week 4	Proms 30–37	£37.50
Week 5	Proms 39–48	£47.50
Week 6	Proms 49–57	£42.50
Week 7	Proms 58–67	£47.50
Week 8	Proms 68–74	£32.50

PROMS CHAMBER MUSIC SERIES PASS (CADOGAN HALL)

Hear all eight Monday-lunchtime Proms Chamber Music concerts for just £30.00, with guaranteed entrance to the Side Gallery until 12.50pm (after which Proms Chamber Music Series Pass-holders may be asked to join the Day Queue). Passes can be purchased from 9.00am on Saturday 11 May online, by phone or in person at the Royal Albert Hall. Two passport-sized photographs must be provided.

Please note: Proms Chamber Music Series Passes cannot be purchased from Cadogan Hall. Proms Chamber Music Series Passes are not valid for Proms Saturday Matinee concerts at Cadogan Hall and are subject to availability.

BOOKING INFORMATION

168

BOOK ONLINE AT BBC.CO.UK/PROMS • BY TELEPHONE 0845 401 5040* • IN PERSON AT THE ROYAL ALBERT HALL • BOOKING OPENS 9.00AM ON 11 MAY

ACCESS AT THE PROMS

PROMS ACCESS INFORMATION LINE:

020 7070 4410

(9.00am–9.00pm daily)

TICKETS AND DISCOUNTS FOR DISABLED CONCERT-GOERS

All disabled concert-goers (and one companion) receive a 50% discount on all ticket prices (except Arena and Gallery areas) for concerts at the Royal Albert Hall and Cadogan Hall. To claim this discount, call the Access Information Line (from Saturday 11 May) if booking by phone. Note that discounts for disabled concert-goers cannot be combined with other ticket offers. Tickets can also be purchased in person from 9.00am on Saturday 11 May at the Royal Albert Hall. The Box Office has ramped access, an induction loop and drop-down counters. Ambulant disabled concert-goers can also book tickets online from 9.00am on Saturday 11 May and use the online Proms Planner from 2.00pm on Thursday 18 April. Please note that the 'Select Your Own Seat' facility will not be available to customers booking online at this time – customers will be offered 'best available' seats within the chosen section. Wheelchair spaces cannot be booked online or via the Proms Planner.

BBC PROMS GUIDE: NON-PRINT VERSIONS

Audio CD and Braille versions of this Guide are available in two parts, 'Articles' and 'Concert Listings/Booking Information', priced £3.00 each. For more information and to order, call RNIB Customer Services on 0845 702 3153*.

BBC PROMS GUIDE: LARGE-PRINT VERSION

A text-only large-print version of the Proms Guide is available, priced £6.50. To order, call 020 7765 3246.

ROYAL ALBERT HALL

Full information on the facilities offered to disabled concert-goers (including car parking) is available online at www.royalalberthall.com.

Information is also available through the Access Information Line.

The Royal Albert Hall has up to 20 spaces bookable for wheelchair-users and their companions. There are two end-of-aisle places in the Centre Stalls and two in the Side Stalls – these places are priced as such; front-row platform places either side of the stage are priced as Side Stalls seats; rear platform places are priced as Front Circle seats. Spaces in the Front Circle are priced as such. Four additional wheelchair spaces are available in the Gallery for Promming. These cannot be pre-booked.

This season an additional six Side Stalls wheelchair spaces will be available for Proms 56–75.

Customer lifts at the Royal Albert Hall are located at Doors 1 and 8. The use of lifts is discouraged during performances.

For information on wheelchair spaces available for the Last Night of the Proms via the Five-Concert Ballot, see page 163.

The Royal Albert Hall has a silver-level award from the Attitude is Everything Charter of Best Practice.

HARD-OF-HEARING AND VISUALLY IMPAIRED CONCERT-GOERS

The Royal Albert Hall has an infra-red system with a number of personal receivers for use with and without hearing aids. To make use of the service, collect a free receiver from the Door 6 Information Desk. Patrons are welcome to use this facility to listen in to the BBC Radio 3 broadcast.

If you have a guide dog, the best place to sit in the Royal Albert Hall is in a box, where your dog may stay with you. If you are sitting elsewhere, stewards will be happy to look after your dog while you enjoy the concert. To organise this, please complete an online Accessibility Request at www.royalalberthall.com or phone the Access Information Line in advance of your visit.

Following the success of the signed Proms in the past three years, Dr Paul Whittaker, Artistic Director of Music and the Deaf, returns to guide you through the Family Prom (Prom 66) on Sunday 1 September. Tickets cost £12; disabled concert-goers (plus one companion) receive a 50% discount. Please book your tickets online in the usual way (see page 166). If you require good visibility of the signer, please choose the 'Stalls Signer Area' online when selecting your tickets, or call the Access Information Line on 020 7070 4410 and request this area.

PROGRAMME-READING SERVICE

Ask at the Door 6 Information Desk if you would like a steward to read your concert programme out to you.

LARGE-PRINT PROGRAMMES & TEXTS

Large-print concert programmes can be made available on the night (at the same price as the standard programme) if ordered not less than five working days in advance. Complimentary large-print texts and opera librettos (where applicable) can also be made available on the night if ordered in advance. To order any large-print programmes or texts, please call 020 7765 3246. They will be left for collection at the Door 6 Information Desk 45 minutes before the start of the concert.

CADOGAN HALL

Cadogan Hall has a range of services to assist disabled customers, including provision for wheelchair-users in the Stalls. There are three wheelchair spaces available for advance booking and one space reserved for sale as a day ticket from 10.00am on the day of the concert. Please note, there is no lift access to the Gallery. For further information, call 020 7730 4500.

ROYAL COLLEGE OF MUSIC

The Amaryllis Fleming Concert Hall at the Royal College of Music has six spaces for wheelchair-users. Step-free access is available from Prince Consort Road, located to the left of the main entrance. For further information, call 020 7591 4314.

FOOD AND DRINK AT THE ROYAL ALBERT HALL

Make the most of your visit and enjoy the full Royal Albert Hall experience with culinary delights from the Hall's caterer "rhubarb". With 14 bars, five dining spaces and box catering, there is a wide range of food and drink for you to choose from.

A contemporary new café bar will be open all day from 7.30am (9.00am weekends) in the Meitar Foyer at Door 12, and Café Consort opens two and a half hours before each concert. Other restaurants and a selection of bars open two and a half hour hours pre-performance. Post-concert dinner is also available on selected dates. Further details will be sent with your tickets; or visit www.royalalberthall.com.

Booking in advance is recommended. Visit www.royalalberthall.com or call the Box Office on 0845 401 5040* to make your reservation.

RESTAURANTS

Coda Restaurant offers an excellent set menu as well as full à la carte dining.

The Elgar Room is modern and stylish, with a vibrant atmosphere and an international menu. A set menu and full à la carte are available. The Elgar Room will stay open late on 18, 25 July, 2, 10, 15, 23 August and 6 September for the informal Proms Plus Late events – see bbc.co.uk/proms for more information.

Café Consort is a casual space that offers a seasonal British menu.

Cloudy Bay Wine Bar is the perfect place to enjoy light seafood and fish dishes alongside complementary wines.

Berry Bros. & Rudd No. 3 Bar serves an excellent selection of seasonal British dishes, sharing plates, wine and cocktails.

The new café bar in the Meitar Foyer at Door 12 will serve food and drink ranging from cakes, pastries and tea to salads, sandwiches and wine.

BOX CATERING

If you have seats in one of the Royal Albert Hall's boxes, you can pre-order food and drinks. The selection ranges from sharing boards to smoked salmon blinis, so you can create a menu perfect for your occasion. Visit boxcatering.royalalberthall.com and please order at least 48 hours before the concert that you are attending.

BARS are located throughout the building, offering a full range of drinks, sandwiches, salads, hot and cold snacks and ice cream. An extensive salad bar is also available in the East Arena Foyer.

INTERVAL ORDERS can be arranged from any bar before the concert.

Please note: the consumption of your own food and drink in the Hall is not permitted. In the interests of health and safety, drinks may only be taken into the auditorium in plastic containers and only cold drinks are allowed in the Promming (standing) areas. Glasses and bottles are permitted in boxes, as part of box catering ordered through "rhubarb".

CAR PARKING A limited number of parking spaces, priced £10.00 each, are available from 6.00pm (or two hours before weekend matinee concerts) in the Imperial College car park. Entrances are located on Prince Consort Road (open daily until 7.00pm) and Exhibition Road. Vouchers are only valid until 45 minutes after the end of the concert. These can be booked online, by phone or in person at the Royal Albert Hall from 9.00am on Saturday 11 May, and planned online via the Proms Planner from 2.00pm on Thursday 18 April. Please note that, if attending both early-evening and late-night concerts on the same day, only one parking fee is payable.

DOORS OPEN 45 minutes before the start of each concert (2½ hours for restaurant and bar access) and 30 minutes before each late-night concert. Tickets will be scanned upon entry. Please have them ready, one per person.

LATECOMERS will not be admitted into the auditorium unless or until there is a suitable break in the music. There is a video screen in the Door 6 foyer with a digital audio relay.

BAGS AND COATS may be left in the cloakrooms at Door 9 (ground level) and at basement level beneath Door 6. A charge of £1.00 per item applies (cloakroom season tickets priced £20.00 are also available). Conditions apply – see www.royalalberthall.com. For reasons of safety and comfort, only small bags are permitted in the Arena. If you bring multiple bags, you may only be allowed to take one bag into the Arena for busy concerts.

SECURITY In the interests of safety, bags may be searched upon entry.

CHILDREN UNDER 5 are not allowed in the auditorium out of consideration for both audience and artists, with the exception of the Family Prom (Prom 66).

DRESS CODE Come as you are: there is no dress code at the Proms.

MOBILE PHONES and other electronic devices are distracting to other audience members. Please ensure they are switched off.

THE USE OF CAMERAS, video cameras and recording equipment is strictly forbidden.

FRONT OF HOUSE TOURS OF THE ROYAL ALBERT HALL run every day during the Proms, except on Sunday 1 September and Saturday 7 September. Tours last approximately one hour. To book and to check availability, call 0845 401 5045* or visit www.royalalberthall.com. Tours cost £11.50 per person, with a number of concessions available.

A selection of **PROMS AND ROYAL ALBERT HALL GIFTS AND MERCHANDISE** is available inside the porches at Doors 6 and 12.

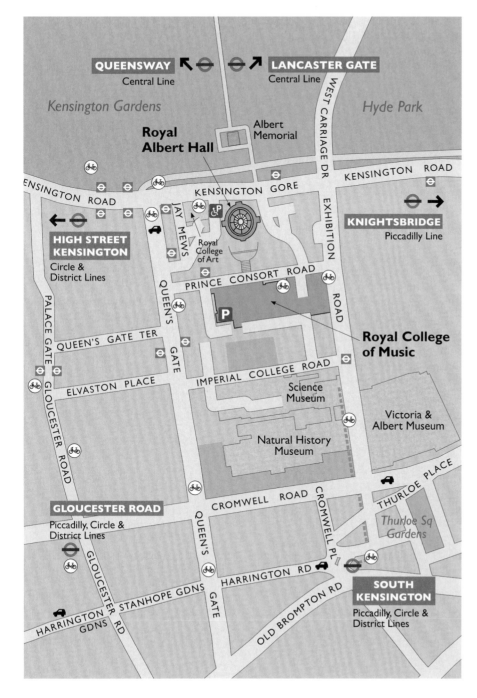

The nearest Tube stations are High Street Kensington (Circle & District Lines) and South Kensington (Piccadilly, Circle & District Lines). These are all a 10- to 15-minute walk from the Hall.

The following buses serve the Royal Albert Hall and Royal College of Music (via Kensington Gore, Queen's Gate, Palace Gate and/or Prince Consort Road): 9/N9, 10 (24-hour service), 49, 52/N52, 70, 360 & 452. Coaches 701 and 702 also serve this area.

The following buses serve Cadogan Hall (via Sloane Street and/or Sloane Square): 11, 19, 22, 137, 170, 211, 319, 360, 452 & C1.

Bicycle racks are near Door 11 of the Royal Albert Hall. (Neither the Hall nor the BBC can accept responsibility for items lost or stolen from these racks.) The Royal Albert Hall has limited cloakroom space and may not be able to accept folding bicycles. Barclays Cycle Hire racks are positioned outside the Royal College of Art, the Royal College of Music and in Cadogan Place.

Please note: the Royal Albert Hall is not within the Congestion Charge zone.

For car parking at the Royal Albert Hall, see opposite.

KEY
- Tube station
- Bus stop
- Taxi rank
- Barclays Cycle Hire
- - - Foot tunnel

VENUE INFORMATION | 171

CADOGAN HALL

5 Sloane Terrace,
London
SW1X 9DQ
www.cadoganhall.com

FOOD AND DRINK AT CADOGAN HALL

The Oakley Bar and Café offers concert-goers a new food experience this season. A selection of light dishes, salads, sandwiches and desserts, all freshly prepared and beautifully presented, will be available from the café and there is a carefully selected wine list to complement the dishes. The café and bar will be open at 11.00am for Proms Chamber Music Concerts and at 1.00pm before Proms Saturday Matinees.

Cadogan Hall's bars offer a large selection of champagne, wines, spirits, beer, soft drinks and tea and coffee.

CAR PARKING

Please check street signs for details. Discounted car parking for Cadogan Hall

performers and customers is available at the NCP Car Park, Cadogan Place, just 10 minutes' walk from Cadogan Hall. Parking vouchers are available on request from the Box Office.

DOORS OPEN at 11.00am for Proms Chamber Music concerts (entrance to the auditorium from 12.30pm); and at 1.00pm for Proms Saturday Matinees (entrance to the auditorium from 2.30pm).

LATECOMERS will not be admitted unless or until there is a suitable break in the music.

BAGS AND COATS may be left in the cloakroom on the lower ground level.

CHILDREN UNDER 5 are not admitted to Cadogan Hall out of consideration for both audience and artists.

DRESS CODE Come as you are: there is no dress code at the Proms.

MOBILE PHONES and other electronic devices are distracting to other audience members. Please ensure they are switched off.

THE USE OF CAMERAS, video cameras and recording equipment is strictly forbidden.

ROYAL COLLEGE OF MUSIC

Prince Consort Road, London SW7 2BS
(see map, page 171) www.rcm.ac.uk

PROMS PLUS

Proms Plus pre-concert events will be held in the Amaryllis Fleming Concert Hall at the Royal College of Music.

Proms Plus events are free of charge and unticketed (seating is unreserved), with the exception of the First Night live *In Tune* event on Friday 12 July, for which free tickets will be available from BBC Studio Audiences (bbc.co.uk/tickets or 0370 901 1227†) and the Proms Plus Storytime events, for which tickets will be available from the Royal Albert Hall (see page 87 for details). Places must be reserved in advance for all Proms Plus Family Orchestra & Chorus events and most Proms Plus Sing events (visit bbc.co.uk/proms or call 020 7765 0557).

Please note: all Proms Plus events are subject to capacity and we advise arriving early for the more popular events. Latecomers will be admitted but, as many of these events are being recorded for broadcast, you may have to wait until a suitable break. The event stewards will guide you.

Prommers who join the Royal Albert Hall queue before the Proms Plus event should make sure they take a numbered slip from one of the Royal Albert Hall stewards to secure their place back in the queue.

If you have special access requirements, see the Royal College of Music information on page 169.

† *Standard geographic charges from landlines and mobiles will apply.*

172 | VENUE INFORMATION

BOOK ONLINE AT **BBC.CO.UK/PROMS** • BY TELEPHONE **0845 401 5040*** • IN PERSON AT THE **ROYAL ALBERT HALL** • BOOKING OPENS 9.00AM ON 11 MAY

TO KILL A MOCKINGBIRD

16 MAY – 15 JUN

Adapted for the stage by **Christopher Sergel**
Based on the novel by **Harper Lee**

PRIDE AND PREJUDICE

20 JUN – 20 JUL

Adapted for the stage by **Simon Reade**
Based on the novel by **Jane Austen**

THE WINTER'S TALE
RE-IMAGINED FOR EVERYONE AGED SIX AND OVER

29 JUN – 20 JUL

By **William Shakespeare**

THE SOUND OF MUSIC

25 JUL – 07 SEP

Music by **Richard Rodgers** Lyrics by **Oscar Hammerstein II**
Book by **Howard Lindsay** and **Russel Crouse**

REGENT'S PARK OPEN AIR THEATRE

"One of the cultural highlights of a London summer

Guardian

Into The Woods 2010. Photo: David Jensen

BOX OFFICE 0844 826 4242
openairtheatre.com

THE ROYAL PARKS

CNBC

magic

INDEX OF ARTISTS

Bold italic figures refer to Prom numbers
PCM indicates Proms Chamber Music concerts at Cadogan Hall
PSM indicates Proms Saturday Matinee concerts at Cadogan Hall
*first appearance at a BBC Henry Wood Promenade Concert
†current / ‡former member of BBC Radio 3's New Generation Artists scheme

INDEX OF WORKS

Bold italic figures refer to Prom numbers
PCM indicates Proms Chamber Music concerts at Cadogan Hall
PSM indicates Proms Saturday Matinee concerts at Cadogan Hall
*first performance at a BBC Henry Wood Promenade Concert

INDEX OF WORKS